VALUE ENGINEERING

A HOW TO MANUAL

STUDENT BOOK STALL
Purohit Arcade, Nr. Iscon Temple,
V. V. NAGAR. Mo.: 98244 46491
Syllabus Change Book Are Not
Taken Back.

VALUE ENGINEERING

A HOW TO MANUAL

(THIRD EDITION)

S.S. Iyer
Management Consultant
and
Certified Value Engineering Specialist

NEW AGE MANAGEMENT

An Imprint of

NEW AGE INTERNATIONAL (P) LIMITED, PUBLISHERS

New Delhi • Bangalore • Chennai • Cochin • Guwahati • Hyderabad
Jalandhar • Kolkata • Lucknow • Mumbai • Ranchi
Visit us at **www.newagepublishers.com**

Published by New Age International (P) Ltd., Publishers
First Edition: 1996
Third Edition: 2009
Reprint: 2012

Branches:

- No. 37/10, 8th Cross (Near Hanuman Temple), Azad Nagar, Chamrajpet, **Bangalore** - 560 018.Tel.: (080) 26756823, Telefax: 26756820 E-mail: bangalore@newagepublishers.com
- 26, Damodaran Street, T. Nagar, **Chennai** - 600 017. Tel.: (044) 24353401, Telefax: 24351463, E-mail: chennai@newagepublishers.com
- CC-39/1016, Carrier Station Road, Ernakulam South, **Cochin** - 682 016. Tel.: (0484) 2377004, Telefax: 4051303, E-mail: cochin@newagepublishers.com
- Hemsen Complex, Mohd. Shah Road, Paltan Bazar, Near Starline Hotel, **Guwahati** - 781 008, Tel.: (0361) 2513881, Telefax: 2543669 E-mail: guwahati@newagepublishers.com
- No. 105, 1st Floor, Madhiray Kaveri Tower, 3-2-19, Azam Jahi Road, Nimboliadda, **Hyderabad** - 500 027. Tel.: (040) 24652456, Telefax: 24652457 E-mail:hyderabad@newagepublishers.com
- RDB Chambers (Formerly Lotus Cinema)106A, 1st Floor, S.N. Banerjee Road, **Kolkata** - 700 014, Tel.: (033) 22273773, Telefax: 22275247 E-mail:kolkata@newagepublishers.com
- 16-A, Jopling Road, **Lucknow** - 226 001. Tel.: (0522) 2209578, 4045297, Telefax: 2204098, E-mail: lucknow@newagepublishers.com
- 142C, Victor House, Ground Floor, N.M. Joshi Marg, Lower Parel, **Mumbai** - 400 013, Tel.: (022) 24927869, Telefax: 24915415 E-mail: mumbai@newagepublishers.com
- 22, Golden House, Daryaganj, **New Delhi** - 110 002. Tel.: (011) 23262370, 23262368, Telefax: 43551305, E-mail: sales@newagepublishers.com

ISBN : 978-81-224-2405-8

₹ 200.00

C-11-09-5893

Printed in India at Parmanand Offset,
Typeset at Pagitek Graphics, Delhi.

PUBLISHING FOR ONE WORLD
NEW AGE INTERNATIONAL (P) LIMITED, PUBLISHERS
4835/24, Ansari Road, Daryaganj, New Delhi-110002
Visit us at **www.newagepublishers.com**

Dedication

This book is dedicated in appreciation and tribute to

Late Mr. LAWRENCE DELOS MILES,
the father of Value Analysis and Value Engineering,
for creating and contributing to the world this management technique;

Mr. ARTHUR E. MUDGE, my GURU,
for teaching me all that I know in Value Engineering;

THE DISTINGUISHED EXECUTIVES
of the House of Tatas, my employers, for graciously encouraging me to
practice the Value Methodology that I had learnt, in my professional career;

Mr. RUDY KEMPTER, my GUIDE,
for enthusing me to teach and propagate what he saw me practicing well;

Mr. SHAHID PRAVIN, my friend,
who started it all, initiating me into the fascinating,
wonderland of management techniques; and

Mrs. SANKARI SITARAM, my wife,
for inspiring and encouraging me to write this book
to share my little expertise for the benefit of posterity.

Late Lawrence Delos Miles, the originator of Value Engineering, (left) with the author, (Second from right), at SAVE International Conference, SACRAMENTO, CA., USA, May 1984

FOREWORD

Value is no new concept. It has been with us from the dawn of civilisation. But, a management methodology based on the value concept, Value Engineering, is rather recent. Value Engineering is a post-World War II development that is currently being extensively and successfully used as a potent and powerful management technique in several countries abroad.

The potential for wide application of Value Engineering in India is tremendous. It could verily be the key management technique and the major contributor for improving our product leadership and cost effectiveness in the days to come. Naturally, it is desirable to have a proper reference material available that deals with not only the basic concepts, but provides more importantly, a practical guide for the systematic, step-by-step application of the Value Engineering methodology to live problems. This need is aptly served by this book, VALUE ENGINEERING–a HOW TO MANUAL. In this book, Mr. S.S. Iyer has, in a concise and lucid manner, dealt with the Value Engineering techniques and demonstrated ways to accomplish better value solutions.

I have known Mr. Iyer for nearly two decades. He is qualified, being one of the few Certified Value Specialists in India today. He has thoroughly understood the Value Engineering technique from the originator, late Mr. Larry Miles himself, as well as some of the world's foremost Value Engineering practitioners. He has extensive experience in the use of this technique in his job in Tata Steel. In fact, he had found it so effective that as a Member of the Society of American Value Engineers and as the founder Secretary of the Indian Value Engineering Society, Eastern Zonal Chapter, he has done pioneering work to spread value awareness in industries of this area, training many industrial managers and successfully conducting Workshops for several projects. Since retirement from Tata Steel and moving to Madras, he is now continuing this drive in the Southern Zone.

For those learners who seek to acquire knowledge and skill in the use of Value Engineering, for the Managers who wish to discharge their responsibility well for accomplishments in their jobs and for the Executives who seek to achieve cost effectiveness, this book can fill an important gap in their supplemental educational experience.

DR. J.J. IRANI
Managing Director, Tata Steel
& National President, INVEST

PREFACE TO THE THIRD EDITION

From the dawn of civilization, the goal of business and industry has been to cater to a **need** and to earn a **reward (profit)** from the customer or the user. He or she will continue to buy and use the item, as long as it provides him or her **VALUE.**

Nothing can have **Value** without utility.

The user buys the item because it will acomplish certain functions efficiently, effectively and well.

All costs incurred by business and industry go for the functions, which satisfies the need. That is why, increasing emphasis is currently being placed, and will continue to be placed, on cost improvement, on all facets that contribute costs.

Managing for Values, for which Value Engineering was specially created by late Larry Miles, ensures that value is improved, both by refining the functions in the item and by preventing all unnecessary use of resources. The skill to manage for values will be vital to succeed henceforth.

I hope that this publication serves the need of all key personnel to build their skill to manage for value, on their day-to-day jobs, and make it a way of life with them.

S.S. IYER

Preface to the Second Edition

The closing decade of the Twentieth Century witnessed several changes, world-wide, in industrial management: re-structuring and down-sizing; global trade and competition; international quality standards; technology and information exchanges; mergers, partnerships and alliances. To find solutions for the challenges of changes, many traditional practices and theories are being thoroughly re-examined; many, scrapped; and, many new approaches, tried. Living centre stage, in USA, for the past few years, I have had the opportunity to observe all that is happening from close proximity and learn what the industry leaders are experiencing. That has enabled me to enrich the original text of the book with appropriate modifications and additional illustrations.

S.S. Iyer

PREFACE TO THE FIRST EDITION

With increasing emphasis now being placed on cost improvement in both industry and government, Value Engineering has become a much needed management tool and technique than ever before. This book is being offered towards meeting this need, as a HOW TO MANUAL.

During the last twenty-nine years I have been involved with Value Engineering, initially as an ardent student, then as part-time practitioner beyond service hours, and more recently, as a trainer and consultant. The more I worked with Value Engineering, the more intensive became my involvement. Now, I have attempted to put on record all that I have learnt in Value Engineering and the experience that I have gained in using that technique.

The book is designed, structured and presented with the objective of providing the neophytes with the theory and methodology of Value Engineering; the value practitioners, with the guidelines, proforma and check-lists for a systematic, step-by-step application of the technique to live problems; and the management men, with a keen and effective means for problem-solving and decision-making.

The book is more in the nature of a compilation. Materials have been drawn and borrowed from a variety of sources. The bulk is, naturally, from the original work of late Larry Miles and the giants who followed in his footsteps, but on whose shoulders I have stood, to see a little more, as applicable to Indian situations. Reflecting, as it does, the technology that I have understood from them, the lessons that I have learnt, their definitions and explanations that I have used for practicing and propogating it, the text has profusion of their thoughts, ideas and writings, the very best on the subject that exist today. For this, I am, for ever truly and sincerely in their debt, irrespective of whether specifically acknowledged in the text or inadvertently missed.

The text is organised in four parts:

PART I — deals with the concept, theory and fundamentals of Value Engineering. Included are the philosophy, purpose and necessity for such an additional technique for developing India.

PART II shows exactly how the methodology is to be applied for problem-solving and making meaningful, time-saving and cost-improving decisions. The various phases of the Value Engineering Job Plan, right from identifying and selecting the problem (or item) for study, to the formation of the study team and performing the study itself, are discussed in detail. Function definition, Function analysis, Function-cost-analysis, Function-cost-worth analysis, creation of alternatives, idea comparison, evaluation, investigation, development, recommendation of change proposals, its implementation and audit to confirm realisation of predicted gains, have all been dealt with in great depth. Wherever appropriate, suitable examples have been used to illustrate the points made.

PART III includes suggested proforma for use in Value Engineering study. The objectives of each phase, the techniques to use, key questions to ask, guidelines to follow and checklists to refer, provided herein, ensure that no link is missed during the actual study, even inadvertentiy.

PART IV contains some actual cases. If a picture is worth a thousand words, then an example should be worth a thousand pictures. The cases should be self-explanatory.

I sincerely hope that this book will prove of immediate practical use to the student and the scholar, trainee and trainer, practitioner and professional.

The contents are based on the syllabus approved by the Society of American Value Engineers for their Module I Training Programmes. Therefore, it should be of help to those who intend to qualify for SAVE Certification as Value Specialist.

I also hope that this publication demonstrates the real potential of this modern management technique and that it is much more than what is being currently experienced in some Indian companies. For those who adopt a real professional approach, the results can be spectacular and breathtaking. And, it is hoped that such professionalism will now develop.

I have benefitted greatly from the reviews and comments by professional colleagues and friends. I thank them for their generous efforts, their time and contribution.

In particular, my tribute to the Tata Iron & Steel Co. Ltd., Jamshedpur, without whose graciousness and generosity, this publication would not have taken shape.

My benefactors are too many for individual mention here, but topping the list are Dr. J.J. Irani, Mr. K.C. Mehra, Mr. H.P. Bodhanwalla, Mr. S.J. Ghandy, Mr. P.N. Roy, Mr. D.P. Kharia and late Mr. Kripal Singh. I am in their debt beyond expression in mere words.

S.S. IYER

TABLE OF CONTENTS

PART I

VALUE ENGINEERING CONCEPT

THEORY & FUNDAMENTALS

INTRODUCTION

Human progress reflects directly the contribution of knowledge and technology to society. Knowledge is expanding. From the start of recorded history to date, it has been meteoring upwards exponentially. Dr. J. Robert Oppenheimer, the famous Atomic Scientist, estimated that the body of knowledge in science has doubled itself between 1950 and 1956; and has been redoubling itself again every six to eight years. Eighty to ninety per cent of the scientists, engineers, etc., who ever lived are alive today. Du Pont Company points out that today 85 per cent of its production is devoted to items which were not on the drawing boards or in the form of experimental hypothesis ten years ago.

Today, we live in an extremely dynamic, fast changing world. Spectacular advances are taking place in science, technology and innovation. The resultant economic growth and development, social progress and well being, are the measure of the skills in intelligently adapting knowledge and technology to secure IMPROVEMENTS. People five decades ago had never heard of jumbo jets, sound barrier, guided missile, application satellite, colour television, video, catscan, laser, micro processor, cellular telephones, xerox or fax, fiber optics and genetically engineered products.

We progress into the future, with escalated endeavours to discover new truths, new technologies, new inventions, new innovations and so on. New products, new processes, new methods, new tools, new techniques, new ways of making current products as well as new products: NEW is the way of life today.

New means CHANGE. To quote Mr. Charles Kittering, the famous inventor, *"The world hates change, but it is the only thing that brings progress."* And the challenge of a Century, and so of the Twenty-first Century, is going to be change: change in products, change in technologies, change in national and inter-national trade, change of every kind, every day. To effectively meet this challenge of change, our job will be to assimilate the scientific discoveries, inventions, technologies and the like, in such a way that practical VALUES will flow to the user and the customer in the most orderly and economical way. The future will be in making it happen. The speed of light is 186,281 miles per second; but that is nothing compared to the speed at which the future is coming at us. And, for making the future happen, it will be the industries, and within the industries, the managements themselves, which will have a vital role to discharge.

The phenomenon of change is just not limited to any one area. We find ourselves today at a point where we must educate, train and develop Managers in what nobody knew yesterday, and prepare them for what they must know tomorrow, and what one knows not yet. What he or she has to become is a jack of all means, methods, tools, techniques, functions and strategies, and master of every one of them. The successful Manager of the future will have to be a change agent, above all else. This is only the beginning. The compulsion is not merely to survive, function and exist, but, more importantly, to grow. GROWTH is about creating and managing opportunities. Growth is selecting particular customer VALUES and mobilizing the entire organisation to deliver those values, time and again. Growth comes from EXCELLENCE. To quote Tata's Chairman, late Mr. J.R.D. Tata, *"always aim at perfection, for only then will you achieve excellence."*

One has to excel at performances. Most measurements of performances are in terms of IMPROVEMENTS. Therefore, there should be no question, but that improvement is a desirable goal. Past success has been closely associated with improvement. Future success will be dependent upon it. But, improvement does not just happen. It is the result of desire and pursuit. It should be pursued by organising for it.

Time-distances between points on earth have diminished, causing escalation of national and inter-national competition in all products and services. ISO 9000 Standards have made trade and commerce global. The spectacular advances in means of communication and transport have made it possible for "more people than ever to collaborate and compete in real time with more other people on more different kinds of work from more different corners of the planet and on an equal footing than at any previous time in the history of the world*." It is now possible to borrow advanced ideas and make painstaking improvements on them. Firms with few years of technical leads today find their products matched (not copied) and bettered in no time. Manufacturing cycle times have declined from years, (3 to 5 years in the past) to months, (3 to 4 months now). Parallel development, developing second and third generation products, catalogue design, high-tech and high-touch have become the key.

There have been many approaches to secure improvements. The traditional thrust has been, and will continue to be, on raising volume of output, i.e., production and productivity. Operations needed for the work are analysed, then synthesised into a process of production; quantities are sought to be controlled; qualities, assured and maintained; and exceptions, acted upon to correct deviations from standards or norms. These perform-

* Friedman L. T., p.8

ance-oriented, efficiency-oriented, incentive-oriented, motivation-oriented approaches would have been taken from, and concentrated on, already attained positions of strength and efficiency. Result: marginal improvements, as the law of diminishing returns governs. Important tasks, no doubt; but, though previously good enough, we need something more.

Global competitors are now a way of life: spectacular examples are in auto, construction equipment, electronics, rubber products, etc. To beat competition, improvements have to be at least a shade better than what competition achieves. But, who are the real competitors? Not only producers of similar products: they may include some of the allies — or even customers. So, to really improve and have an edge over competition, one has to devote painstaking attention to the needs of the customers; analyse the company's freedom to respond completely to those needs; re-think on a fundamental level what the current products are and what they do; and make improvements in where all the customer finds VALUE.

Doing better what is being done is efficiency. It is a condition for survival after success has been achieved. What is needed today is EFFECTIVENESS: doing what is right. The need is for performance effectiveness, cost effectiveness, quality per cost, reliability per cost, etc. Effectiveness is more than efficiency, or aims, or outputs, or minimum costs, although it includes all of them. To quote Peter Drucker (1974), *"Efficiency is concerned with doing things right. Effectiveness is doing the right things."*

Once, the key was slick production techniques, matching technical leads and painstaking improvements. Now, the most effective weapon is rapid innovation. The successful firm of the future will be an innovation machine characterised by speed and flexibility. Manufacturing is in the throes of a technological revolution. In the lead is programmable automation, or flexible manufacturing systems (FMS) that can turn out a wide range of products on the same line, shifting instantly from one model to the next. With FMS, it is claimed that the efficiency of both capital and labour can be doubled (or even trebled) and defects reduced considerably. It can reduce the time it takes to introduce new products by as much as 90% which will mean EFFECTIVENESS in EFFICIENTLY MEETING the CUSTOMER'S NEEDS.

What is needed today is a step beyond cost control and cost reduction: it is cost prevention and cost avoidance. The target is not merely to conserve resources; but also, more importantly, to PREVENT UNNECESSARY USE OF RESOURCES and UNNECESSARY COSTS.

These are, indeed, a great many new and difficult tasks. The tasks will be more and more difficult as days progress; and more will be required, and expected, of the Managers. That is a challenge they should be prepared to take.

To successfully tackle the tasks, from time to time, many new concepts, ideas, tools and techniques are developed. The earliest such development came from Frederick Taylor, who suggested scientific management, to find the best way to do anything. He concentrated on job content, job method and fair wages. Then came the Gilbreths, who provided the tools of time and motion study to measure work. Next, Henry Fayol postulated the principles of administration. The behavioural scientists followed, working on the area of human relations, focussing attention on people as the greatest management resource. Fordism was a template for mass production and mass marketing to achieve economies of scale. Peter Drucker suggested results-oriented approach. Herzberg recommended job enrichment. In this series, Larry Miles concentrated on Functions and Cross-functional Team Approach.

Of all such developments, perhaps, the most effective, promising and rewarding modern technique is VALUE ENGINEERING, late Larry Miles's contribution.

Relevance of Value Engineering to Indian Scenario

After years of Independence, all the planned developments we could achieve through several successive Five Year Plans and the significant advances made in a variety of areas, economic progress in India and the productivity levels are way below what has been achieved, not only in industrially advanced countries in the West, but also by some of the near neighbours in the East. Indeed, India has a long, long way to go to catch up with them, let alone surpass them. The task is further compounded by the fact that significant advances are predicted for the South East Asian countries.

Per capita status of India compared to some other countries is revealing, as seen from Table 1.

The growth of Gross Domestic Product (GDP) in India, in real terms, in 1985-93 was a mere 3%, sarcastically referred as Hindu Rate of Growth.

Indian economy is facing a formidable challenge as never before in its history. An economic survey showed the following facts. The growth of industrial production has been stagnating between 8.4% and 8.7% per year in a past period. There has also been wide variations among industry groups. Basic goods growth has more than halved from 9.9% in 1988-89 to 4.8% in 1990-91. Capital goods growth has more than tripled in the same period (7% to 21.9 %). Consumer durables, which dipped sharply in 1989-90 boomed back to 10.9% in 1990-91, although it is still lower than the rate that was achieved in 1988-89 (12.0%). Consumer non-durables, which rose from 2.5% in 1988-89 to 7.5% in 1989-90, dropped to 5.2% in 1990-91. The growth rate of intermediates dropped by nearly half, though there was some improvement in 1990-91. From 1986-87 to 1989-90, export volume growth had been running at a strong 10% average annual rate. So, there was a growth in exports by 29.1% in 1988-89 over the previous year and by 36.8% in 1989-90. But, the accelerated growth turned to a decline to 17.5% in 1990-91 and the trade gap shot upto, an all time record at Rs. 10,644 crores. The composition of India's exports has undergone significant change since mid-sixties. Manufactured goods exports today constitute over 70% of the total exports, a price-sensitive area.

Table 1: Per capita status

Item \ Country	India	Canada	China	Japan	South Korea	U.K.	U.S.A.	USSR	West Germany
Food Grain (kg)	215	2,240	309	129	196	427	1,184	635	364
Electricity (kwh)	355	18,846	489	5,440	1,549	5,664	10,964	6,010	6,245
Coal (kg)	272	1,487	857	91	534	1,818	3,590	2,112	1,296
Crude Petroleum (kg)	41	3,054	124	5	40	2,080	1,537	2,217	64
Cement (kg)	59	459	185	590	704	207	290	486	515
Pig iron, Ferro alloys (kg)	15	366	53	656	304	219	178	403	514
Newsprint (kg)	0.4	384	0.2	25	9	9.7	22	4.4	14

(As in 1988)

Fortunately, food grains production continues to increase, providing a solid base for growth.

The population is predicted to reach a billion resulting in severe pressure on the land and other physical resources. Ecological imbalances, energy crisis, under-capacity production, and so on: there are several items of vital importance that need careful addressing in the coming decade.

The Public Sector Undertakings are, by and large, still in the red. Scarcely one or two are performing in the competitive sectors, while some others in the monopoly or semi-monopoly sectors are showing profits through administered prices. The total investments in the infra-structure and public sector undertakings in the national economy account for over Rs. 2,215,000 crores. Their return is barely 1.5%, which is clearly unsustainable.

The Commerce Minister is on record, pointing out that India today required on an average Rs. 45,000 crores of foreign exchange annually — an amount of staggering magnitude — for meeting its import requirements. Import of "essential and vital" commodities, such as petroleum products, fertilizers, drugs, edible oils and the like, would cost approximately Rs. 20,000 crores. An additional Rs. 25,000 crores would be required in hard currency for importing requisite raw materials and components. If this requirement has to be met, the country's exports have to increase considerably. And, for that, "radical" changes have to be effected and the industry and the Government would have to acquit themselves far better than they have done so far. What is needed is total attention: from the stage of raw material, through production, to packaging and marketing. Solutions can be found only with a new "mind set" and an attitude of problem-solving, innovations, experimentations and professionalism — says an international management consultant.

In contrast to the heavy emphasis in the past 35 years on import substitution and growing domestic market supplies, there is now urgent need to develop an export ethos, to face severely escalating competition in inter-national markets. India's exports are a mere 0.6% of the world trade. At the beginning of the sixties, India was the second largest exporting country in Asia, next only to Japan. Thereafter, India lost place steadily, to Iran, Saudi Arabia, Hongkong, South Korea and so on. Today, Indian exports rank 38th in the world, according to World Competitiveness Year Book. Other near Asian neighbours have outstripped India, as reflected in their rankings - Singapore 2nd, Hongkong 3rd, Taiwan 18th, China 26th, etc. The quality of export goods (and home consumption goods too) suffers and consequently Indian goods are not competitive abroad. Telco vehicles are a classic exception — the result of their cult of excellence, engineering quality in the product before it is inspected. To earn foreign exchange, we have to compete for it. We have to be competitive both quality-wise and price-wise.

Unemployment has been, and continues to be, one of India's most serious problems. The rate of industrial expansion has not been fast enough to absorb even a fraction of the addition to the labour force. The oft repeated excuse has been that capital is scarce. But, foreign investments are attracted with liberalization in Governmental policy and changes in procedures. However, this alone cannot solve the problem. It has to be remembered that such investments will always go to lower cost places—for which India has yet to qualify. Unemployment levels are 3.4% in Japan, 6% in USA, 9% in Germany, inspite of ongoing action for re-engineering, restructuring, down-sizing, and so on, all in single digits, whereas the corresponding figure for India is in double digits. In USA, they have created, in the past 3 years, 8.4 million new jobs, many of which pay higher than average wages, and, significantly, as many as 60% of them in managerial or professional cadres. Culled from the studies conducted by International Labour Organisation, Table 2 shows the alarming trend in India as compared to some other select countries.

There has to be a significant increase in employment. The annual increase in labour market is around 3 million. There are already 42 millions of educated adult population, with a total work force of about 632 million.

Table 2: Unemployment (thousands)

Country	*1989*	*1990*	*1991*	*1992*
Egypt	1107.9 (6.9 %)	1346.5 (8.6 %)	NA	NA
Canada	1018 (7.5 %)	1109 (8.1 %)	1417 (10.3 %)	1556 (11.3 %)
USA	6528.0 (5.2 %)	6874.0 (5.4 %)	8426.0 (6.6 %)	9384.0 (7.3 %)
Venezuela	621.1 (9.2 %)	741.7 (10.4 %)	701.0 (9.5 %)	NA
India	32776.0	34632.0	36300.0	36758.0
Israel	142.5 (8.9 %)	158.0 (9.6 %)	187.4 (10.6 %)	207.5 (11.2 %)
Japan	1420.0 (2.3 %)	1340.0 (2.1 %)	1370.0 (2.1 %)	1420.0 (2.2 %)
Italy	2865.0 (12.0 %)	2621.0 (11.0 %)	2653.0 (10.9 %)	2799.0 (11.5 %)
UK	2063.0 (7.2 %)	1949.0 (6.5 %)	2385.0 (8.3 %)	2732.0 (9.6 %)
Yugoslavia	1201.2 (14.9 %)	1308.5 (16.4 %)	NA	NA

Source: Statistical Year Book, UN 1994, pp. 303–315.

By the turn of the century, this is likely to go up to 65 million and 790 million respectively. The social cost of unemployment will be staggering. To quote from "Scientific American", September 1982, "*given the rate of technological advance, the creation of one additional job that 20 years ago would have required an investment of $50,000 now demands $100,000 and in 20 years hence will demand even $500,000, (even with inflation discounted).*" The small-medium sector accounts for around 80% of the employment and 50% of the production in the industrial sector. This sector also accounts for 40% of the exports. A country like India, which is long on labour and short on capital, will have to increasingly develop and strengthen this sector. But, here, many are deficient in managerial effectiveness.

We have not yet been able to conquer poverty, eradicate disease, banish illiteracy or contain social disparities. We have yet to fulfill many needs, both quantitatively and qualitatively.

In the case of resource utilisation, we have a long way to go. For instance, it is estimated that about 35% of energy is lost before the final end use. Freight is moved both by rail and road. Hereagain, it is assessed that for every billion TKm of freight traffic diverted from road to rail 30,000 t of diesel will be saved. This will mean corresponding saving in import as well. As compared to the international average, the same capacity road transport in India consumes 8 to 15% more fuel.

In 1947, before gaining Independence, it was said that "Industrialisation is the key to India's success." The question then was EITHER INDUSTRIALISE OR PERISH. Today, more than a half century later, we still need a strong industrial base, which we sought to build to produce the physical goods that create wealth. Besides, we have to sustain a comparably high standard of living; create the jobs needed for the millions of our adult, educated, unemployed; and provide a lot of other good things in the society. So, industry continues, and will continue, to be the key. Only, the question has slightly enlarged to INDUSTRIALISE AND MANAGE IT FOR EXCELLENCE, OR PERISH. It now rests squarely on the industries to rise up to the need of the hour and play their vital role: expand, modernise, improve production and productivity, reduce costs, raise qualities, efficiencies and effectiveness, escalate in volume and value of exports, etc. Better use of existing facilities and re-organisation of patterns of production are imperatives.

That is, in essence, the Indian scenario today.

What is the prospect for the Indian Manager, now and henceforth? To quote our Prime Minister from his address to the National Development Council on Novemeber 8, 1985, "*a tremendous effort to mobilise resources, absorption of technology, reduction of costs, greater competition, increasing efficiency, improving quality.*"

In the coming decades, the following would be promising areas of thrust and logical priorities for the Indian Managers:

- *Material Conservation*
- *Product Improvement*
- *Performance Maximisation*
- *Energy Saving*
- *Quality Improvement*
- *Safety Assurance - both health and hazards*
- *Cost Reduction - both immediate and life-cycle*
- *Manpower Optimisation*
- *Quality of Work life*

The Indian Managers will have to raise production and productivity many-fold and achieve far greater performance levels than ever before. These will have to come from even existing technology, old worn out equipment and facilities, and inspite of scarcity of capital, lack of requisite skills in labour, socio-economic and mandatory pressures, poor infrastraucture, etc. Scarcity of resources coupled with high rate of their consumption would make imperative not only conservation of all available resources, but, more importantly, prevention of unnecessary use of resources. This is where VALUE ENGINEERING will secure results, as it is created for this specific purpose.

Until fairly recently, Indian companies were more than happy to operate in the highly protected domestic environment. Indian executives also operated with the assumption that they enjoyed limitless resources and plenty of time to build profitable enterprises; but today, finite resources, new technology and escalating change are placing unprecedented pressure on every organisation. Managements have reached a point when reliance on old experiences, old concepts and techniques as well as established ways of doing things will not help either the organisation to function and compete effectively; or the Manager, to successfully meet the ever increasing demands on his capacity, capability and skills. In fact, their very survival will depend on how well and how quick they respond to the new and rapidly changing demands. Which enjoins that there is urgent need to adopt new theories, new approaches, new techniques; to develop new skills and new practices; as well as to assimilate the modern tools and techniques as soon as these are developed. The Manager's capacity to think, to plan strategies, to organise logistics and to control inputs are extended and strengthened in direct relation to his (or her) proficiency in the choice and strategic application as warranted. The Indian Manager will be no exception; he or she will need every tool and technique, approach and what not, to better what he or she has achieved so far. This is where VALUE ENGINEERING will have a vital and critical role.

Measures have to be taken to make Indian industries competitive and growing export-wise. The Government had initiated some bold steps to overcome the ill-effects of lop-sided industrial growth of the earlier years and discarded the four decades of economic restrictions in industrial policy. Measures have also to be taken to reduce dependence on imports, even for raw materials. Extend it for those who earn foreign exchange through exports.

The poorly performing public sector plants are being divested. But, the progress has been slow.

Indigenous materials will have to be used to a much more extensive extent than hithertofore. The core of VALUE ENGINEERING is substitution by equivalents at lower costs.

When Man Mohan Singh, who unexpectedly took office as the Prime Minister sometime back, it was expected that the pace of the reforms would pick up. For, he had, as Finance Minister, initiated them. But, this did not happen. So, although India still needs a large doze of economic reforms, and although Mr. Singh's credentials as a reformer are unimpeachable, the government has yet to produce the changes so badly needed by her to catch up with her neighbor and competitor–China. The service sector and information technology have been doing well. If only, it would add manufacturing of equal performance, then, economic uplift would have been substantial. That is, perhaps, a job for the future for his government.

Fortunately, the IITs and the management Institutes have already established a reputation worldwide, for training and developing the best of best Managers, even at the entry levels of corporate jobs. Their success has been in delivering **values**, as perceived by the customers, from time to time. They will find in Value engineering the much needed skill of the future.

Most products or services that are offered cost us much more than they should do. Often they do not perform the needed functions satisfactorily. They include a lot of frills that are of no use. For a definite and predetermined requirement, the product or service should be most appropriate. It should meet all requirements fully, no more and no less; and at the least cost possible. Though a universal truth, it is more of a challenge to the Indian Manager to invariably break even. In accomplishing these requirements, VALUE ENGINEERING has no parallels or equals.

Competitiveness depends on the ability to improve product design and quality. It also depends on how quickly the industry reacts to market changes and takes advantage of the often short life-cycle of high technology products. To accomplish these goals it would require the necessary skills and tools to get the job done cost effectively. Again, that is what VALUE ENGINEERING helps to accomplish.

Internationalisation or globalisation has come to stay, due to removal of trade barriers, free flow of capital, progress in information technology, intensity of market competition, changing life styles and demand for new products and services. To promote exports and to compete in global bids, world quality standards, prescribed vide ISO 9000 series, will have to be met, by our products and services. From 1993, all manufacturers are expected by their customers to produce evidence that they operate to the ISO 9000 Standards. Adoption of ISO 9000 philosophy on quality and installation of the system for quality management, accreditation and maintenance of registration for certification involve a series of steps, akin to the phases of Value Engineering Job Plan (see Chapter on Value Engineering and Quality). Quality is value. In VALUE ENGINEERING, the Indian Managers will find the crash technique they need today for gearing up to Total Quality Management and ISO 9000 series accreditation.

Value Analysis was a luxury for General Electric; but for Indian managements, it is a NECESSITY. Particularly so, if India is to become the world's fourth largest economy by the year 2010. In this context, the potential for application of Value Engineering in Indian industries is tremendous. Value Engineering is most relevant to accelerate the pace, nature and content of development in the country.

Verily, VALUE ENGINEERING will be the key for India for production, productivity, cost effectiveness, competitiveness and prosperity.

VALUE

The Greeks believed that value is an indwelling property of goods and services. That idea of value dwelling in goods and services still pervades our thinking. However, it is also seen as a force that governs our behavior. It is centered in the people and the goods and services that they desire. Changes in their needs alter the value of the goods and services.

Perhaps, value is best understood from *Bhagawat Gita*. Chapter xiii, verses 7–11, enumerates twenty values that Krishna, the God incarnate, teaches Arjuna, a human hero. Though part of an important text of religious beliefs and norms of human behavior, they contribute the basic determinants of much of our material world decision-making. As Swami Dayananda Saraswathy eruditely explains, value here means *"the regard for a thing, situation or attitude, which, for some reason, is esteemed or prized by the value holder."*

Thing includes product, service or communication–those that can be seen, touched, felt or handled. They all have value. They derive value from their inherent properties and characteristics: like, life, performance, use, strength, composition, weight, configuration, etc.

Situation includes subjective attributes: like ability, capability, condition, capacity, circumstance, position, location, context, quality, reliability, complexity, simplicity, intricacy, equality, congruence, surfeit, abundance, dearth, scarcity, rarity, harmony, suitability, inter-changeability, maintainability, reparability, serviceability, possibility, probability, feasibility, maneuverability, etc.

Attitude is mental, emotional and ephemeral: like, appropriateness, desirability, difficulty, facility, ease, comfort, euphoria, delight, pleasing, esteem, etc.

By *value holder* is meant the recipient. Value is what the recipient gets out of what is received.

Value is an abstract concept. It is as old as mankind or civilisation itself.

Remember our childhood days. We began analysing value when we first decided that a bottle of warm milk was MORE DESIRABLE than a teddy bear or a rattle. We have been analysing values ever since.

Aristotle, more than two thousand years ago, described seven classes of value: Economic, Moral, Aesthetic, Social, Political, Religious and Judicial. Value Analysts and Value Engineers are most concerned with ECONOMIC VALUE.

What is value ?

We all have used this term — and continue to use it — many times and under different contexts.

Everyone seems to understand it. But, most cannot define it clearly.

The term is also used in variety of ways, and, therefore, has many different meanings.

Dictionary meanings include: WORTH, A FAIR EQUIVALENT, ESTEEM, EFFICACY, EXCELLENCE, THAT WHICH RENDERS ANYTHING USEFUL OR DESIRABLE, and so on.

Because it is applied to both subjective qualities:

> STYLING, APPEARANCE, SHAPE etc.,
> determined by the emotions,

and objective qualities:

> LIFE, PERFORMANCE, RELIABILITY, LIGHT WEIGHT, etc.,
> determined by properties and characteristics,

it is a difficult word to define.

The wide scope of definitions permits its extensive usage; and, so, compounds confusion and mis-understanding (Fig. 1).

Value is established by comparison. *"That a thing may have any value, it must be of some USE and it must satisfy some DESIRE. Besides, there must be some DIFFICULTY in its acquisition, possession or attainment. When something is both desirable and difficult to get, some one has a problem (the user); and some one else has an opportunity (the producer). The item is made and sold to the user for the difference in difficulty in its acquisition, possession, or attainment. The difference between what the item means to the customer (worth) and what he or she has to pay for it (price), is the measure of the customer's value for the item."**

Different customers will demand different things. That is, value means MANY THINGS TO MANY PEOPLE.

For instance, in the case of the car market are people who buy for economy and personal needs, who discriminate on aesthetic concept, who buy the best product for their money, or who want to keep up with the

---

* Fallon, p. 13, 14

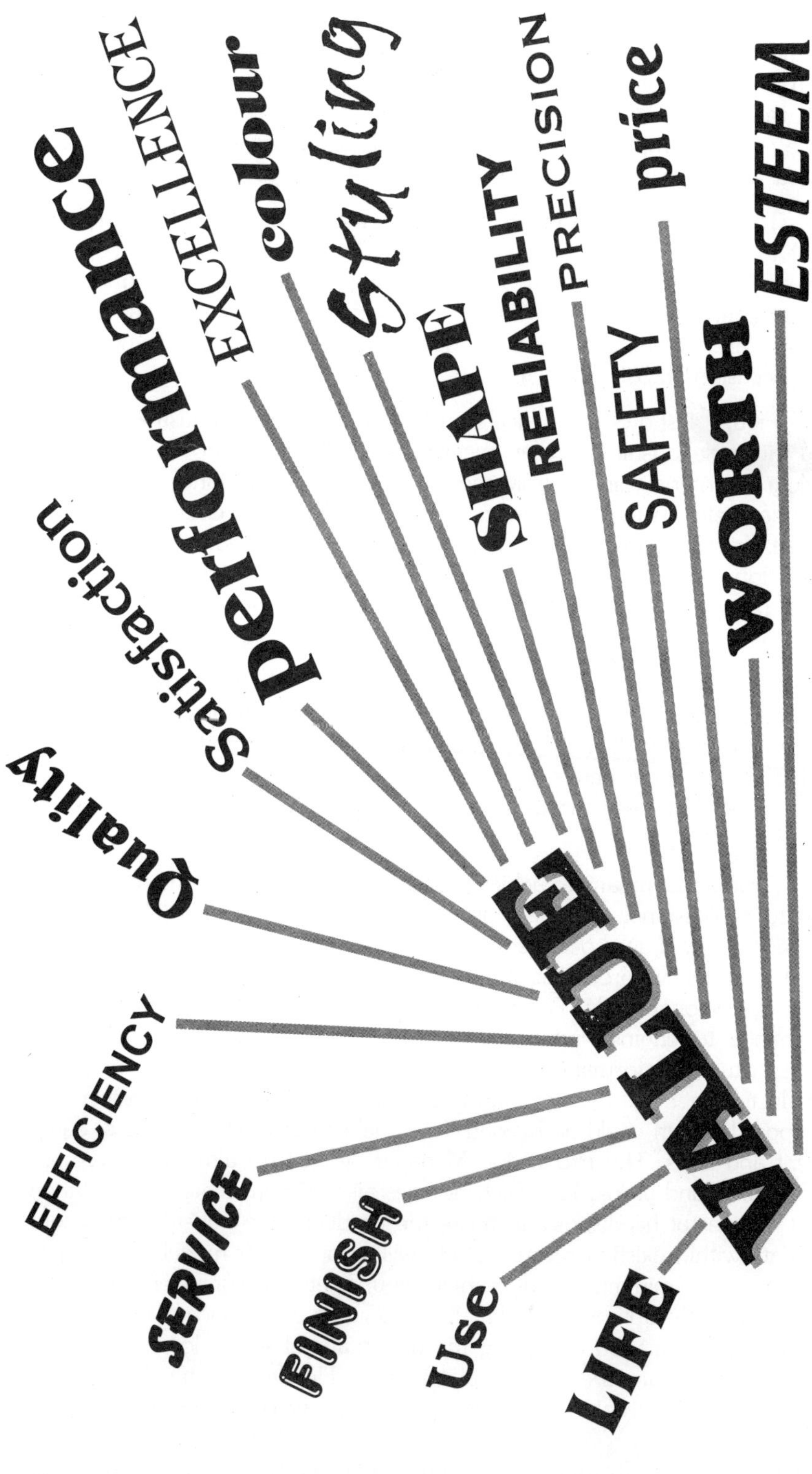

Fig. 1. Abstract concept, many meanings

Joneses. When you want to trade your car, it will be a solid gold Cadillac for the price that you will demand. The buyer may see it as a ramshackle contraption, fit only for the scrap heap. As your neighbour sees it, it moves with man-power, and not motive power. Your wife views it as a museum piece, when compared to the new model. After the first scratch, it has ruined a vintage piece, for the fuss you make about it (Fig. 2).

To take another example, the watch market consists of people who want to buy the lowest priced watch that works reasonably well (25% as per one survey), who prefer watches with long life, good workmanship, good material, and good styling (50%), and who look for useful product features and meaningful emotional qualities, say, to symbolise some important occasions (25%) (Fig. 3).

Figure 4 shows ten typical items of customer and industrial products and inter-relationship between these products and market segments. The variety of criteria will be easily seen — purpose, needs, fancies, fragrance, attitudes, etc. Truly, the customer behaviour is inner-directed, other-directed, tradition-directed, autonomous and even unpredictable! Everyone has a long list of things that they want, but each item has a comparative value rating.

In business world, everyone is often working at legitimate cross purposes, governed by self interest and own sub-goals. Customers look for lower prices; suppliers ask higher prices. Unions demand higher wages; stock holders expect more and more earnings. The competition is always trying to market a better product or a product with more features at a lower cost. Business success depends on managing all these and some more.

Traditional means to achieve results are to assign specific responsibilities to professional specialists: like Sales, Production, Materials, Finance, Personnel, etc. Each specialist and his department then endeavour to study, analyse and solve problems of its own area of responsibility, optimising on own operational goals. For example, the Designer equates his best performance to engineering excellence in terms of materials, precision in manufacture, performance, strength and reliability. He tends to make the products larger and heavier than necessary and consequently, costlier. The proposed design could be beyond the capability of existing process, equipment and skills. The Production Manager defines his aim as to maximise efficiencies and yields, for which he uses all the men, material, machinery and minutes at his disposal to make the products. He will strive to accommodate within existing resources. He will favour fewer models, larger production runs, minimum and simpler set-ups, etc. It fosters efficiency, but not necessarily optimum combination and cost to produce. The Materials Manager sees his job as getting the best material at the lowest price and best delivery from the registered suppliers. He will not be exploiting to advantage a different, but equally good and low cost specification or an

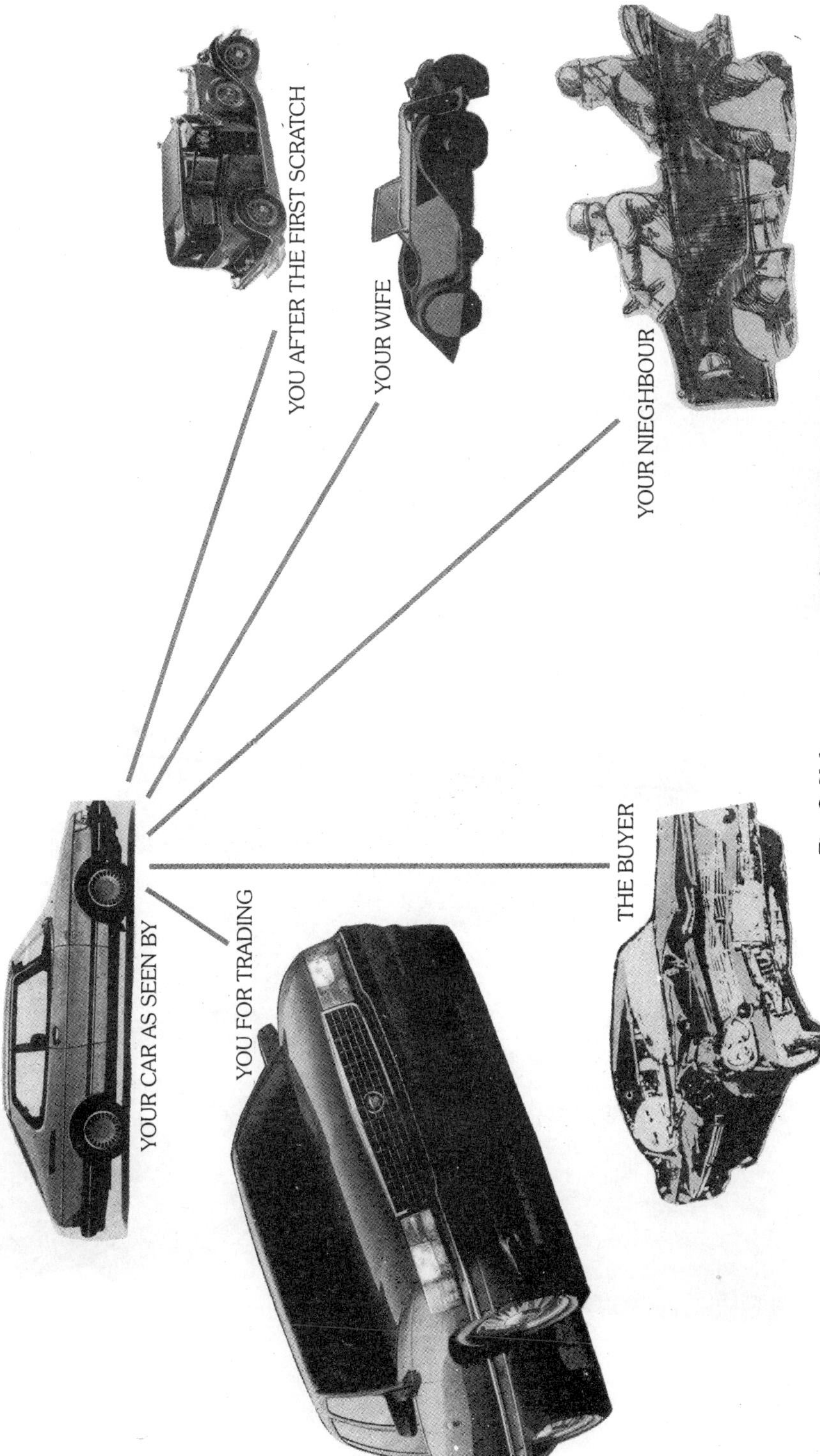

Fig. 2. Value means many things to many people

Fig. 3. A typical watch market

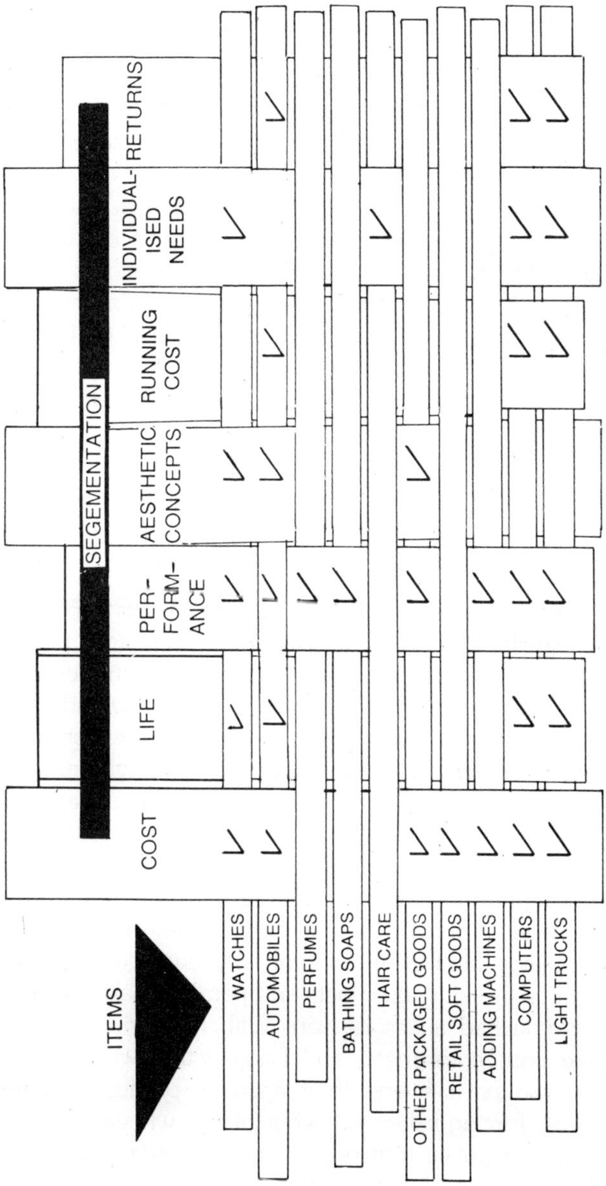
ITEMS
SEGEMENTATION
COST
LIFE
PER-FORM-ANCE
AESTHETIC CONCEPTS
RUNNING COST
INDIVIDUAL-ISED NEEDS
RETURNS
WATCHES
AUTOMOBILES
PERFUMES
BATHING SOAPS
HAIR CARE
OTHER PACKAGED GOODS
RETAIL SOFT GOODS
ADDING MACHINES
COMPUTERS
LIGHT TRUCKS

Fig. 4.

unregistered but better supplier. He would like to place larger orders to get price discounts and limit replenishment effort. The Finance executive looks to securing a large difference between sales income and revenue expenditure: the means, not important. He discourages high inventories. The Chairman and Managing Director seek better returns on investment. Their focus is on profits. The Sales seek to maximise orders by accepting what the customer is willing to pay. They give away discounts and promise ex-stock deliveries to pile up orders, paying little, if any, consideration to the adverse effect it makes on cost of production, work schedule and even quality (while rushing orders through the system), to redeem their promises. Traditionally, each pursues his or her operational goal with ardour, but, sub-optimises. Each operational goal makes demand on the limited resources available. Advancement to achieve one operational goal is generally secured at the expense of others. Thus, concentrating too much effort on excelling on sub-goals, would adversely affect overall performances. So, the sum total of all their endeavours need not, and does not, add up to the goals and expectations of the organisation, i.e., to the customers' value, which is THE BEST BUY FOR THE MONEY PAID, or the LOWEST PRICE FOR A FUNCTION OR SERVICE, at the desired place, time and with the essential quality (Fig. 5). Truly the customer is the arbiter of value, besides being the value hunter. He or she seeks to maximise the value return for the money spent.

Value also changes. The SAME ITEM MAY HAVE DIFFERENT VALUES TO THE SAME PERSON, depending on the time, place, demand and supply position, availability of substitute items, extraneous pressures, and so on (Fig. 6). Recall the days when you were a boy and day-dreaming as to what you will do when you graduate, enter a profession and start life. On an item for transport, you may have then thought of a top-down, sports cabriolt, with enough and more horsepower to drive past the local girls and impress them. When you got married, the sedan would have represented better value for the protection it would afford to your wife and her costly Kancheepuram saree from unpredictable rains, the characteristic of our towns. Raising a family — and if you are of the old school of thought, wanting large families around you — you would have found it hard to accommodate all the kids, their pets and paraphernalia, besides bag and baggage, unless you had an estate van. With meteoring prices, inflation, having to make both ends meet, and living within whatever is available easily, values would have swung to indigenous products. Soaring petrol prices are similarly forcing values in favour of two wheeler for you and taxi for family rides, or a public transport. The same item, a means of transport, and you over a period of time, under pressure of circumstances: the change in value should be obvious.

Will not an ice box have less value in the Arctics than in the tropical climate? Similarly, toys and halo lights will sell during festival times; and rain coats and umbrellas, during monsoons: not other months.

Fig. 5. Traditional Industry effort

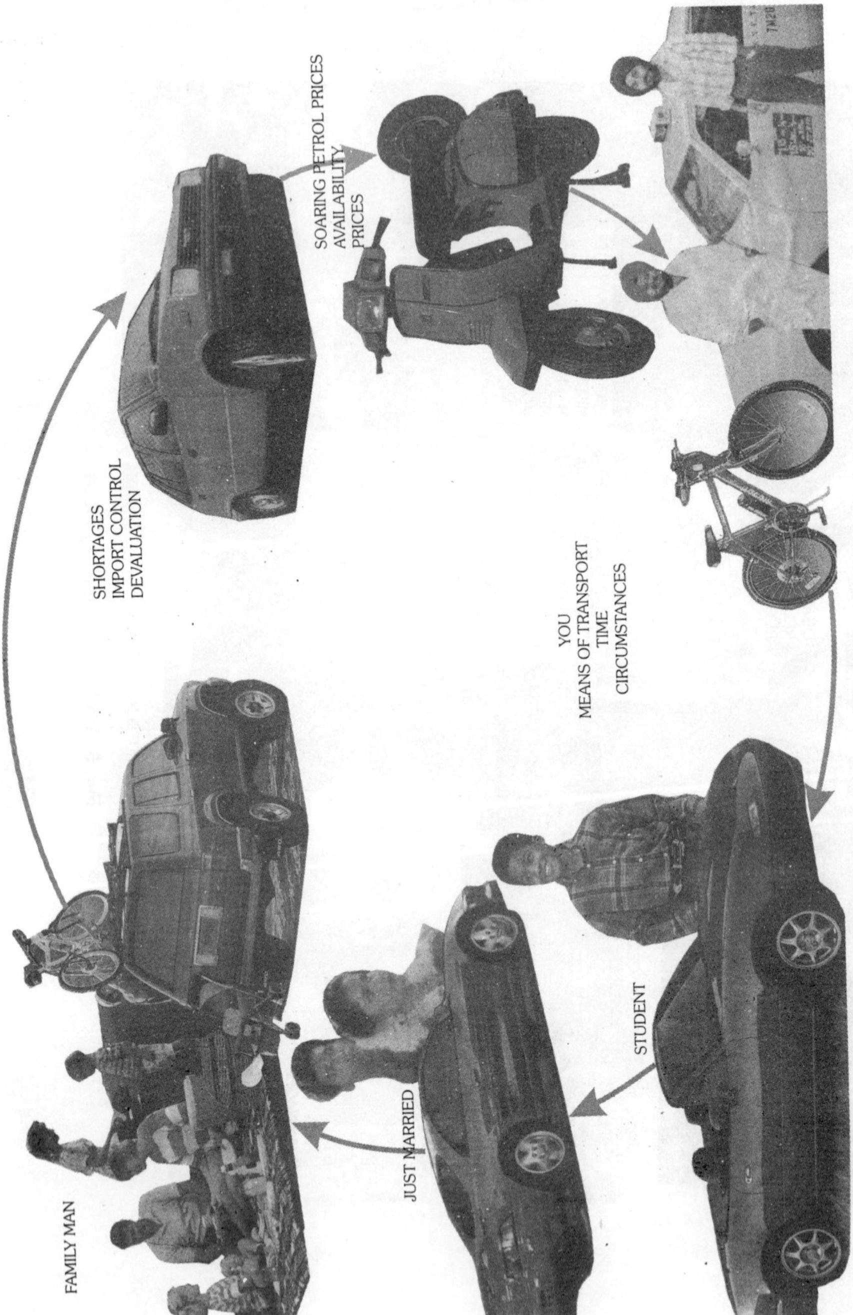

Fig. 6. Same item, same person, different values

Imagine the task, then to provide the best buy for the price paid to a seething, disparate, infinitely varied conglomeration of human beings with very wide and contrasting differences in value measures. Therefore, the unlimited opportunity that the industry has to provide a variety of products and services that meet the needed functions effectively and well, and at costs covering an equally wide range.

The objective of a firm is to supply a product or service of economic value to the customer in order to make a profit. A user purchases an item or service because it will accomplish certain functions at a cost he or she is willing to pay. He or she interprets its value to be good, if it satisfies the needed function for low cost; poor, if it costs too much, or if it does not perform the required function, or if it creates problems while performing. That is, as Mr. Miles stressed, *"a product or service is generally considered to have good value, if that product or service has the appropriate PERFORMANCE AND COST."**

Value is determined by two major considerations: PERFORMANCE and COST.

FOUR BASIC KINDS OF VALUE

We may classify economic value into four kinds:

1. USE VALUE	The properties, features and qualities which accomplish the use, the work or the service — causing the item to perform or serve an end.
2. ESTEEM VALUE	The properties, features or attractiveness which cause us to yearn to possess it — causing the item to sell.
3. EXCHANGE VALUE	The properties or qualities which enable us to exchange an item for something else we want.
4. COST VALUE	The total of material, labour and other costs that have to be incurred to produce an item.

* Miles, p 4.

Value can be quantitatively treated, if, identifying the various values possessed by the item, an appropriate monetary measure is established for these values. When the sum of these monetary measures for values offered by the item approximates to the price, the purchaser or user would deem that "this is fair price".

Use value, being derived from the delivered function and representing the properties and qualities which perform the function, can be quantified. Other values, in abstract form, are difficult to quantify.

For instance, the use value of a motor car bumper is approximately 13% of its cost, being equivalent to a piece of single steel angle section of equal length. The remaining 87% has been added to enhance the appearance, customer appeal and acceptance. The use value of the manufacturer's label on dress-ware is virtually nil. It does very little to add to its performance — say to keep the woollens warm, or the cottons in crease. But, without it, the prestige attached to owning and wearing the dress will be very much reduced and the product will lose the esteem value of the complete dress.

The customer is interested in maximizing the return for his money. The more the return, the better. The quicker the return, it is even better still. And, if it is also a sure return, it is the best. So, the three quantifiers of value are HOW MUCH, HOW SOON, and HOW SURE. The customer or user is especially interested in the accomplishment of the necessary or required function. Therefore, an item is of no value, if it does not accomplish the function for which the user intends it. The opportunity here is to IDENTIFY THE BASIC FUNCTION AND TO FIND THE BEST MEANS TO ACCOMPLISH IT, COST EFFECTIVELY, RELIABLY AND WELL. The customer does not care what else it does — i.e., what additional, secondary or support functions it accomplishes. The opportunity here is to IDENTIFY THE UNNECESSARY, ADDITIONAL FUNCTIONS AND ALL SECONDARY AND SUPPORT FUNCTIONS. ELIMINATION of all of them would be ideal; but for practical reasons some secondary or support functions would be inevitable. The next to ideal solution is to KEEP THEIR COST AND NUMBERS AS LOW AS POSSIBLE.

Fortunately, the customer or user is not concerned with how the necessary or required function is accomplished, so long as it is accomplished effectively, reliably and well.

An item: i.e., a product, a service, a project, etc., is intended to accomplish a purpose, serve a use, perform a job and provide a facility; to remain durable, reliable and reasonably trouble-free; to provide satisfaction through a shape, a finish, a colour, texture, a style, an appearance, a quality, etc. (Fig. 7.)

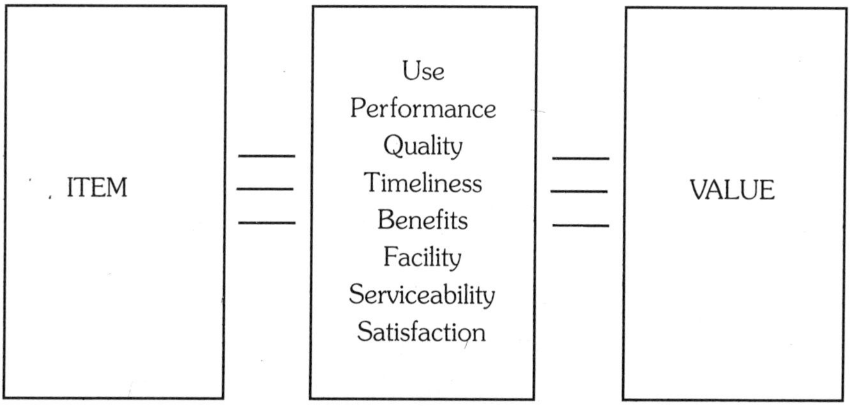
ITEM
Use
Performance
Quality
Timeliness
Benefits
Facility
Serviceability
Satisfaction
VALUE

Fig. 7.

From what we have discussed so far, Value can be seen as:

$$\text{VALUE} = \frac{\text{ITEM}}{\text{MONEY}}$$

$$= \frac{\text{USE} + \text{ESTEEM}}{\text{PRICE}}$$

$$= \frac{\text{USE FUNCTION} + \text{ESTEEM FUNCTION}}{\text{COST}}$$

$$= \frac{\text{BASIC FUNCTION} + \text{SECONDARY OR SUPPORT FUNCTION}}{\text{COST}}$$

$$= \frac{\text{NECESSARY FUNCTION} + \text{UN-NECESSARY FUNCTION}}{\text{COST}}$$

Fig. 8.

Value varies inversely with cost, function remaining the same. Also, an increase in value does not demand a reduction in cost, as it can also be accompanied by an increase in function (provided that an increase in function is also desirable).

Karl Marx had stated that *"nothing can have value without being an object of utility."* Surely, if an item does not do its job effectively and well, (i.e. what it is intended to do) it is of no use to the customer and naturally no amount of cost reduction will improve its value to the user. Not only high cost, but also anything done which adversely affects the needed utility of an item, will reduce the value to the user. By the same token, anything done to increase the functional capacity of an item beyond that which is needed will also be of little value to the user. That is, *"anything less than the necessary functional capability is unacceptable; and anything more is unnecessary and wasteful."** Or, real value lies in providing JUST RIGHT and NOTHING MORE.

DEFINITIONS

Some of the standard definitions used in value Engineering are:

VALUE	The lowest cost at which a function, by any means, can be accomplished effectively, reliably and well.
VALUE	*"The lowest cost to reliably provide the required functions or services at the desired time and place and with the essential quality."***
FUNCTION	*"That which makes a product work or sell."*** It is the natural or characteristic action performed by a product or service.
BASIC FUNCTION PRIMARY FUNCTION USE FUNCTION	Those for which the customer or user buys the item or service; the primary purpose, the utilitarian characteristic, or the feature that fulfils the need of the customer or user. It is the most important action performed by a product or service.
SECONDARY FUNCTION SUPPORT FUNCTION	Those functions required to cause or allow the designer's choice of means for accomplishing the primary purpose. Other functions not directly accomplishing that primary purpose, but supporting it, or resulting from the design approach chosen.

* Tufty, p. 7

** Mudge, p 13, 16.

	An additional function for helping the item to work or sell better.
	A Secondary function is not as important as the Basic function.
NECESSARY FUNCTION	That which must be performed by the item to accomplish the user need.
UN-NECESSARY FUNCTION	That which is superfluous or additional to the primary need of the user.
AESTHETIC FUNCTION	That which is for the purpose of pleasing the buyer through colour, shape, or feature, causing the person to buy.
VALUE INDEX	The ratio of WORTH over COST.
WORTH	The least cost that is required to perform a function or a group of functions.
	The value of a function is often referred to as worth.
VALUE GAP	The difference between Cost and Worth.
VALUE MISMATCH	Value Mismatch is when function cost does not match user/customer function needs and attitudes; high cost — low worth: high worth — low cost.
COST	The total of material, labour, design and overheads allocated to the product or service.
LIFE CYCLE COST	LCC is the cost of the product or service over the life of the item minus a trade-in value at the completion.
DESIGN TO COSTS/ VALUE CONTROL	Value control is a cost avoidance procedure which establishes an estimated total cost objective for each new product or service, then designs and manufactures to this cost objective a functional and reliable product or service.
FUNCTION ANALYSIS SYSTEM TECHNIQUE	FAST is a diagramming technique which shows graphically the relationships and inter-relationships of all functions. It is a method of analysing, organising and recording the functions of a system, product, plan, process, procedure, etc., to stimulate thinking and creativity.

How to Add Value

To know how to add value to a product or service, first and foremost, one should know the reasons for poor value. Then, an analysis can be made to gauge the complexity of the problem and determine the effort required to investigate and evaluate for value. Meaningful decisions for building or adding value to the item will then be possible.

REASONS FOR POOR VALUE

Reasons for poor value are many. The most important ones are listed below: They are:

1. Lack of Information.
2. Lack of Ideas.
3. Lack of Time.
4. Lack of Attention.
5. Lack of Listening.
6. Lack of Problem Ownership.
7. Lack of Experience.
8. Poor Quality.
9. Honest Wrong Beliefs.
10. Habitual Thinking.
11. Risk of Personal Loss.
12. Reluctance to Seek Advice.
13. Habits and Attitudes.
14. Unrealistic Requirements.
15. Changed Circumstances.
16. Changing Technology.

17. Poor Communications.
18. Prejudice.
19. Misconceptions.
20. Desire to Conform.
21. Poor Inter-action Among Contributing Disciplines.
22. Comfortable High Cost Activities.
23. Creep.
24. Non-Value-Adding Work.
25. Waste.

These are discussed in the following:

1. LACK OF INFORMATION

Failure to get sufficient relevant facts. This can be caused by lack of knowledge or mis-understanding of the full requirements of the original project plan, non-availability of full information, non-transmittal of information in suitable form, mis-interpretation of available information or inaccurate definition of the problem/project itself. Limited information causes mis-perception. The type of information most frequently lacking is the comparable costs of various solutions to a given problem. Usually, it is neither compiled, nor kept up-dated. Especially when new processes and new methods are being tried out for the first time. New products, new processes and new materials are constantly entering the market. It is a difficult task to remain knowledgeable on all these changes. To investigate a number of different processes or materials, to look for standard parts, to compare costs, etc., need time (refer also item 3 following) — the lack of which breeds unnecessary costs. A reference to Fig. 9 and Fig. 10 will show the order of magnitude of costs for different surface finishes and tolerance limits. *"Lack of information and the relative costs thereof in these cases can add something like 25% to the cost of a component."**

One of the early jobs that Miles had undertaken was value study of Westinghouse Hot Point Refrigerator. On its Thermostat control, the wire clip to hold the cover was made of phosphor bronze, at a heavy cost for the component ($7,000 a year). The Designer had specified the best material for the part — non-corrosive, flexing without breakage, etc. But, had he the information that the clip needed to flex only an average 6 times in its life, he would not have specified phosphor bronze with the characteristic of flexing ten thousand times before breakage, for this component,

* Raven, p. 32

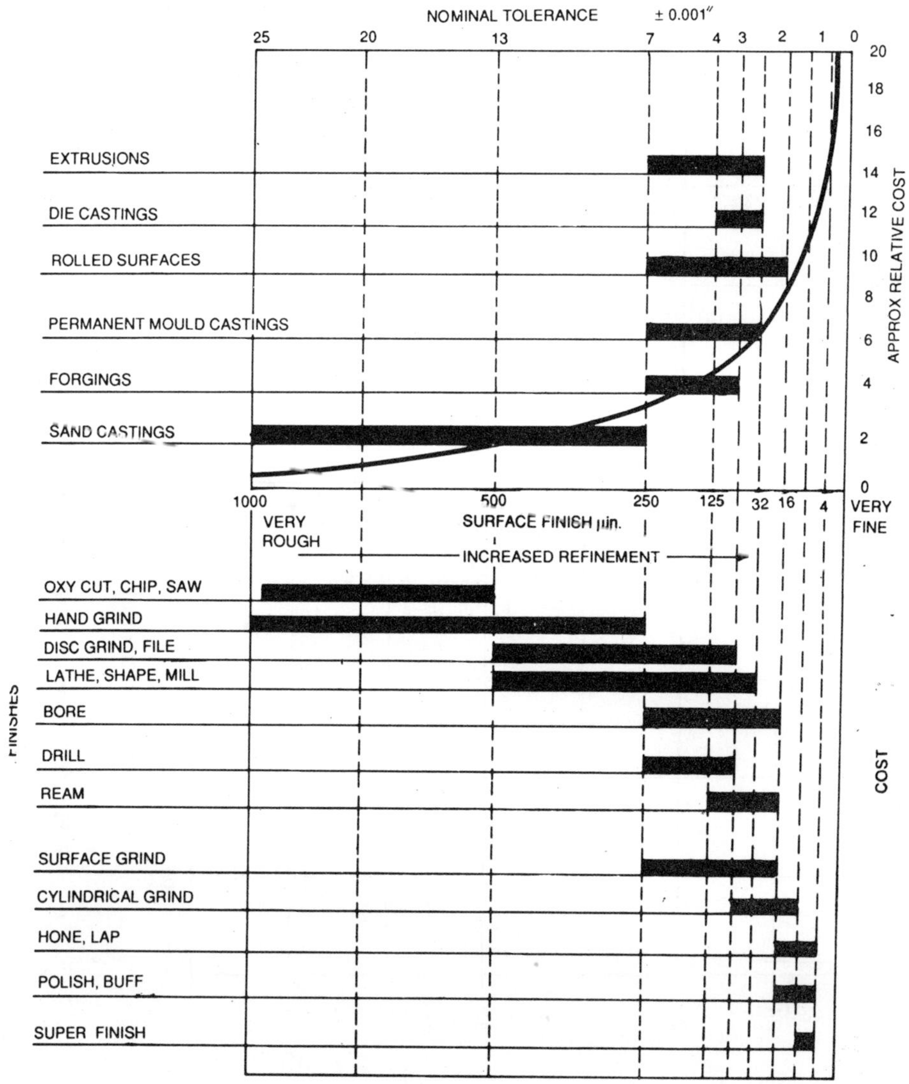

Fig. 9. Relationship Between Cost and Surface Finish

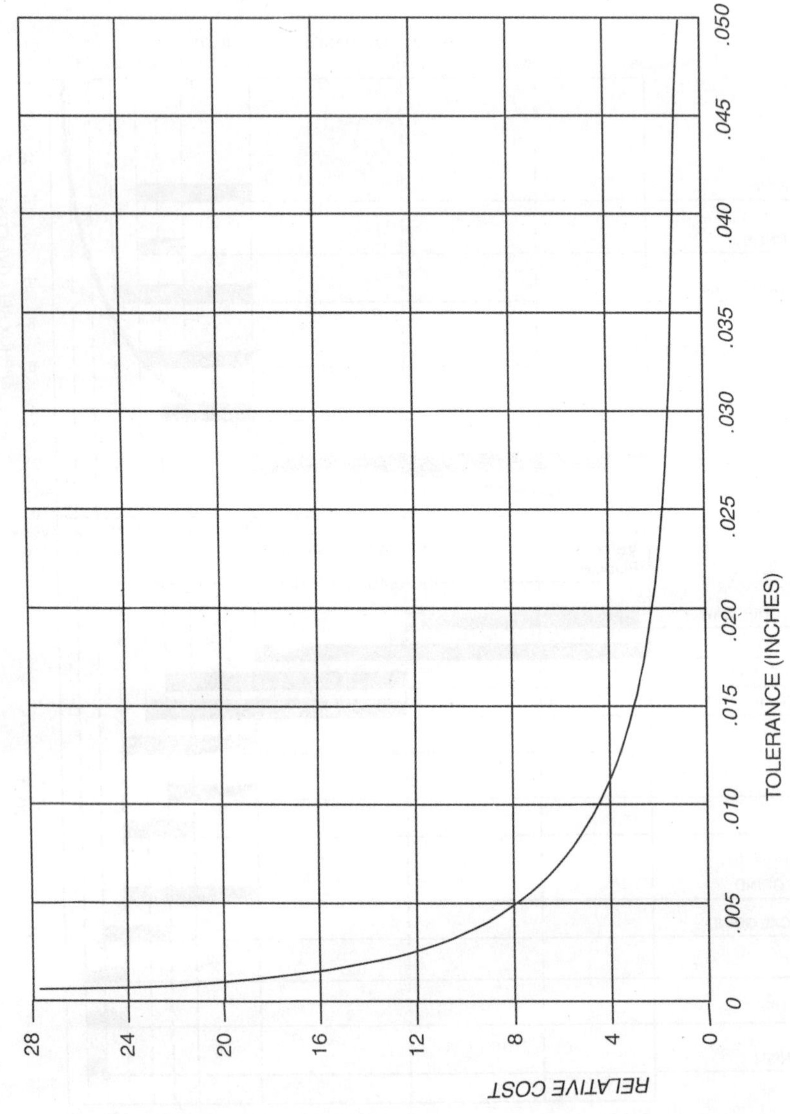

Fig. 10. Cost Comparison of Various Tolerances

(By changing to spring brass, the same job could be done for $3,000 a year).

Competition is a fact of life. Deregulation, globalization of trade and adoption of international standards opened unlimited opportunities for business and industries. They are now able to produce a variety of goods and services, with little to differentiate between them. That has shrunk today's competitive advantage to matters of knowledge and skill. For, it has become necessary not merely to find, but also invent, new competitive advantages. Therefore, knowing the competition is just as important as knowing the customer, or your product or service. Immediate competitor, distant competitor, current competitor, and potential competitor, others in the same line of business, any business whatsoever: there is no end to the coverage needed for information. A steel plant has to worry about not only other steel plants, but also aluminum plants, engineered plastics, etc. The need is to know not only others strengths and weaknesses, but more importantly, their objectives in technology leadership, strategies in costs, and response patterns. The goal is for one to deliver extra-ordinary levels of distinctive value, and more of it, as compared to the competitors.

The best way is to gather what information can be got and then act, or plan the action required. Telecommunications, micro electronics, fiber optics and information highways are being used in creative ways, to bring information age capabilities to everyone. It is possible now to simultaneously transmit voice, data, video and graphics over a single copper telephone wire, and soon, over fiber optic cable.

Vital information to modify the product or service to suit the customer comes from interaction among internal functions, external suppliers, distributors, and customers themselves.

Customers are on the move too. Their needs and tastes are changing. They seek greater variety and quality, durability, convenience and customized alternatives with special features suiting individual requirements. To remain responsive to their changing needs, to add customer friendly features, widespread availability of information is necessary. For effective, day-to-day, problem-solving, visual display of information speeds up dissemination and spurs action.

Knowing how to focus or re-focus information to improve performance is equally important. Few companies do. Too often their Managers are mired in the complexity of their tasks. They believe that every employee understands the basic building blocks of how their business works. Most do. However, many do not. They do not realize how important the fundamentals – cash, margin, velocity, improvement and growth – are. Unless, of course, the Manager explains them, in the context of the entire business–and, often. This is a cost-free opportunity for prospering, especially when the economy is in the doldrums.

To quote a Nigerian proverb, "not knowing is bad; not wanting to know is worse." How true!

2. LACK OF IDEAS

Reason, scant use and application of knowledge and skills, be it available in the organisation, outside the organisation, in standards, with specialists and professional forums. No one can think of everything. This makes creative ideas a rarity.

Piping in ships used to run overhead, around bulkheads and across the decks. At 30 knots, the pipes vibrate and rattle, with terrific noise, if they are not well secured. So, each support used to be moulded in plastic clay and then tailor-made in metal and bolted on different. A creative idea was to change to metal strapping and then tightening. (A saving of $ 200,000 per ship accrued.)

3. LACK OF TIME

When a prospectus is finally approved, there is always pressure to provide it as quickly as possible. Time is not available to make every study or comparison desired. There is a due date to deliver, staring at you.

The time pressure is so great that the Designer's prime objective becomes getting a solution off the board within the allocated time. His decision-making works on the principle of what Simon calls "satisficing," the search stopping when coming across the first solution that is good enough. He makes little effort to consider properly, if at all, the value of the design approach being developed, or to optimise the many possible solutions to a given design on the basis of cost. Seldom is there time to sit back and contemplate ideas, or to design or develop alternative approaches on solutions.

The first workable solution to the problem is accepted: it usually is the one which had succeeded in the past. The design proposed is either a scaled-up or scaled-down version of the successful predecessor. Naturally, it will be including the faults of the previous design, difficulties of assembly, high scrap rates, wrong choice of materials, its servicing difficulties, and so on.

Deadlines generally do not permit complete searching, testing, and seeing and utilising information which would enable accomplishing customer needs at the lowest cost — be it in design, engineering, purchasing or manufacturing. *"Lack of time aspect of unnecessary cost could add up to 15% or more of the ex-works cost of a product."**

* Raven, p. 36

4. LACK OF ATTENTION

The conventional approach is to accept that a certain amount of error is normal. For instance, you expect the plane or train to be late; the mail to go astray and not get delivered; the equipment would breakdown; etc. You expect things to go wrong all the time. This is all right for planning and estimating; but not for execution. Whereas, by paying serious attention to every detail, you can be prepared for every exigency, even for the most unlikely events. It is obsessive; but, at the final reckoning, you would be a winner, having thought of everything and being in complete control.

At Tokyo Railway Station, you can stand at a marked spot on the platform and when the train arrives, the doors will open right in front of you. Trains are on time. Bags are not lost. Connections are not missed. Here everything works, as the Japanese have paid, and continue to pay, attention to precision and detail. The clothier, Lands' End, remembers your last order, your family members' sizes, etc.

TV, riches to rags saga in USA, is another classic, but different type of example. There was a time when every TV manufacturer was US based. Every job for TV, from Research and Development and Design through manufacturing and marketing, was American. Nevertheless, no more. Reason: they targeted only American customers, offered others the same products designed for American customers, and failed to devote attention to modify the product and match the specific needs of overseas customers. To the list can be added left-handed drive cars, huge refrigerators, items made to BSS, exported from USA.

Conventional management routine includes spending time to check and control production plans, schedules and progress, maintenance and service, cost, and such like items. However, the agenda for any of the meetings, (at plant level, management level or board level), does not include checks and controls on the **value** of the product or service. Only revising the priorities can solve this lack of attention: showing that value is what the management is most concerned about. The message is on time spent (see also item 3, Lack of Time).

5. LACK OF LISTENING

Listening, like many things simple, is not so simple. It has five main objectives:

- as a practical means to gather information and applicable ideas;
- to keep in touch with several sources – employees, suppliers, distributors, customers, etc.
- to collect quickly all information, especially on things concerning the product or service that trouble the customers.

- to motivate everyone in the organization to correlate the information gathered with result-oriented opportunities;
- to share, and disseminate widely, ideas and information.

Effective listening is engaged listening. It means paying attention. The best way to do so is to use all listening techniques – listening systematically, listening carefully, listening for facts, listening for perceptions, listening naively, and so on.

Many do not listen. On the other hand, what starts out as listening often deteriorates to getting in touch with; then, making others understand; and ends up, talking, telling and educating. The fact is you never learn anything talking.

The more closely you looked, you will see more examples of senior executives failing to listen to their middle managers. Middle Managers are close to day-to-day operations, customers and front line employees. They are more diverse in functional area, work experience, geography, gender and ethnic background. Thus, they are fertile ground for creative ideas. However, for want of listening, good ideas routinely die before they even see the light of the day.

In listening studies, women used both the left (analytical) and right (feeling) sides of the brain. Men used the left side of the brain. Value management encourages use of both sides of the brain – the right, for blasting creative ideas and the left, for later judicial analysis.

Many simply assume that they know better than the customers, co-workers, etc. Whereas, most ideas are rooted in workers' practical needs, or in the minds of service people and customers, waiting for someone to listen. Most unsuccessful products are not technically deficient, but too much technology, at far too high a price. It is common to consider feed back from customers, service people and Sales as wish lists to make their lives easier. Functional barriers are too many. Successful companies had better, faster, inter-actions that create, make and market values.

Both Tom Peters, with his idea of *"managing by walking round"* and Rene McPherson, with his emphasis on *"managing from the bottom up"* base their approaches on true listening.

Melville Shoe, a small, undistinguished shoe chain of 1960s, became one of the fastest growing and most profitable fashion retailers in America, listening to customers and exploring their values.

6. LACK OF PROBLEM OWNERSHIP

The lack of problem ownership, particularly where job specialization is strict and severe, causes many problems (solvable in a very simple way), to stay unresolved. Often in situations, the employee would say, it is not his or her problem; let the other person fix it. In many cases, he or she would say what is being done wrong; he or she could show how to do it right. His or her excuse for not doing so: he or she would neither get credit; nor any monetary benefit; nor recognition.

An example from auto air conditioning. They should not be too noisy, as, otherwise, it would mar listening to the stereo. Quick cooling would require high-speed blowers. If the blower is too noisy, the Air conditioning Technician cannot say, "it is not my problem. I only want to cool the car." Similarly, the Audio Technician cannot say, "it is not my problem, my units are ok." Both have to look at the problem as the total system of the car and set it right.

Group Technology, practiced by some industries, has tried to overcome this problem. Each group completes all the tasks required to complete an item.

Semco, Brazil, is considered the best plant in that country. It is run on participatory management principles and profits are shared with the workers. They have no job descriptions. The shop floor level personnel are either Associates or Coordinators. Associates do research, design, sales and manufacturing. Coordinators lead teams and tasks. Most people can do several jobs. They take on more and more tasks, as needed – security, cleaning, driving vehicles, cooking food in the canteens, etc.

7. LACK OF EXPERIENCE

Often when we talk of 25 year's experience, it actually is one year's experience multiplied twentyfive times.

Real experience is a process of discovering and learning something new, which somehow leads to a growing cumulative capability. In this sense, even failures will add to one's storehouse of experience, if the venture was creative. When Du Pont was working on polymer chemistry, the aim was to manipulate the structure of large, organic molecules. But, one failure found the stuff in the kettle congealed into fibers — Nylon. A Chemist accidentally broke a bottle containing a liquid plastic substance and ushered in shatterproof glass, in another company.

8. POOR QUALITY

Quality has always been a criterion for value — be it in Defence, consumer products, or service. But, until recently, customers lacked the means to objectively evaluate product performance. Conditions have changed. Now, manufacturers have to contend with better educated customers and consumer advocate/protection groups, who assess global markets and rate product quality by relative comparison.

Without quality, there is no value. Quality adds value at each step of the product creation. It is something that has to be measured at the customers' end and not in the manufacturing plants. Quality is to be built during the production phase, and not by just eliminating what is not good. Many characteristics of unacceptable quality in manufacture are traceable to the absence of this approach in design and in the management of the business process. The least cost remedy lies before the fact, during design. However, it can also be had after the fact, during manufacture and service, though to a lesser degree of return.

Quality does not mean quality of the product and service alone. It means total quality. That is, it includes such items as quality of communication, quality of relationships, quality of guarantees, etc. Conformance to specifications is only the beginning. The real test of quality will be how the customer perceives the specifications and what it means to him to work with products and services conforming to those specifications. If there are no complaints on quality from the customers, it may not prove that the quality offered is the best. The customer may be living with the quality problems created by your product or service, and not complaining. Interaction with the customer will open out wide vista of quality improvement that are possible and desirable. Value can be added through appropriate, but small changes or improvements, costing little money — and many such. "Kaizen," as the Japanese say — and not "Kayo."

To improve quality while at the same time cutting costs is a big headache that few executives only find systematic methods to solve.

9. HONEST WRONG BELIEFS

Some decisions are based on erroneous beliefs, rather than on facts. A situation is often assumed to be impossible, for erroneous but sincere reasons. For example, Planners who make decisions on what a design should accomplish may not have properly gauged the public's needs. Designers who make decisions on what material, process, fastener, or factor of safety to use, may be biased against some specific items, because of one or more unfortunate experiences of failure (personal or from hearsay). Design decisions could be based on wrong beliefs. For example, spheroidal graphitic iron was considered too brittle; Electric Overhead Travelling Crane gear breakdown was attributed to poor hardness of the gear teeth. Half truths compound the problem.

A sound improvement may be abandoned, because it was thought it might cost too much. It could be due to either honest wrong belief or lack of time to check the costs. An equally sound reduction in cost could be turned down because it was thought it could hurt performance; again for similar reasons. Conversely, product worth is improved in the sincere belief that the added cost would be reasonable. And, the product cost is reduced with the fervent hope that the reduction would not lower the product worth. These are daily occurrences — but could be guarded against.

10. HABITUAL THINKING

Thinking and doing things in the same way is a frequent cause of poor value. Most people have a tendency to re-use what worked the last time or to copy a standard set by others. They duplicate a success, repeat a good experience and avoid a bad one. This is a defensive measure calculated to minimise risks, and is promoted by managements through rigid use of standards designs, set procedures, customs, traditions, etc., without consideration of changing needs or technology. Keeping updated with the state-of-the-art is essential in today's complex world.

11. RISK OF PERSONAL LOSS

Any good Engineer or Manager knows that nothing is FOR SURE.

But, they also know that anything that is done over and over again has less probability of failures as compared to something new and unknown. Failure of a new approach could cause personal loss of face to the suggester and/or decision-maker. People fear the consequent ridicule or humiliation.

12. RELUCTANCE TO SEEK ADVICE

Designers and Planners are often very reluctant to seek advice from others, as well as to admit that, may be, they don't know the answer. Architects, Planners and Engineers should seek the advice of competent experts if maximum design value is to be achieved, with the information-explosion reaching unprecedented limits.

13. HABITS AND ATTITUDES

"The deepest law of human nature is HABIT," wrote Carlyle. It *"works more constantly and with greater force than reason,"* remarks Locke, *"which is seldom fairly consulted and more rarely obeyed."*

Often the force of habit results in developing a pattern in thinking, doing things, solving problems, and so on.

Habit solutions are often obsolete solutions. No doubt, the advantages gained are speedier preparation of drawings and easier meeting of time schedules. However, the disadvantages are not immediately known, as the unnecessary cost that the habit solution breeds does not manifest until much later and is, often, unknown to the Designer.

Traditions and habits are hard to break. *"Habit is rigid, unbending, unchanging, ungiving, unyielding." "Knowledge,"* which *"is diametrically opposite, is fluid, always changing and always growing."** Habits are what we use to build basic skills, and, so, many are beneficial. What are disadvantageous are habits supported by attitudes and becoming road blocks.

The attitude you have is yours by choice, whether it is positive or negative. You control your attitude. With a positive attitude, you will get positive results and develop the habit of searching for alternatives and possibilities. With a negative attitude, on the other hand, you will get negative results and develop a habit of blocking alternatives. Attitudes play a big part in our decision-making process. They are tough and difficult to change. During our progression in life, we develop an attitude screen. At birth our attitude screens are clear. As years go by, clouds begin to develop within the attitude screen, tempered by experience.

Some people become reluctant to change of any kind regardless of the merits of the proposal, especially if the change directly affects their plan or design. Perhaps it is the natural fear of the unknown; but more often than not, the point is over-stretched for the slightest excuse. Some others feel that they, and only they, always provide for the best in their approaches. Over the years, this feeling cumulates to form a negative attitude of resistance to change.

Charles Kittering once stated that nine hundred and ninety nine people out of a thousand, when presented with a new idea, will immediately give the proposer all the reasons why it shouldn't work. The sole exception will give reasons why he thinks it would work.

14. UNREALISTIC "REQUIREMENTS"

Requirements are often unrealistically specified or grossly overstated with reference to performance, materials, safety, or procedures. People like to "play safe." Sometimes requirements are assumed by the Planner or Designer when none are specifically indicated. Traditionally, Designers have concentrated on development of reliable systems exceeding all known and assumed requirements. The net result is over-design, with attendant excess cost. Requirements are not usually challenged to determine actual needs.

15. CHANGED CIRCUMSTANCES

When pressed for a decision, we take to a temporary expedient, fondly

---

* Zimmerman and Hart, p. 20

hoping to get back to it later and make a review. Only, this getting back to a review seldom happens. For example, in a Steel Mill, the electric overhead travelling crane, the principal material handling equipment, is given in service during an emergency short circuiting a relay, to avoid the down time to replace it, when the Mill is on a production drive. It is more likely that the crane would continue to be in operation for a long time thereafter without a scheduled shut down to effect the replacement. Similarly, a cable fault is solved drawing in parallel a temporary new line. The likelihood is that the new line stays permanant thereafter.

A customer may no longer require all the features of the product originally specified. Certain operations, finishes or tolerances may have been added to correct a temporary situation or an emergency. The emergency may have disappeared, but the operations are continued. For example, a forging may have been specified for a crane shaft, which necessitates certain amount of machining to finish. With the development in rolling practices, it could have been changed to rolled round, but missed as far as correcting the drawing or specification. Result, continued procurement of rolled round with surface machining. Or, when in an emergency, to offset die wear, certain machining operations could have been specified to remove excess material and to maintain surface finish. Even after change of die, the machining could be continuing unaltered.

The areas of unnecessary costs caused by temporary circumstances are painfully obvious, but only after they are revealed.

It is surprising how difficult it is to discern these situations from an apparently innocent looking piece of equipment or part. Under normal conditions, anyone very familiar with the item, would not be able to detach himself from the problem to discover these inconsistencies.

Beware of temporary solutions. They tend to become permanent.

16. CHANGING TECHNOLOGY

Once every century or so, the way of making things changes with a sweeping flourish. Developments of processes, products and materials make available constantly changing and many times lower cost ways of performing the necessary functions. Right now, the world is on the cusp of the next such major reformation, which will make yet another addition to the list of developments. Therefore, it should be no surprise that an individual finds it difficult to keep up, be completely current, even in his own field of specialisation.

When a revolutionary new technology arrives, it will be wise to scrap the old. If this is not possible, at least, we should spot when the outer performance limits of a successful product have been reached and then abandon it at that point.

17. POOR COMMUNICATIONS

Lack of good communications, mis-understanding, jealousy and normal friction between human beings are frequent sources of unncessary costs. Mis-communication results in others interpreting it as they desire; or assuming that they have understood.

An average Manager spends *"9% of his time writing, 16% in reading, 30% talking, 35% listening and the rest (10%) on other activities."** It should be obvious that faulty communication is not only expensive, but also time-consuming. They surely are a major source of poor actions and wrong decisions and, so, poor value.

18. PREJUDICE

Everyone is prejudiced in some way or the other. Prejudice influences opinions and attitudes — against a material, a certain method, a process, a person or an idea.

For years, the Indian Railways used to specify high grade Acid Steel for their axles. This steel had to be made in Acid Bessemer, Basic Open Hearth and Acid Open Hearth combination, in accordance with the best modern principles of steel making. Simultaneously, the Railways were using the less expensive, less time consuming Basic Steel for their wheels. They were prejudiced against the process of making steel by blowing air through molten pig iron for causing rapid oxidation of metallics: the Bessemer Convertor. Therefore the insistence on high grade Acid Steel for axles. It took quite some research, development, experimentation and negotiations (involving considerable time and money) before a change could be made to use Basic Steel for axles also.

19. MISCONCEPTIONS

All of us have misconceptions: but they may be few or many, depending on our alertness or lack of it, to assimilate new developments as they occur and correct our earlier experience.

Iron ships were thought to sink in water because of their weight: they would not float. They would damage more than wooden ships when grounded. Besides, they would be difficult to protect from rust. The navigational aid, the compass, would be deflected by the steel, making it impossible for navigation.

Another example: for years steel was considered the only strong reinforcement, until polymers of equal strength were developed.

---

* Mudge, p. 10

20. DESIRE TO CONFORM

Normal industry work and day-to-day duties involve conformance to practices, procedures and policies. Conformity stems from the fear of the unknown. A known devil is better than the unknown friend; so, conform. Non-conformity, both intellectually and personally, appears to be a central characteristic of high creatives.

21. POOR INTERACTION AMONG CONTRIBUTING DISCIPLINES

Traditionally, companies specialize in their industry and individuals, in their careers. To achieve right results to a given purpose (product or production), specific responsibilities are assigned to specialist professionals: like, production, materials, finance, engineering, markets, personnel, etc. They are set into conflicted work units or organizational blocks. This block concept is so deeply rooted that each specialist and his department then endeavor to take responsibility for that area alone. They work at legitimate cross-purposes, governed by self-interest and own sub-goals. For example, the Designer, equating his best performance to engineering excellence in terms of materials, precision in manufacture, performance, strength and reliability, would tend to make the product stronger, larger and heavier than necessary; and, consequently, costlier. He does not look at the design from the standpoint of the production work. The proposed design could be beyond the capacity and capability of existing equipment, process and skills. The Production Manager, in his zeal to maximize efficiency, would avoid idling of men and machinery, and wastage of material and minutes (time). He would favor fewer models, longer production runs, minimum and simpler set-ups, etc. to keep his cost low. It may not be the optimum combination or cost to produce, or the source of excellent opportunities for selling. The Materials Manager, seeing his job as getting the best material at the lowest price and best delivery from the registered suppliers, would not exploit to advantage equally good or better alternatives in specification or supplier. He would like to place larger orders to get price discounts and save on replenishment costs; and incur increased inventory cost. The sales would give away discounts and promise ex-stock deliveries to fatten their order books. These affect adversely cost of production, work schedule and even quality (while rushing orders through the system), to redeem their promises. Traditionally, each specialist would pursue his sub goal with ardor, but the sum total of all such pursuits may not, and need not, add up to the goals and expectations of the organization: customers' value.

Their approaches may not be in synergy. Each department works on its own logic and wants to protect that logic. For example, Research may wish to develop the best-engineered products; but those products may not sell at that high quality level and prices. The Materials manager may look for "the lowest price" for "good enough supplies," to specification; but Production would have problems to manufacture with them; or the customers, to maintain. Transportation may like rail over air as the lower-cost shipping mode; but, the customers will be forced to wait longer for the items. Marketing may hold something the customers would not like. The Divisional Head, at the middle level, would look for "profitable solutions to a cost problem or a revenue generating opportunity." Top management would be less interested in solutions to problems than profits it can add or the improvement in productivity of corporate assets that it will permit. Accounts would press for reduction in support services or substitution of a lower cost ingredient "to save on costs." Which, the Sales, Production and Quality Control may see as "leading to more operation/repair problems" and "increasing customer discontent".

Their performance measures may not be aligned. Planning may emphasize growth; budgeting, earnings; and incentives, production. Their priorities may differ. One month production, another quality, next on labor saving or inventory control. Coupled with constraints like time horizons, uncertainty and limited resources, these tend to dilute focus.

Their satisfaction measures may differ. Employees would demand higher wages and perquisites; Customers would look for lower prices; shareholders would ask for higher prices.

Possessing advanced skills and spending their entire career with own specialty, they tend to develop sub-goals devoted to their specialties. They may lack system understanding. They do not appreciate enough the subtleties of other jobs; nor readily see the inter-dependencies. They may not know either the people or their problems to help others. A major process would involve several departments and professional specialists. If they do not work towards a common goal, precious time would be lost. Acts of omissions and commissions abound. Cooperation and coordination between specialties, if any exist, are only in a distant and formal manner. Mistrust, withholding of information, defensive communication and unwillingness to change are common.

Sharing information is considered an affront to their expertise. Result, decisions, which could have been easily made, postponed. Because somebody thought that somebody else could not comply. Or, what could have been done; what could have been done easily; what was the obvious thing to do; was not done. On the other hand, Ford has one of the most successful, tried-and-proven schemes for knowledge sharing, called Best Practices Replication Process. In almost 5 years, more than 2,800 proven superior practices have been shared across Ford's manufacturing operations. It has netted a billion-dollar benefit for the auto maker. Royal Dutch/Shell and Nabisco have licensed the process.

* Miles, p. 6

As the market grows, companies try to satisfy every single customer (user) through the same product or service, adding progressively feature after feature, to become multi-purpose performer. In the process, they maximize what the product can do, rather than optimize for meeting a specific customer request. Simultaneously, the product or service costs more, becomes hard to use, maintain, repair and service-loss in value.

Larger the organization, more complex it becomes; one part undoing what another part is doing. Contributing disciplines work without common direction, setting priorities to suit expediency, consuming resources (sometimes at the cost of others) and becoming mutually incompatible over a range of work and non-work related issues.

22. COMFORTABLE HIGH COST ACTIVITIES

When some activities that go on well have remained in vogue for a long time, they become established as part of the organization. Especially, if they intrinsically cost not too much. Nobody wants to, or has the time to, bother with them. Consequently, even if there are equivalent lower cost activities, they are not replaced. The unnecessary costs continue year after year.

23. CREEP

As the company ages, creep sets in. The company could become involved in several businesses, not originally planned to be in. The company could be making, in-house, many items, which were originally not available in the market. Currently, they may have become common items, and, at lower costs. Age old, obsolete machinery, may be producing items "temporarily." Similar temporary changes made to solve some exigencies, or special needs, may have tightened specifications; and come to stay. Change in the normal operating procedures, made as temporary expedients, coupled with loose planning and/or lack of proper controls, cause creep to become permanent. Even, some side activities, or departments, edge into the main business, with consequent long-range effects. Looking closely into creep discloses operations, which should be outsourced.

Creep in product features and product cost occurs when designers and approving authorities add something so that the product will be so much better or safer (and cost only a little more). Or, when the fits are tightened a little bit, to err on the safe side.

24. NON-VALUE—ADDING WORK

Just less than half the time spent on traditional design work is actually non – value – adding, as the work itself is caused by engineering changes. Parts are, on an average, designed twice: once, as an initial release and second time, as a changed design. The changes usually snow ball. Yet, most are unnecessary. Recently, McKinsey analyzed and found two thirds, in a company unnecessary.

Poor procedures add up in cost. The number of approvals needed on documents would bear re-study and would be profitable. GE once did a post-mortem on a sampling of big mistakes. The review found that not one of them would have been prevented by an extra managerial signature.

Proverbial non-value—adding work, leading to high costs, are in the Defense Services. Last year, Pentagon spent $ 409 on a sink that should have cost only $ 39. There were numerous other over priced items, like electric bells, springs, screws, screw thread inserts, etc.

Because cross company processes are not coordinated, a vast number of activities end up being duplicated. Same information is entered repeatedly into systems, same forms filled out and passed around many times, same checks, verifications and approvals, done over and over again, etc. This leads to inconsistencies, errors, misunderstandings, and wasted effort.

25. WASTE

During the last two centuries, vigorous industrialization vastly enriched our world. However, in doing so, it also produced a rising tide of scrap, discards and waste. As everything created must go somewhere, industry's traditional response was to recycle to the extent possible and dispose of the rest by incineration or releases into the atmosphere. They relied on waste disposal technologies, end-of-pipe controls, recycling and reuse, as well as redesigning products to make them easier to reuse, recycle or incinerate. Good enough so far, but of poor value, today. 'Environmental protection has supplanted 'cleanliness' and value has shifted to 'industrial ecology'.

Common practice is to find use for the bye products. Air pollution equipment produce powdery residue of calcium sulphate and fly ash. The former can find use vice gypsum in wall boards. Fly ash is used in concrete. Similarly boiler slag is used for abrasives. Beyond it, industry is now beginning to find that it makes sense to pass energy, waste water and some products back and forth between a number of plants (Kalundborg, Denmark); design products that are eco-friendly, and so on. Value has shifted to elimination of releases that are hazardous and pollutants.

The notion that environment is just an expensive cost is out of date. Value based action proves that risking environmental benefits can be also profitable. Starbucks, the coffee par excellence, are growing coffee plants under a forest canopy (and not in open ground), saving trees that would normally be cut and preventing rain forest carnage. The coffee beans so grown add to quality of the beverage. Nova Chemicals set aside 11.5 acres out of its 60 acre plot, for a habitat for migratory birds. The one time cost is about $ 8,000 to plant 24 species of trees and fruit bearing shrubs. The unanticipated savings, in not mowing those 11.5 acres, is $ 16,000.

Returns have become an inevitable nuisance, especially with the growth in e-commerce. On an average 6 % of retail sales are returned by American customers, per year. The lowest is 2 % for automobile parts; and the highest, 40 % for women's apparel. In the past, it was enough for the return centers to recycle them, to salvage, repair and re-use to the maximum extent possible. Additional value is found by some by selling in outlet centers or abroad or by re-boxing them for the next season or sale theme. However, now value here has shifted to cost prevention – by providing testing and analysis to determine why the product has a high rate of return.

Estimates vary on what money is wasted buying unnecessary insurance. Such wastage can occur in two ways – paying too much; and buying policies that are not needed. Because of unrealistic fears and inadvertent duplication of what is already covered unwanted policies are purchased..

HOW TO BUILD OR ADD VALUE

Every cause of poor value that has been discussed in the foregoing provides an opportunity for solution and an area for efforts to build or add value. The Value Engineering methodology covers all the causes and indicates the way the efforts are to be canalised for achieving results. It secures addition to value by:

1. Accomplishing equivalent or better performance at same or lower costs i.e., upgrading product performance.
2. Providing the shape, appearance, attractiveness and the features the customer wants — i.e., improving product esteem.
3. Holding (or raising) quality at reduced (or same) costs or both.
4. Identifying, isolating and removing unnecessary costs and non-essential elements from the products and services — i.e., cost prevention or cost avoidance, in addition to cost reduction.
5. Exploiting the technological development, the expanding knowledge and the creation of "new" items — in short all the current changes — to advantage, i.e., innovation and creativity.
6. Preventing the unnecessary use of resources. It is a fallacy to think that one should outspend competition to gain comparable or better results. Resources, through their concentrated application, accumulation, combination, conservation, re-use and rapid recovery, can be made to yield better return.

7. Controlling Value-to-Price Ratios. Finding the break even points for cost, quality, reliability, etc., and providing just right and nothing more. Beyond this point, the added costs, quality, reliability, etc., will begin to unbalance the Value-to-Price relationship.

8. Making yourself partner material for your customer. Expanding customers' gains (by displacing, constraining or reducing his variable costs), revenue (by high volume), earnings (improving margins by adding new features and benefits to their products, services or systems), or market share (adding to productivity, contributing realised values that confer competitive advantage).

It is fundamental that *"an acceptable product must serve the customers' needs and wishes to the degree that he or she expects."* Miles terms this PERFORMANCE CAPABILITY. Performance is the specific combination of FUNCTIONAL abilities and properties that make it suitable (and saleable) for a specific purpose. Appropriate performance requires that the product (or service) have a pre-determined level of quality, reliability, durability, inter-changeability, appearance and maintainability; and that it satisfy all of these requirements of that level at a reasonable cost. For a desired function there could be several combinations of design concept, material, product and process, or multiple solutions; each with its cost characteristics. The choices are very many as will be seen from Fig. 11.

Analyse the item you have (or the proposal) and find out what functions are being satisfied. Generate multiple solutions to satisfy them. Then you can choose how to derive equivalent performance, note what the costs will be, what changes — minor or major — will be required, and take appropriate decisions. Fig. 11 shows the range of possibilities.

Just as function is thus analysed, the quality aspect can also be similarly studied.

Process for making the part depends primarily on the shape. Basic shapes of metal parts can be grouped into a few categories for which processes for size limitations, material, surface finish, and cost can be compiled. Using such guide charts, applicable alternative processes can be read and the final selection made. Additional data and updating are important to ensure that the guide does not become obsolete.

Unnecessary costs are those *"that provide neither quality, nor use, nor life, nor appearance, nor customer features."** As proven by Miles, it varies from 25% to 75% of the cost of a product. Though large, it is difficult to identify, isolate and/or reduce it, if not totally eliminate it. It is more likely to be hidden. So, it has to be searched out and found.

---

* Miles, p. 6

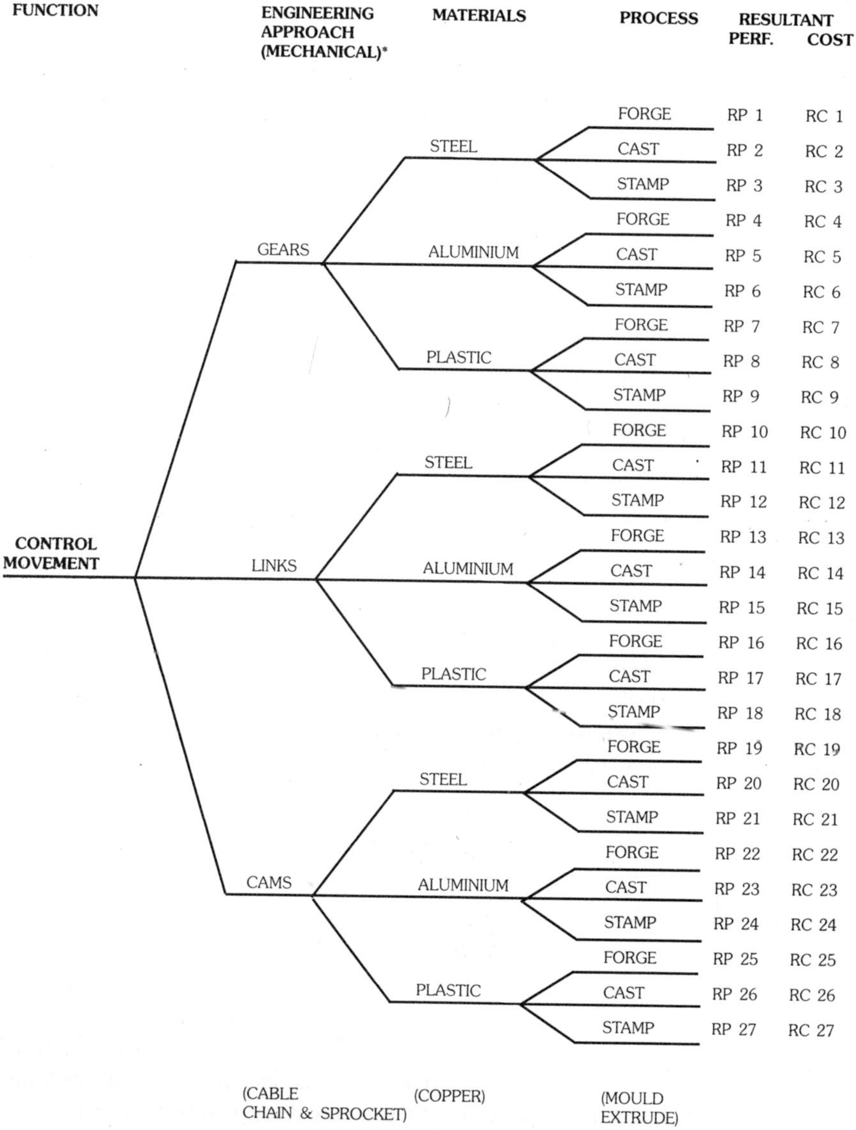

Note: No. of choices–3^n

* Additional choices are shown in paranthesis.

Fig. 11.

Unnecessary and hidden costs can be due to at least nine identifiable reasons, as we have already seen:

1. Lack of information
2. Lack of creative ideas
3. Lack of time
4. Honest wrong beliefs
5. Habits, attitudes and prejudices
6. Temporary circumstances
7. Poor communication
8. One solution fixation
9. Non-value-adding work.

The first four are causative. The rest compound the problem.

It is but common, in industrial situations to make decisions without sufficient information — be it due to nonavailability, lack of knowledge of its existence, lack of knowledge of how to obtain it, lack of means to accumulate, sort, select, store and retrieve it, or lack of time to collect it. Additionally, available information may not be updated either. Also, temporary circumstances may cause or force a decision for expediency's sake, irrespective of data or not.

We seldom realise how much of our active life is controlled by habit. To break work habits, we have to be understanding, patient, but firm and persevering.

Waste is comparatively easily recognized, but non-value-adding work is more difficult to identify. A set of principles, laid down two hundred years back, has shaped, and continues to shape, the structure, management and performance of industries. Conventional processes are replete with fragmentation of tasks, re-work and iteration, checking and control steps, etc., all adding no value; but are included because of tradition, mistrust, inadequate feed back and to prevent wrong things from happening. Extensive information exchange, data redundancy and re-keying are a natural outcome of fragmentation of work. All these take time, effort, labour and money to do, but do not contribute value to the product or service or the customer. It should be the aim to enhance those things that bring value and change or eliminate those that do not.

The ultimate aim is the maximation of end item value through the control of USE VALUE, ESTEEM VALUE, COST VALUE; and the elimination of costs associated with any other value not related to performance of the needed function(s). As we have seen in the previous chapter, value can be improved by reducing or eliminating unnecessary costs, which is one way. Another way is to review the functions themselves. Hereagain, as we will see in a later Chapter, every item has a Basic Function and a number of Secondary or Support Functions. In the Secondary or Support Functions lie a significant potential for improvement, in terms of costs, choice of the Secondary or Support Function itself and its numbers. Ideally, in the best value solution, there should be no Secondary or Support Functions. However, this is not practical. So, the next best alternative is to restrict the Secondary or Support Functions to the minimum, both number-wise and cost-wise.

A trained full-time Value Specialist, using the established techniques and following the Value Engineering Job Plan can (and can alone easily) eliminate all types of unnecessary and hidden costs, not normally identified and isolated by other methods.

TRAINING

Training of value specialists is necessary for them to be able to apply the technique of **Value Engineering** efficiently, effectively and well.

Training is also recommended for all managers, decision-makers and key personnel, for them to perform their jobs well when included as Team Leaders and Team Members.

It would be in the interest of the company to train everyone, so that they could apply the technique as a way of life, on all jobs. For, the ultimate objective, if attainable, is to have all members of the organization applying the technique on their jobs as routine. It is to help them think value, innovate value and ensure value in all that they do.

Origin and History of Value Engineering Technology

Origin of Value Engineering Technology, as we know it today, can be traced back to the World War II efforts to maintain and increase production of all items against scarcity of traditional strategic inputs. It was a survival period when some critical materials were difficult to obtain. Shortages forced a great many subsitutions of materials. Such substitution, while it ensured availability, also reduced costs, satisfied requirements and in many cases, improved the products and their performance. Conclusion: a well organised study of alternative materials, processes, procedures, and the like, could produce cost and quality improvements that were hitherto overlooked.

Mr. Henry Erlicher, Vice President, Purchasing, in General Electric Company, USA, observed that an organised approach could make this phenomenon of improvements occur on purpose, instead of by chance and emergent compulsions. He assigned Mr. Lawrence D. Miles, a Purchasing Agent, with both Engineering and Education degrees, to undertake this study. Result: the methodology and technique called VALUE ANALYSIS.

MILESTONES

1947	Value Analysis Programme formally ushered in at General Electric Company, USA. A one-man operation under Mr. Miles.
1952	Mr. Miles conducted the first Value Analysis Workshop Seminar. It was considered Company confidential.
1954	US Navy Bureau of Ships adopted this concept to cost improvement during design in their organisation under the name VALUE ENGINEERING.
1956	Watervliet Arsenal, under US Army Ordnance Corps initiated a Value Engineering program.

1958 Mr. Miles was awarded the US Navy's highest civilian honour, the Navy Distinguished Public Service Award, for his assistance to the Bureau of Ships in Value Engineering.

1959 American Machinist Special Report No. 475, dated July 13 — Success story at G.E.

SOCIETY OF AMERICAN VALUE ENGINEERS (SAVE) was founded in Washington D.C., USA, to unite all practitioners and promote the growth of the profession.

1961 Value Engineering contract clauses were established in US Armed Services Procurement Regulations (ASPR), permitting contractor incentive sharing in Value Engineering contract cost reductions.

1962 US Department of Defense made Value Engineering contract incentive clause a pre-requisite for all procurement contracts in excess of $ 100,000.

Value Engineering Ltd., founded in London.

1963 US Navy Bureau of Yards and Docks began applying Value Engineering incentive clause in their contracts.

1964 US Army Corps of Engineers Value Engineering programme started.

1965 Society of Japanese Value Engineers (SJVE) formed as a voluntary Society.

Value Engineering Pty. Co. formed in Australia.

1966 Fifth Annual Convention of SAVE. Affiliation of Societies outside USA and international affiliation of SJVE.

Secretary of Defense hires first Senior Value Engineer to head a program — Mr. Rudy Kempter.

1967 Working Committees were started in:

Canada — Canadian Society of Value Engineering.

Scotland — Scottish Association of Value Engineering

	Norway Denmark Sweden] Scandinavian Association of Value Engineering
	South Africa — Value Engineering Management Society of Africa.
	VE introduced by the Chinese Productivity Council.
	Twentieth Anniversary National Convention and Seventh Annual Conference of SAVE held in Chicago, III., USA.
1969	US National Aeronautics and Space Administration, Office of Facilities, began conducting Value Engineering studies and training.
1970	General Services Administration (GSA) began its Building Contractor Value Engineering program.
1973	SAVE launched a programme to recognise as CERTIFIED VALUE SPECIALISTS (CVS) those individuals who have attained specified levels of proficiency in professional use of Value Engineering. Federal Government of USA immediately accepted it as a measure of competence to render Value Engineering services in USA.
	VE introduced by CPC.
1977	The Indian Value Engineering Society (INVEST) was founded in October. First National Conference held in New Delhi.
1978	China forms Shanghai Value Engineering Society (SVES).
1980	Government of Japan (MITI) accredits SJVE as independent incorporated society.
	First International Seminar on Value Engineering for Developing Countries held at National Metallurgical Laboratory, Jamshedpur, on June 2-4, under the aegies of Jamshedpur Productivity Council.
1981	Second INVEST National Conference, New Delhi.
1982	Third INVEST National Conference, Bangalore.
	Invest Eastern Zonal Chapter inaugurated, at Jamshedpur.

1983	Society of Japanese Value Engineering honors Miles by establishing two awards — the Miles Award, Department and the Miles Award, Corporate, for outstanding Value Engineering work.
	Fourth INVEST National Conference, New Delhi.
	INVEST Andhra Pradesh State Chapter inaugurated.
	Korea started SKVE.
1984	Twentyfifth Anniversary of SAVE, Sacremanto, CA, USA, attend by the author.
	Fifth INVEST National Conference, New Delhi.
1985	Sixth INVEST National Conference, Jamshedpur.
1986	General Directorate of Military Works, Saudi Arabia establishes Value Engineering Programme.
	Association Francaise pour l' Analyse de la Valeur (AFAV) convenes Fourth International Conference in Value Engineering in Paris.
	The Society of Indian Value Management (SIVAM) founded in Bangalore.
1987	First International Congress on Value Analysis, Milano, Italy.
1988	Pacific Basin Value Engineering Conference, Honolulu, Hawai.
1989	SIVAM convenes First Value Engineering Conference, Bangalore.
1990	Seventh INVEST National Conference, New Delhi.
	Commonwealth of Virginia, USA, on July 1, 1990, became the first State in USA to require Value Engineering during design on all highway projects over $ 2 million.
	The first European Conference on Value Management held in Paris, attended by representatives of AIAV, Italy; AFAV, France; APAP, Portugal; AVD, Belgium; ZWA, Austria; and ZWA, Federal Republic of Germany.
1991	Eighth INVEST National Conference, Bombay.
	VE practiced in Taipai.
1992	World Federation of Value Societies, formed.

1993	President S. Korea mandated use of VE in industries.
1995	First VE workshop conducted for Aircraft Industries in Taiwan.
1996	Name changed to SAVE International: the Value Society.

At the beginning of the 1970s, Russian enterprises did not practice value analysis. But, this soon changed when value analysis became mandatory under the Soviet Centrally Planned System. Ministries within the government implemented value analysis. There was a boom in interest in 1982, when the supreme ruling body made it mandatory for all economic bodies. The crisis in 1990, led to the formation of the society of Russian Value Analysts.

Value Engineering has come a long way since Miles first propounded the concept and organised its methodology. The technique was originally applied quite successfully on engineering items — i.e., small components and assemblies. That was where it took roots. However, such was the measure of success that accrued from its use that it quickly crossed all bounds. Today, it has emerged as the most potent, most effective, modern management technique, successfully applied to any ECONOMIC ACTIVITY — in trade, industry, commerce, education, transport, civic administration, health care, hospitals, police work, government, etc; to any LEVEL OF WORK — at the shop-floor, department, executive offices, corporate headquarters; to any PRODUCT OR SERVICE — be it tiny or massive, simple or complex, custom-built or mass-produced; to any JOB — planning, design, construction, operation, production, maintenance, service, administration; to any PROCESS, PROCEDURE or PRACTICE; and in any COUNTRY — USA, UK, EUROPE, RUSSIA, AUSTRALIA, SCANDINAVIA, MIDDLE EAST, SOUTH AFRICA, BELGIUM, GERMANY, FRANCE, ITALY, ISRAEL, PAKISTAN, PORTUGAL, HUNGARY, BRAZIL, KOREA, HONGKONG, SAUDI ARABIA and JAPAN, besides INDIA.

THE SOCIETY OF AMERICAN VALUE ENGINEERS (SAVE)

The Society of American Value Engineers, acronym SAVE, is a professional technical society, dedicated to the advancement of Value Engineering through a better understanding of the principles, methods and concepts involved in value technology. A small group of early enthusiasts recognised the need to organise to develop and improve communications among themselves and to obtain recognition to spread the concept to others. Thus was born the Society of American Value Engineers, at Smyrna, Georgia, USA. It was incorporated on October 22, 1959. Name changed to SAVE International, the Value Society.

Charter membership cards were issued to 20 people on March 1, 1960. Mr. L.D. Miles was elected first President of SAVE, on December 5, 1960. It has membership, today, of international affiliates, institutions, corporate bodies, and over 1,208 individuals, spread over 35 Chapters in USA, 8 international affiliates and a number of foreign countries. The membership of SAVE is widely diverse, consisting of Educators, Executives, Scientists, Lawyers, Managers, Doctors, Contract Administrators, Engineers, Designers, Businessmen, Manufacturers and Salesmen. All who share a common interest in improving the value of products and services are admitted.

Key membership benefits include Certification with SAVE's Certification programme, which is respected, and often required by employers; opportunities to participate in SAVE Seminars, Workshops, Conventions, and meetings to keep one abreast of trends and developments within the Value Engineering community; help to develop business opportunities; getting and giving advice on national and inter-national levels; exchange of ideas and information related to Value Engineering; publications at discounted prices; and so on.

In 1973, SAVE launched a programme to recognise as CERTIFIED VALUE SPECIALISTS (CVS), those individuals who have attained specific levels of professional competence. The objective of the certification programme is to ensure individual ability and create professionalism in the field of Value Engineering by establishing the range and depth of application of the concept, uniformity in the technique and methodology, continuing advancement and education, as well as attesting the proficiency in complying with certification standards. This certificate was immediately recognised by the Federal Government of USA as a measure to render VE service. Today, this certificate is recognised all over the world. Three grades of Specialists are certified: CVS, AVS and VMP. There are 423 current active Certified Value Specialists (CVS), 19 current Associate Value Specialists (AVS), and 11 Value Methodology Practitioners (VMP).

The SAVE CVS Certification Board examines the qualifications and experience of people seeking certification, holds periodic examinations and issues certificates to Value Engineers, valid for four years, and renewable thereafter by recertification. The Board has also approved organisations like the Japanese Society of Value Engineering (SJVE), the South Korean Society of Value Engineering (SKVE) and the Indian Value Engineering Society (INVEST) to administer under licence the certification programmes. Those who are active in value work and have taken the SAVE approved MOD. I Workshop and MOD. II Advanced Seminar are qualified to apply for certification.

Value Engineering

Value Analysis, Value Engineering, Value Management, Value Control, Value Assurance, call it by any name, it is a highly potent and powerful management technique created to effect IMPROVEMENTS.

Improvements from what it was hithertofore to what it should be. Improvements in design, performance, life, producibility, maintainability, service and warranty. Improvements in size, shape, features, style, appearance, characteristics. Improvements in quality, reliability, quality-reliability, quality per cost. Improvements in cost of production, use, maintenance, and ownership. Improvements of all kinds, all types, in all areas, and on all facets. Continuous and continuing improvements.

Its core is the value concept: that an item is intented for a purpose (called FUNCTION), the user or the customer buys it for this purpose, and it is of value for him if it accomplishes the purpose efficiently, effectively, and well, at the lowest cost.

It is the belief and conviction that there is a better way to do anything: its mission is therefore, finding it. Its work is a systematic approach, comprising a number of techniques: some old, some modified, and some new. Its aim is the greatest value return for the money spent. It ensures this by supervising for value at all stages — design, specification, manufacturing, purchase, packaging, transportation, sales, servicing, etc. It analyses the function of the product, service or system, with the purpose of achieving the required functions at the lowest costs, consistent with the requirements which comprise its value — such as performance, life, reliability, usability, quality, maintainability, salability, appearance, etc. It ensures that every feature, tolerance, allowance, fit, finish, treatment, piece of material or part of the service is vetted to see that none of them is adding to the total cost without serving a necessary purpose.

It increases the value of the item through making functional improvements, stimulated by creative ideas. It enables determination of how the part could be made at lower cost, without sacrificing essential attributes and performance. It ensures examination from the stand point of functions, allowing the decision-maker to decide which function the user really wants — which is basic or almost so — and which he or she can do without. It is a tool for making intelligent choices.

Lawrence Delos Miles, the founder of Value Engineering, wrote in his book — "*Value Analysis,* (as he then christened his methodology), *is a problem-solving system implemented by the use of a specific set of techniques, a body of knowledge, and a group of learned skills. It is an organized creative approach that has for its purpose the efficient identification of unnecessary cost: i.e., cost that provides neither quality, nor use, nor life, nor appearance, nor customer features.*"**

The Society of American Value Engineers define Value Engineering as *"the systematic application of recognised techniques which identify the function of a product or service, establish a monetary value for that function, and provide the necessary function reliably at the lowest overall cost."*

The objective of value work is, as stated by Miles himself, *"to make possible a degree of effectiveness in identifying and removing unnecessary cost, that approaches the effectiveness of identifying performance improvements for the product or service and incorporating them into it."****

Value Engineering ensures COST EFFECTIVENESS, by identifying unnecessary costs and avoiding the use of resources unnecessarily. Value Engineering serves *"to define and segregate the NECESSARY from the UNNECESSARY and thereby develop alternative means of accomplishing the necessary."** It means that the complete potential in improvement is garnered in full. *"Anything less than the necessary FUNCTIONAL capacity is unacceptable; anything more is unnecessary and wasteful."***** Perhaps there is no tool or technique other than Value Engineering which speedily locates all frills and gold plating, providing the way for eliminating them. Value Engineering is a unique combination of many proven tools and techniques, the co-ordinated use of all available internal expertise and the systematic, step-by-step approach to problems, *"to balance infinite wants with finite resources"****** and ensure rich dividends in quick time.

In Value Engineering, we are concerned with the USE VALUE as the lowest cost of providing the reliable performance of a FUNCTION and with the ESTEEM VALUE as the lowest cost of providing the shape, appearance, attractiveness and features which the customer wants and/or the product or service needs for its sale. In combining these, the aim is to arrive at the minimum expenditure which must be made in manufacturing and selling the product or the service, to create the appropriate use and

---

* Miles, p. 3

** Miles, Preface xvii

*** Mudge, p. 5

**** Tufty, p. 7

***** Fallon, p. 8

esteem factors. In other words, to obtain the maximum sales in the product, every usable idea, process, material, method, shaping, packaging, and approach to problems have to be exploited to secure the best combinations, involving the least expenditure of time, money and other resources. The purpose of the special knowledge and special technique of Value Engineering is to bring into focus this combination.

Value Engineering is no new technique. In fact, it is not a single technique either. It is an organised approach, an extension of the commonsense approach, to a job or problem, using a specific set of techniques — some old and some new — a compendium of knowledge and collection of skills, to analyse all phases of production from raw material specifications to the end products and after-sales services, to synthesise the best combination of concepts, ideas, processes, materials, methods and procedures, involving the least expenditure of resources, time and money. Therefore, it is concerned with the study of the relationship of design, function and cost of any product, material or action, with the object of reducing cost by modified design, or material specification, more efficient processes, or change in source of supply (external or internal), elimination or combination. Value Engineering creates values in terms of essential function, performance, life, appearance, reliability, quality assurance, size, maintainability, ease of operation, ease of assembly, on-costs, operating costs, warranty, and after-sales service costs. It is supplementary and complimentary to all other conventional management techniques.

The concept, the design, the prototype, the product or even the service is first analysed to identify the REQUIRED FUNCTION(S). The next step is to establish the worth of the function, each one of them, and relate it to its function cost. This will reveal the VALUE INDEX (Worth divided by Cost), the VALUE GAP (Cost minus Worth) and VALUE MISMATCH (High Cost — Low Worth). Continuing, we find out several alternatives to provide the required functions, creating such alternatives on the basis of function alone. We assess the cost of each alternative. Then, we synthesise the selected alternatives providing the needed functions that ensure the required performance and user/customer acceptance at the lowest overall cost.

Value Engineering is change. It creates change on purpose to manage cost and performance needs. It is unconventional, non-conforming.

Value Engineering is team work. It makes use of a small multi-disciplined group of company's own personnel. Their value efforts follow a job plan that guides the group step-by-step through the Value Engineering process.

Value Engineering is ENGINEERING FOR VALUE.

VALUE ENGINEERING JOB PLAN

The Value Engineering Job Plan includes an array of approaches and actions required to get better answers to the problem, more efficiently and more effectively.

The Job Plan, as used and recommended for use by Arthur E. Mudge, CVS, FSAVE, Senior Associate, Value Associates, Bethel Park, PA., USA, comprise seven steps*. They are:

General Phase.

Information Phase.

Function Phase.

Creation Phase.

Evaluation Phase.

Investigation Phase.

Recommendation Phase.

The Value Engineering systematic approach is a relatively simple and proven methodology, usable by any individual, who has learnt the fine points of its application and acquired a fair measure of skill in its use; and by an enterprise, irrespective of its size or output. It closely follows the steps used by inventors when they develop new ideas and procedures. Following the Job Plan ensures that the project studies accomplish MORE IN A SHORT TIME. It forces a concise and succinct description of the purpose and therefore, a good definition of the requirements and the true function. It highlights high cost areas, and, therefore, identifies areas for value efforts. It forces the team to think deeper and incisively than normal, and, therefore, secures creative solutions. It is built on facts and therefore, fosters objective decision-making.

Thomas Snodgrass, Director of the Centre for Value Engineering Research at the University of Wisconsin, Madison, USA, says that *"If the*

---

* Mudge, p. 30

object of your focus has a function, then you can perform value analysis on it."

As long as there is a function required and a financial decision to be taken on the money to be spent to accomplish that function, the Job Plan will provide the best value solution. Value Engineering establishes an analytical framework for determining the function(s) of a project, product, process, service or operation. Once the functions are agreed upon, Value Engineering uses a methodology for reducing cost at the same time that the performance, quality and acceptance of the product or service are enhanced, or the efficiency of the process or operations, improved.

Over the years, the Job Plan has matured into a powerful tool, capable of solving all product and cost improvement problems. It is today universal in its approach and application. Each phase of the Job Plan comprises, or is supported by, one or more techniques — some new, others already in wide use in industrial situations — all organised into a systematic plan for deriving the best advantage of each. In all, some twentyfive techniques are employed. Whilst brief references are made to these techniques in the following discussion of the Job Plan Phases, their theory and application are discussed in depth in subsequent chapters.

During the GENERAL PHASE, the stage is set by organising the task force, identifying the decision-maker, selecting the areas of effort, assigning specific tasks to each member of the team and inspiring them for coordinated team work. Value Engineering work means problem solving for the decision-maker. It needs considerable personal contact, so use of good human relations would mean the difference between assistance and resistance. The ground rules for the value effort are explained, laying emphasis on controlling opinions and feelings, as well as applying good business judgements based on facts.

In the INFORMATION PHASE, the problem is broken into specifics, avoiding generalities. All relevant, accurate and meaningful data are collected for helping the decision-making. Facts are ascertained. Costs are determined. Money value is put on each finish, tolerance, allowance and specification. It will be natural to meet with road blocks, which have to be identified and overcome.

The FUNCTION PHASE is the key to the value effort. One of the basic problems a manufacturer faces is that of providing a function. An item is a means to the end of providing a function – not the end itself. In this phase, the function needed is first identified, then defined and classified as the BASIC and SUPPORT FUNCTIONS. The keystone of Value Engineering lies in stating the function in a TWO WORD, VERB NOUN combination, the former to indicate the action the item performs and the latter, what is acted upon or the object of the action. Work functions are always expressed in active verbs and measurable nouns, which establish quantitative statements; Sell functions, in passive verbs and non-measurable nouns, which establish qualitative statements. It sounds simple; but it is not easy to accomplish. Costs are determined. (For detailed discussion, refer subsequent chapter).

In the CREATION PHASE, creative ideation techniques are used to generate a multitude of ideas, products, processes, methods, etc., to accomplish the defined function(s). It involves two mental processes: the creative and the judicial. Suppressing the judicial, a quantity of ideas providing for the defined functions are generated. Refining, evaluation, etc., come in the next phase.

In the EVALUATION PHASE, the judicial mind is brought into active use. The quantity of ideas generated in the Creation Phase are now appraised, modified, refined and combined to generate the Change Proposal. Function alternatives are developed, compared and estimated for costs. The best ideas are selected.

The creative ideas so refined, evaluated and compared are then subject to investigation in the INVESTIGATION PHASE. Vendor consultations, assistance of company and industrial specialists, and use of company standards, industrial and national standards that are applicable, lead to the most reasonable, practical, low cost, high value solutions, without impairing the use and esteem factors, quality, safety, reliability, durability, etc.

Several tests are applied, including the vital question, "would you spend your money this way?" before the value alternative of merit is finally decided upon. Unless the answers from all the functional specialists in all areas of decision-making can affirmatively meet these tests, it should be seriously questioned if a good degree of value exists.

The value change alternative of merit is now ready for recommendation, approval and due implementation. Some value practitioners stress the recommendation aspect, how to prepare it for motivating positive action and how to gear it for the need of the decision-maker to approve. Some others, like Mr. Rudy Kempter, like to stress the implementation part, who will take positive action, what he will need — resources, budget, time, personnel, assistance, etc. They prefer to call this phase Implementation Phase (as I do).

Fig. 12 shows the phases in sequence.

Although at first glance this Job Plan looks like a straight line approach, it is not. The ideas created are refined, evaluated and investigated, during which process some new information or data, inadvertently missed, or not originally collected or considered, would emerge. This will

GENERAL PHASE

INFORMATION PHASE

FUNCTION PHASE

CREATION PHASE

EVALUATION PHASE

INVESTIGATION PHASE

IMPLEMENTATION PHASE

Fig. 12

entail passing through the cycle again. When this happens, all of the following phases in their logical sequence are reiterated. Re-creating, re-refining, re-evaluating, re-investigating, the steps are continued in sequence, until finally the lowest cost, most sound solution emerges, to secure in the item same or better performance, worth and esteem. The modified chart of the phases, showing the value circle and re-iteration of phases is given in Fig. 13.

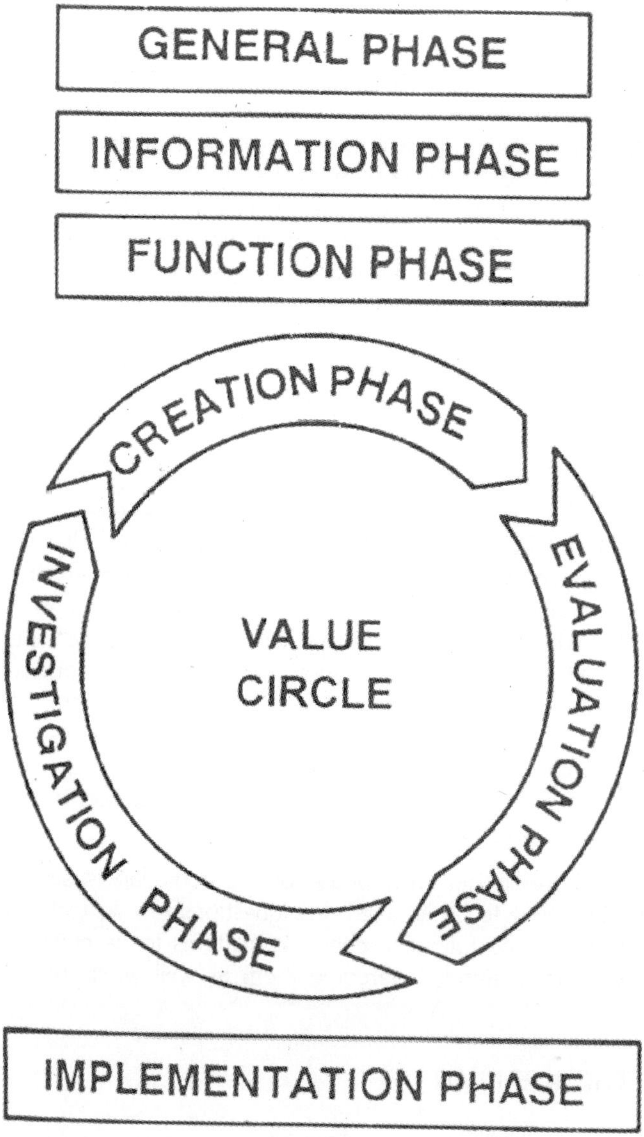

Fig. 13.

Each phase is completed with thoroughness, using the appropriate techniques, before the next phase is started. In pursuing a step, ground work is laid for the next. Therefore, some overlapping is inevitable.

Since the time Miles originally created the concepts of Value Analysis in the early 1940s, extensive advances have been made. Originally, the Job Plan was established for value studies on existing hardware; to find new ways to do things out of sheer necessity and during war and post-war era; and to find substitutes for certain strategic materials which were unavailable at that time. Cost reduction was one of the many benefits realized by applying the methodology. Spurred by the spectacular successes, when the use of the methodology spread among major industries and US Government agencies, the primary focus continued to be on cost reduction, manufacturing tasks, product problems and procurement. However, in the years that followed came extensive refinements of the original job plan and techniques, development of additional techniques to be used within the framework of the original job plan, and application to non-manufacturing tasks. Defining 'product' as anything that is the result of some one's labour or mental application, opened the way for application of the job plan beyond hardware to software, system and procedures, construction, buildings, highways, hospitals, government, etc., wherever an economic activity was involved. And so, it is the reason why a number of Job Plans, fundamentally the same, but structured a little differently, have been successfully used by eminent Value Engineering specialists. A comparison of all known such Job Plans can be seen in Fig. 14.

In the IMPLEMENTATION PHASE, the value change alternative of merit, selected, is presented as a VALUE ENGINEERING CHANGE PLAN (VECP) to the management, for final approval and implementation. Just as the work started with facts, it is concluded with facts, which will speak for themselves. VECPs would be concise, show before and after comparisons, costs, advantages, disadvantages (if any), how to overcome them, plan for implementation (authority, cost, and time frame for it), as well as acknowledgement of assistance received from others. It would contain sufficient data for the decision-maker to determine the course of action to be taken as well as for post-implementation audit.

In Part II of this book, each phase of the Job Plan is discussed in greater detail. Objective to be attained, key questions to ask, techniques to be used, guidelines to be followed, checklist of items to be covered, possible pitfalls and the means to overcome them as well as illustrations are included.

LOGIC OF THE JOB PLAN

The logic of the method is given in Fig. 15.

The key is EVALUATE BY COMPARISON. This technique shows how to use imagination and skill to improve value and reduce cost of high cost items. The underlying assumption is simple: if two similar items are compared in a prescribed manner, and one is costlier than the other, the low cost item will suggest ways to improve the value of the higher cost item. Fig. 15 will illustrate.

Job Plan	Steps	No. of steps
MILES ORIGINAL	ORIENTATION, INFORMATION, SPECULATION, ANALYSIS, PROGRAM PLANNING, PROGRAM EXECUTION, SUMMARY AND CONCLUSION	(7)
MILES 1972	INFORMATION, ANALYSIS, CREATIVE, JUDGEMENT, DEVELOPMENT	(5)
MUDGE	GENERAL, INFORMATION, FUNCTION, CREATION, EVALUATION, INVESTIGATION, RECOMENDATION	(7)
KEMPTER	SELECTION, INVESTIGATION, SPECULATION, EVALUATION, DEVELOPMENT, PRESENTATION, IMPLEMENTATION, AUDIT	(8)
FALLON	INFORMATION, ANALYTIC, CREATIVE, EVALUATION, PRESENTATION, IMPLEMENTATION	(6)
DELL ISOLA	INFORMATION, SPECULATIVE, ANALYTICAL, PROPOSAL	(4)
US - DOD / GSA - PBS / TUFTY	ORIENTATION, INFORMATION, SPECULATION, ANALYSIS, JUDICIAL, DEVELOPMENT, PRESENTATION, IMPLEMENTATION, FOLLOW UP	(9)
ATTWOOD	DATA COLLECTION, ANALYSIS, RECORD OF IDEAS, SPECULATION, INVESTIGATION, RECOMMENDATION, IMPLEMENTATION	(7)

Fig. 14. Comparing Job Plans

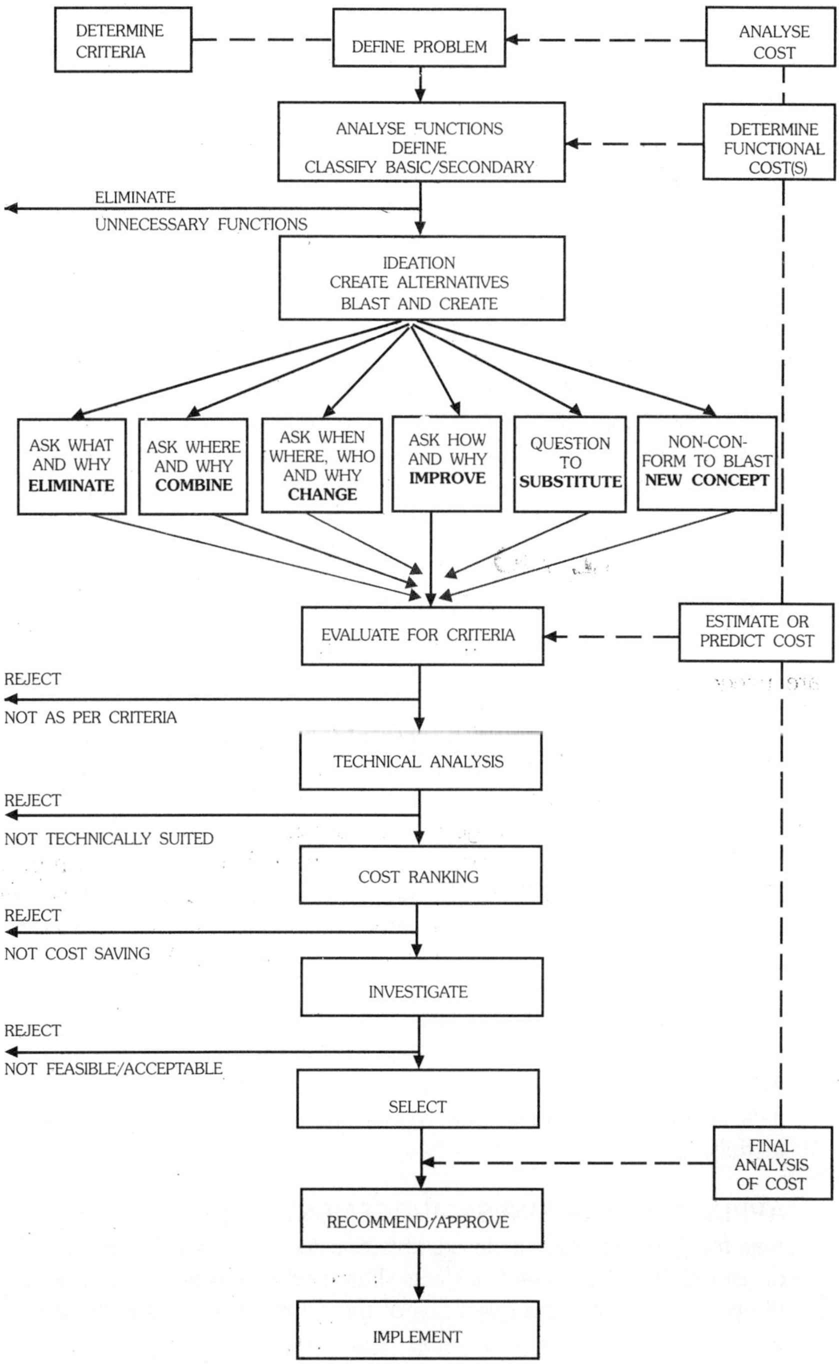
DETERMINE CRITERIA
DEFINE PROBLEM
ANALYSE COST
ANALYSE FUNCTIONS DEFINE CLASSIFY BASIC/SECONDARY
DETERMINE FUNCTIONAL COST(S)
ELIMINATE UNNECESSARY FUNCTIONS
IDEATION CREATE ALTERNATIVES BLAST AND CREATE
ASK WHAT AND WHY ELIMINATE
ASK WHERE AND WHY COMBINE
ASK WHEN WHERE, WHO AND WHY CHANGE
ASK HOW AND WHY IMPROVE
QUESTION TO SUBSTITUTE
NON-CON-FORM TO BLAST NEW CONCEPT
EVALUATE FOR CRITERIA
ESTIMATE OR PREDICT COST
REJECT NOT AS PER CRITERIA
TECHNICAL ANALYSIS
REJECT NOT TECHNICALLY SUITED
COST RANKING
REJECT NOT COST SAVING
INVESTIGATE
REJECT NOT FEASIBLE/ACCEPTABLE
SELECT
FINAL ANALYSIS OF COST
RECOMMEND/APPROVE
IMPLEMENT

Fig. 15.

Techniques Employed

The traditional tools and techniques suffice only to guarantee the minimum condition for survival. We need something more: to grow by design. Value Engineering Job Plan will show that some twentyfive techniques are employed. The provisions of the Job Plan, the process itself and the techniques applied are meant for an objective, action-oriented, searching study of the item or the problem for value improvement. For the sake of effectiveness, each technique should be well understood and appropriately applied. The success or failure of the value study depends on this.

1. **USE GOOD HUMAN RELATIONS:** Value Engineering is team effort, and, therefore, has to be developed, nurtured and applied. Particularly, under existing conditions in India. It means understanding and working with people. It involves considerable personal contact, both within the team and outside of it, for collection of information, studies, discussions, investigations, etc. Therefore *"the use of good human relations throughout will mean the difference between assistance and resistance."**

2. **AVOID GENERALITIES:** The key is to work on specifics. It produces results. *"Only opinions, views and hearsay can be expected when talking in generalities."**

3. **OVERCOME ROADBLOCKS:** Value Engineering means change to improve. Resistance to change is but natural. There will be many, who, deliberately or unwittingly, use all means possible to resist change. It is important that these roadblocks are identified, recognised and tactfully overcome.

4. **APPLY GOOD BUSINESS JUDGEMENT:** It goes without saying that for good results, unbiased objective judgements are critical. All decisions should be based on facts. Past performances should primarily be aids to solve the questions of the future. Failures should serve as a burning stimulus to develop better products.

---

* Mudge, p. 30

5. **INSPIRE TEAM WORK:** Individuals working together accomplish more than what they could, singly. Experience has shown that good performance is the result of not only individual competence. The need for team building is acute in India, where Indians are said to be excellent individually, but ineffective in a group.

6. **SECURE FACTS:** It should be ensured that the data/information collected are all facts and nothing else. For, there are apparent facts, assumed facts, reported facts, hoped for facts and facts so labelled and accepted as facts. Most of these are not facts at all. To secure facts and opinions backed up by facts, answers are sought from the best sources and the right sources.

   Facts are power. They are critical to good management.

7. **CONSTRUCTIVELY CHALLENGE EVERYTHING:** The cardinal rule in Value Engineering is not to accept anything on mere face value, but to understand and gather facts. The questioning approach is particularly useful during development of function alternatives.

8. **DETERMINE THE COSTS:** The need is for accurate data on costs. Also, since the cost data usually available with the company accounts are based on statutory dictats, it would necessitate understanding their build-up for each item, so that meaningful cost data for value work can then be determined.

9. **FIX MONEY VALUE FOR ALL SPECIFICATIONS, TOLERANCES, FITS, AND FINISHES:** Costs are related truely and accurately to specifications, tolerances, fits, finishes, reliability indices and so on. This is a potent area of unnecessary and hidden costs.

10. **DEFINE AND CLASSIFY FUNCTIONS:** Defining the function in a two word combination and classifying the function into basic, support, and secondary levels of priority are the heart of Value Engineering.

11. **BLAST AND CREATE:** With experience, it should be possible to bring to the fore creative faculties, suppressing the judicial part of the mind. Then, one can blast and create innumerable ideas and approaches for accomplishing the function(s). This is the soul of Value Engineering.

12. **SIMPLIFY:** Complexity, exceptions, special cases, etc., are all the result of additions, modifications and changes made during the growth of the product, service or organisation. Restore the original, as far as practicable.

13. **REFINE AND COMBINE IDEAS:** Once a number of ideas are

created, these are refined using continued creativity, to ensure that they are workable, feasible, saleable, etc. It has to be done on all ideas and combinations of ideas.

14. **ESTABLISH COST FOR ALL IDEAS:** As value is the ratio of function to cost, the potential cost of applying each idea and the expected savings must be computed.

15. **DEVELOP FUNCTION ALTERNATIVES:** This is the building block approach of developing combinations, to mould various needed functions into the whole product, process or service.

16. **USE STANDARDS:** Use of standard items — company standard, industrial standard, national standard and international standard—for all possible items, ensures lowest cost, best availability, etc.

17. **CONSULT SPECIALISTS, VENDORS, CUSTOMERS, ETC.** Their expertise in their fields of specialities are valuable, and would be most updated.

18. **USE SPECIALTY PRODUCTS, PROCESSES, PROCEDURES:** Instead of your generating own designs for certain items, starting from scratch, the use of off-the-shelf components ensures equal performance and quality reliability as when designed yourself, if not better, as well as almost 50% cost advantage. It also saves time.

19. **EVALUATE BY COMPARISON:** When the total solutions and their predicted costs are known, they are compared to determine which will provide the greatest possibility of attaining the target value level. No idea is ignored. Those showing maximum promise are selected for further development first, and the others take their turns in order of priority. The unused ideas are recorded for future use, if needed.

20. **SPEND MONEY AS IF IT IS YOUR OWN:** Ask this question, "if you are spending your own money and (not a company's, would you spend it on the suggested solution?" If the answer is YES, the solution is the best.

21. **USE GROUND RULES**

22. **RECOMMEND SOLUTION WITH ENOUGH DATA FOR DECISION-MAKERS TO DECIDE:** Value Engineering Change Proposal (VECP) would be brief, concise, factual, showing before and after costs, advantages and disadvantages, plan for implementation. It should facilitate the decision-maker to decide on action to be taken. The work sheets may form annexures.

23. **DEVELOP TWO SOLUTIONS, IF POSSIBLE:** By developing the best value solution and the second best value solution, the decision-maker is given the opportunity to exercise his prerogative to make the final decision. It indirectly improves the chances of approval and/or quick implementation.

24. **USE INDEPENDENT AUDIT TO VERIFY PREDICTED SAVINGS:** The solutions are no good unless implemented and the predicted savings are realised in actuality. An independent audit enhances the veracity.

25. **ACKNOWLEDGE ASSISTANCE:** Value Engineering is no single man's job. It is team work which means assistance in various forms, from several sources, within the team and otherwise. It is wisdom to acknowledge them, and an investment for future assistance.

WHO WILL DO VALUE ENGINEERING

Value Engineering is a technique for use when better than normal results are needed.

Traditionally, management used to delegate functional responsibilities and hold the functional specialists accountable for the accomplishments in their assigned areas. This meant not only performance-oriented improvements, but also getting some good costs automatically, to the extent that such normal performance improvements impacted on costs. The normal management believes that value is everyone's business and so, an acceptable degree of value will be achieved in the product or service, as a matter of routine. However, with the increase in competition, the expansion of knowledge, development of technologies, turbulent changes that sweep the earth today, it does not happen automatically. Managements now realise that value returns have to be specific responsibilities, assigned specifically to selected individuals for achievement of value targets.

Value Engineering is teamwork. A successful Value Engineering study requires:

(i) a knowledge and expertise in the technical field of study, and

(ii) a solid background in the principles of Value Engineering.

Such a combination is provided by using own officers, with multidisciplinary skills, who have a minimum of 40-hours training in Value Engineering Module I programme, where a diversity of talents (idea people, communicators, developers and organisers) and technical expertise in the area of study are brought together.

The degree of knowledge and abilities required to maintain a successful value program varies with the type, size and structure of the organisation, product complexity, product cost content, product volatility, life-cycle cost, etc. Teams engaged in full-time value work and teams assigned part-time, engaged in value studies in addition to their normal work, have both returned good results. Outside Value Engineering Consultants are necessary, particularly when training the teams and when they are learning the application of Value Engineering methodology, as well as when formulating and introducing the Value Engineering programme. They can also help to prepare the climate in the company for value effort, by conducting appreciation programmes for the top and middle management group, who ultimately control the destiny of Value Engineering programmes.

It is common practice to assign the responsibility of organising and leading the Value Engineering studies to Value Engineering Team Coordinators. The American practice is to assign one individual full time, if the company has a sales between \$2 million and \$5 million per year. However, large engineering groups employ on an average 5 to 10 Value Engineering Specialists, that is one Value Engineering specialist for every 15 to 20 Engineers in the company. British practice is one full time Value Engineer when the turnover is about £ 500,000. Hitachi is reported to have all their Design Engineers trained in Value Engineering. They do value studies, as routine, on every design.

Organising the Value Engineering Study

It is being increasingly realised now that, ideally, by imbuing a function-oriented philosophy throughout the plant, all personnel would be made to use the Value Engineering techniques in solving problems and making decisions — particularly those that affect costs — deriving lasting, substantial benefits and possibly in far greater measure than otherwise.

Value Engineering does not necessarily mean a new department; but only a new, organised activity, a part of the culture of the organisation. Imperative for its success is its smooth integration into the existing organisation, with least possible disruption and without sacrificing any of its effectiveness. A model is suggested in Fig. 16.

For lasting results, Value Engineering must become a way of life throughout the organisation. It should become integral with the culture of the organisation. It should be a continuous and continuing activity.

Suggested patterns of Value management activity for large, medium and small industries are given in Figs. 17, 18 and 19.

If there is no Value Engineering set up in an organisation, it is suggested that they introduce the Value Engineering concept with training key personnel, have them conduct a Seminar to select some problems or projects for value study, hold a workshop on these items, preferably engaging the help of a qualified Value Specialist, and see the results. It could be followed up with organising a Value Engineering Group in the company on trial basis, for a year or two. At the end of the trial period, a decision could be taken about placing the Value Engineering activity on a permanent basis in the company. Fig. 20 shows an approach that succeeded in a large industry.

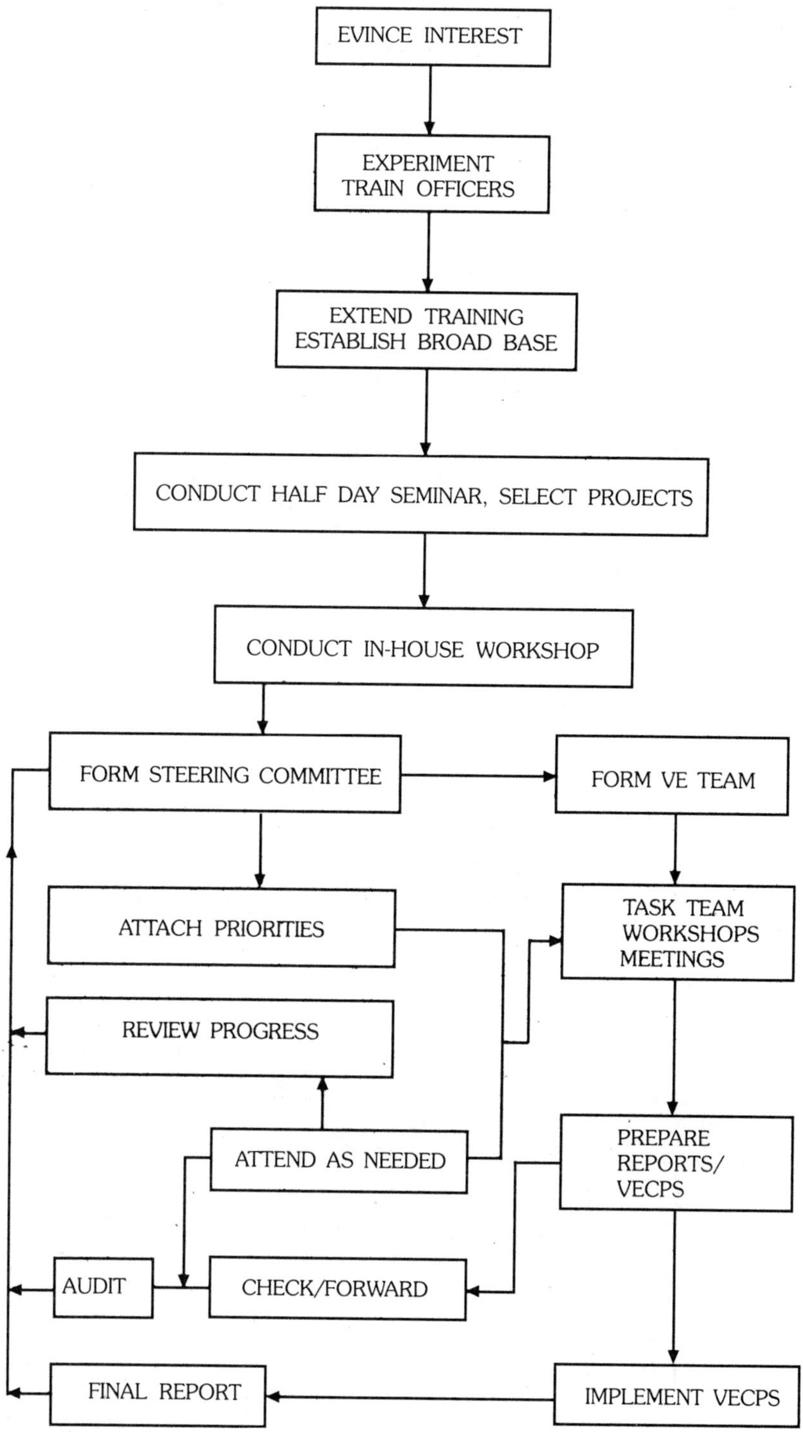
EVINCE INTEREST
EXPERIMENT
TRAIN OFFICERS
EXTEND TRAINING
ESTABLISH BROAD BASE
CONDUCT HALF DAY SEMINAR, SELECT PROJECTS
CONDUCT IN-HOUSE WORKSHOP
FORM STEERING COMMITTEE
FORM VE TEAM
ATTACH PRIORITIES
TASK TEAM
WORKSHOPS
MEETINGS
REVIEW PROGRESS
ATTEND AS NEEDED
PREPARE
REPORTS/
VECPS
AUDIT
CHECK/FORWARD
FINAL REPORT
IMPLEMENT VECPS

Fig. 16.

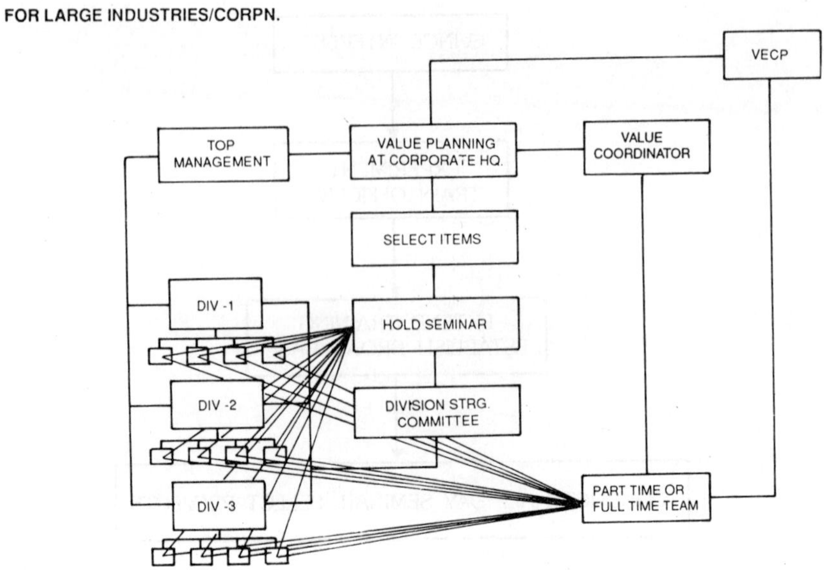

Fig. 17. For Large Industries/Corporations

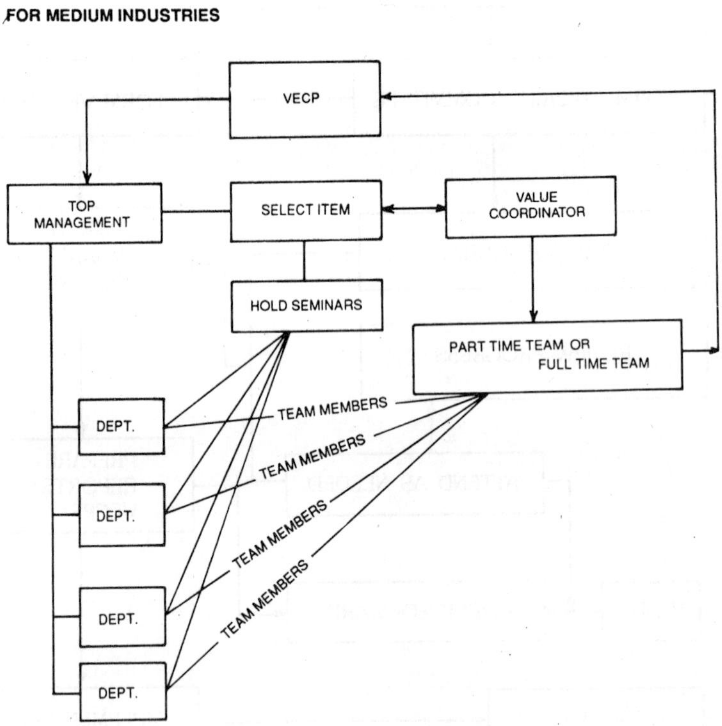

Fig. 18. For Medium Industries

FOR SMALL INDUSTRIES

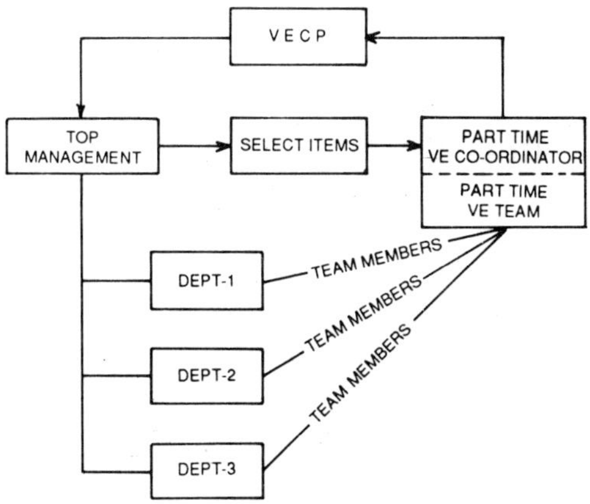

Fig. 19. For Small Industries

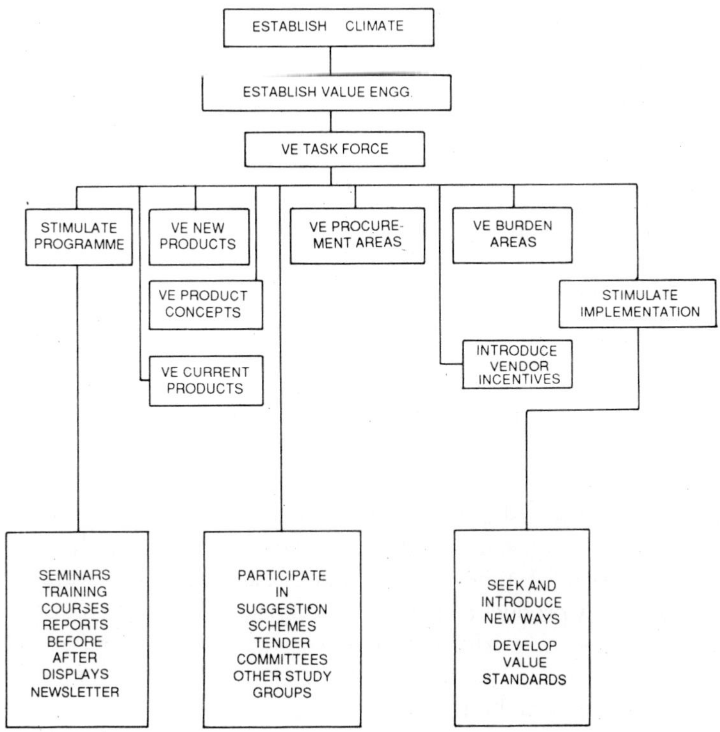

Fig. 20.

TECHNIQUE WITH A DIFFERENCE

1. Traditionally, a product, service or project is born to be of some use to the customer or to satisfy some desire. A survey finds out what the needs are. The chances are that the data obtained at that point of time are neither clear, nor reliable enough. So much so, what gets translated as specifications for the item would more likely be the DESIRES and not the actual NEEDS or what are MUSTS. Result, over-specification, leading to heavy unnecessary expenditure. Predicted cost will be much higher than the budget/estimate. A series of exercises then begin to cut costs — which ultimately end up with arbitary chopping off and compromises on needs. The customer's needs would not be met effectively and well. In Value Engineering there are no compromises. The real needs are well met.

2. Having produced the product or service accepted by the market, the company now enters into business from a position of strength. Soon competition starts. Then it will be a race to retain customers satisfied. It would require all the expertise that can be mustered, all the management techniques, all the sales gimmicks and what not, to continue to perform, survive and prosper. Performance-oriented, efficiency-oriented, incentive-oriented, motivation-oriented approaches that are conventional, would have been exploited to the full. Besides, they would yield only marginal returns. Value Engineering is function-oriented and finds the least cost means to provide the needed functions.

3. Product leadership is a function of performance equality or leadership and value equality or leadership, when compared with competition at any point of time. Performance itself includes several aspects of values. A product can perform a function better, it can perform more functions, or perform with fewer demands on the operator. Value Engineering is getting equivalent or better performance at same or lower costs or both.

4. Product cost is determined by the particular combination of designs, materials, methods, manufacturing processes, and finishing opera-

tions selected. Each has its performance and cost characteristic. Since there are actually several options in any one category, and in addition, a large number of parts in a product, the possible permutations and combinations are almost astronomical. Most designers and manufacturers investigate only a relatively small number of possible combinations before the first acceptable solution is found and the product or industry is established. Value Engineering job plan enforces thorough and complete search of all alternatives, enabling selecting the best solution. Value Engineering enables design to cost.

5. Once an item is designed, its life cycle cost is also fixed. However much the user tries to improve the utilisation of the item, efficiency, service or maintenance, because the design has already fixed the characteristics and life cycle, the potential for improvement during the use of the item is severely limited. Even to reap benefits from this limited scope, the cost of making changes rises exponentially with time. With use of Value Engineering in the design stage, the maximum potential in savings is realised.

6. Today we live in an extremely dynamic era of spectacular advances in science, technology and inventions. The smart manager will have to assimilate all these new changes in such a way that improvements are progressively secured in his product or service, keeping the quality up and lowering the cost. It means a second look at everything. Or, for that matter, a third look, a fourth look and so on — which is Value Engineering, a continuous and continuing activity for securing progressive improvements.

7. It has been proven that, at any point of time, based on then current knowledge, experience, information, etc., a product or service is brought into existence, without being aware that it yet contains potential for cost improvements upto 25%. If it were a rush product, the potential is as high as 50%. Cost improvement becomes necessary for success, growth or survival. Value Engineering focussing on high cost areas, identifies areas and items for action to cut costs.

8. The conventional tools and techniques are all valuable, useful and powerful. But, these tools are essentially "how-to-do-better" tools. In most cases, they will help to do things better — but, as it is not certain that every thing being done are the right things, they may also help to do wrong things better. Contrast it with what Value Engineering produces, usually a totally different item, part, or procedure, which is more appropriate and more fruitful. What people really want is FUNCTION and not the material.

9. Conventional approach to improvements is one of trade off. The

decisions justifying trade offs are based on cost estimates and estimated cost benefits. Seldom they represent meaningful costs. Value Engineering is based on meaningful costs.

10. A team can achieve much more than the sum total of its individual members. It takes advantage of the skills and strength of each member to beget success for the whole group. Contrast it with committee work, keeping minutes and wasting hours and avoiding decisions. Value Engineering is team work.

11. It is but human to show resistance to change. It is also natural to be afraid of censure, criticism and personal loss of face, likely to result from a change being introduced or a new idea being implemented comparing unfavourably with what existed so long. For this reason, many good ideas/suggestions never get implemented. With Value Engineering, it makes you a party to the solution: such situations are avoided. Moreover, it helps in speedier acceptance and implementation of the solution.

12. To make the future happen requires work, rather than genius. The individual with creative imagination will have more imaginative ideas. In any organisation there are many such individuals and more such ideas than put to use. We often overlook the goldmine in the knowledge, experience and creative talents of our people. Value Engineering seeks out these talents, welcomes — in fact, solicits ideas, and makes them work.

13. The Value Engineering Change Proposal is prepared by the organisation's own people. Who else will know better where and what the problems are and how to solve it (or how they have been solving it so far).

14. Value Engineering means raising the skills of the company personnel to practice Value Engineering as a way of life. It is an endowment.

15. Value Engineering is permissive, appreciating and showing regard to all in-house specialists, but involving them in the team work for the common good of the organisation.

16. The proof of the pudding is in the eating. Truly, results are the most important thing. With Value Engineering the job is not complete until the proposal is implemented and the results verified.

17. In Value Engineering there is a target to reach — the WORTH, the VALUE INDEX; or the VALUE GAP to fill. It also serves as a measure to appraise how good the work of the team has been.

18. Even if the full potential value is not attained at the first look, you can have second look, a third look and so on, until the best value results are obtained.

19. A minimum average of 10% return on investment is normally achieved.

20. The cost cutting abilities of ordinary workers in a firm is about 5%. In the case of trained Engineers (Industrial Engineers), it is about 10 to 15%. That by Value Engineering is more than 30%.

21. In Value Engineering, NOTHING IS TAKEN FOR GRANTED, no matter for how long it has been practiced. Every item is examined and re-examined continuously. The cardinal rule is CHALLENGE EVERYTHING.

22. Value Engineering believes in partnership between the individual and the technique for success. It recognises the reality of the old Chinese proverb, *"Tell me, I forget; show me, I remember; involve me, I understand."* Therefore it is that the 40-hr MOD I Value Engineering WORKSHOP prescribes inputs half the time and working on live, own projects, the other half; ensuring learning by work and involvement.

Verily, Value Engineering is a technique with a difference, and beneficial difference.

VALUE ENGINEERING AND QUALITY: CONFLICT OR COMPLEMENT ?

Today's watchword is QUALITY. As late Dr. Edward W. Deming, the Quality Guru, describes it, quality means what will sell, what the customer needs, what is presented in a way that he or she can use it, and what will do him or her some good — or at least try to. To quote Dr. Armand Feigenbaum, the international implementer of quality systems, quality is what the customer says it is.

The era of quality has sired an endless parade of standards and awards. There are national standards, international standards, top ranked European Quality, Deming and Baldrige awards, competitions and a seemingly infinite list of supplier-based certifications administered by corporations. These truly form the basis for a practical working foundation for world-class management.

The following table compares and contrasts conventional management thinking and total quality management thinking:

Conventional Management thinking	Total Quality Management thinking
# Quality improvement costs money and time.	# Quality improvement SAVES money and time.
# Work is a series of events: marketing, operations, finance, etc.	# Work is an integrated process.
# Quantity is as important as quality.	# Without quality, quantity is irrelevant.
# 95% is great.	# Only 100% will do.
# Quality is the result of better inspection.	# Quality is built from the start.
# Suppliers must be kept on their toes.	# Suppliers must feel like they are partners.
# To achieve quality we need more and better people.	# Quality can be achieved with the people we have right now — simply by leading and training them.

Truly, it is quality that begets customer satisfaction, customer delight and an edge over competition. Customer satisfaction is gained by focusing attention on all aspects of the product or service that are meaningful to him or her. It is a measure of applied values. It takes place at the customers' premises. It reflects how much more competitive one is, how much less of a high-cost producer, or how much more of a cost-effective, high-share marketer. Once on the road to customer satisfaction, the next logical step on the continuum is delighting them. Customer delight means positioning the purchase decision as just one small step in a long lasting and profitable relationship. Pitney Bowes Inc. survey of 80,000 of its customers reveal that only 20% of its satisfied customers would commit to definitely do business with it again. About 79% of its very satisfied customers, on the other hand, definitely would buy again with the intent of making it the vendor of its choice. What distinguishes the very satisfied from the satisfied is neither the product quality, nor response time, nor billing accuracy, and the like; but the contact person!

There are several facets to quality. Strictly having a product-focus is not enough. Consumers expect manufacturers to have mastered the basics of what they are in the business to provide. The cost of poor quality is substantial. In manufacturing, it is estimated at 25% to 50% of sales. In service industry, it is as much as 40% of operating costs. Government estimates run 30% to 40%.

Of equal importance are distribution packaging, ownership process, and post acquisition experience. Distribution packaging is what the customer sees first, even before the product is revealed. It is his or her first impresssion on the quality of the product. Here the options are many, but so also is the confusion about which material, machine or method will do the job. However, the principle guiding the choice has to be customer service, balancing cost and time against customer satisfaction. Obviously, no company can make satisfaction. But, it can, and should, make the best means to attain satisfaction.

The way the customer perceives the product is a measure of quality in the eyes of the customer. The first annual Bozell-Gallup World-wide poll surveyed 200 countries to show how others rate the quality of ones manufactured goods. In the quality profile revealed by this poll, Japan's glittering quality halo is evident, though excellent ratings were also secured by Germany, USA, Britain and France.

The way the customer receives the product or service (or the ownership process) also influences the quality rating. To the extent there are difficulties, hassles, stresses and frights associated with its acquisition, the rating is clouded. Similarly, the post-acquisition experience, i.e., the running in, service during use, maintenance and repairs, the availability of spares, warranties and how the company handles complaints and claims, also impact the quality rating favourably or unfavourably. The customers evaluate the willingness of a company to fix its mistakes. Besides, at a time when they have so much complexity in their lives and so much caution about spending money, things like warranty become differentiators in purchase decisions.

Interestingly, although quality is largely a matter of opinion on the part of the customer, few are able to give a clear definition of quality. Further, different people define quality differently, depending on their background. For instance, the Designer may define quality as meeting the concept objectives; the Quality Manager, producing within tolerances; and the customer, relating quality to appearance and performance. Even what the manufacturer thinks is the best quality of the product, may be of little interest to the customer. In fact, business leaders are widely divided about how to approach quality; those on the far left preach the gospel of quality as a philosophy and the right wingers put their money on tools and training.

Quality is the major influence in consumer buying decisions. Dr. Joseph M. Juran defines quality as FITNESS FOR USE. Philip Crosby, who is well known for the expression, "Quality is free," defines quality as conformance to requirements. Quality is one of the many factors that make a product; but perhaps an important factor in that it makes the product more desirable to the customer. In the consumer hierarchy of values, the basic criteria are accomplishing a purpose and affordability. The consumer deems something as good value if it satisfies well his purpose or product-use goals. But that is only one step towards acceptance of the item. The next check is reasonableness of cost. Then, they move up the hierarchy to focus on certain product esteem, but supplementary, functions — such as timeliness, serviceability, convenience, reliability, appearance, satisfaction, appeal, etc., though not in the same order. Consumers want the products they buy to be reliably the same day after day, week after week. Industries will have to keep all these questions: philosophy, purpose, intention, conditions, etc. in mind, as they develop and design products and services, manufacture them, and supply them to the market.

The product or service is created for a purpose. It is endowed by the creators of the design with concepts of purposive actions. These transform abstract customer demands of product-use functions and product-esteem functions into plans, specific forms, basic components and assemblies. Production is the transformation process for generating output (such as products and services) from the inputs of various resources (like people, information, material, energy, etc.) under given conditions of quality, cost and delivery schedules. Quality control is the system of traditional measures taken by managements to secure conformance to the design and to accomplish economic manufacture of products and services, whose quality matches the demands of the customers.

With the best of traditional design made to serve the users' parameters, and the best of conventional production and managerial systems devised, installed and operated to secure conformance, a QUALITY GAP exists between the users and the company. Prof. Kaneo Akiyama[*] describes this as follows:

Quality according to users	*Quality controlled by the company*
• *What they think is good*	• *Physical properties*
• *What is reported to be good*	• *Mechanical properties*
• *What experience says is good*	• Actual performance

GAP

Fig. 21.

The reasons are many. First, in defining quality. The difficulty in defining quality is to translate the expectations and needs of the user into measurable characteristics, so that the product can be designed and made to give satisfaction at a price that the user will pay. The traditional methods for identifying customer demands relating to quality are not always adequate for grasping fully the nature of quality needs. Besides, the customer may not be able to articulate his needs or requirements. The customer's judgement may take time to crystallise; it may vary; and it may change with time. Consequently, even the best developed designs may leave much to be desired to meet the customers' present needs, as well as future needs.

Second, in the productive system following the quality of design with fidelity and achieving conformance to the design prescribed. There are four basic elements affecting the production of the item so as to conform to the designated quality: materials, machinery, methods and men. Conventional approach is to measure and control variability in the properties of parts and products and determine quality by the number of defects in a product. These may be divided into major and minor categories, acceptable combinations and levels, etc. This control is still applied largely at the manufacturing stage and principally to quantifiable physical products and parts. The system would be either or a combination of Quality Control (QC), Statistical Quality Control (SQC), Quality Management (QM), Total Quality Management (TQM), Zero Defects (ZD) drives, and so on.

Third, the emphasis is on acceptance function as distinct from preventive function. Quality Assurance provides fair guarantee from defects reaching the customer. But, it is largely hind-sight; keeping informed about the amount of defective products made, or re-work/salvage done, week by week (or suitable other periods); or comparisons of levels of quality; cost

* Akiyama, p. 32.

of warranty; etc. Approximately 87% of the costs go to product failures — e.g. waste, full rejects, rectify faults, and servicing goods returned by customers. The remaining 13% only goes for preventing failures.

Fourth, as Dr. Edwards Deming states in his book, OUT OF THE CRISIS, page 465, *"efforts and methods for improvement of quality and productivity are... fragmented, with... no integrated system for continual improvement."*

Fifth, it is not enough to improve quality. Lots of people can do that. The challenge is improving quality from the customers' perspective — meeting their expectations — by following them closely and consistently, by anticipating them, and by leading them. Whether you choose to satisfy, serve, or delight the customers, or even to turn them into raving fans, understanding what the customer wants is a never ending task. The relationship between the company and the customer is for life.

Sixth, it is often the minor defects that establish the customers' opinion of the quality level of the product. In many cases, the measure of quality of the product may be based on performance of a minor function, not affecting the life or performance of the product. For example, the Washing Machine would be considered a better quality equipment if it runs silently. Correcting the minor defect could be a major cost problem.

Seventh, many organizations have been implementing quality improvement efforts like QC, QA, QR, TQC, QM and TQM as just any other quick fix, specialized attempt at improving what is broken in that which exists. But, almost invariably, every such single effort has failed to make a lasting difference. The key is continuous improvement of the whole system, and not merely, the quality system.

Eighth, the silent killers of continuous — or radical — improvement, deeply ingrained in old, existing, large, bureaucratic, autocratic and formal organisation processes. More important among them are the cultural blocks like mistrust, with-holding information, unwillingness to change: deficiencies in skills like (defensive communication, deficient approaches to resolving problems); groupism like (little or no cooperation, absence of team work within and between departments); poor organisation structure like (conflicted work units, divisions by steep functional boundaries; poor reward) system that ignores performance and improvements. Ralph H. Killman, in his Holographic Quality Management suggests identifying these barriers and removing them by conducting periodic workshop sessions along five tracks: culture, skill, team, strategy-structure and reward system.

As a means to close, or at least drastically reduce the Quality Gap, Quality Function Deployment, acronym QFD, developed in the late 1960s to help design super tankers in Mistubishi's ship yards in Kobe, Japan, is gaining popularity. Properly used, QFD articulates and ranks customer desires, details the technical requirements needed to fulfill those desires, and provides an organized plan that serves to focus and guide everyone involved in the project from design to delivery. QFD is ranked fourth among 26 programs to receive attention in the future by American, Japanese and European manufacturers. Properly conducted, QFD projects require the use of a number of other techniques, including Value Engineering and the seven basic quality tools. While the most obvious application for QFD is product development, it can be used in any number of ways, as its benefits range from 30% to 50% reduction in engineering charges, 30% to 50% shorter design cycles, 20% to 60% reduction in start-up costs, 20% to 50% reduction in warranty costs, 30% to 50% improvements in time to market, and fair reductions in life-cycle costs.

In the 1980s, industries learned that investments in pursuit of better quality can save money as well as improve the product. But, there are limits to how far and fast a firm should push toward reducing defects in the product and/or the process. Zero defects cannot be everybody's ultimate goal. An exaggerated program of defect reduction may reduce a firm's competitiveness. While most firms still underinvest in quality, some firms have now reached a point at which over-investment appears possible.

The survival, growth and functioning of business are because of customers: customers that are satisfied with the product or service; that boast about it and compliment it; and that bring friends with them. There was a time when the approach was to cram products and services with better and better quality materials, processes, finishes, etc. It was thought that the discriminating customer will look for the better quality and willingly pay the costs to buy it. But conditions have changed. Today's customer is still wanting better and better qualities, but at lower and lower costs. In other words, he is looking for quality per cost, performance per cost, life per cost, reliability per cost and lowest cost of possession, use, upkeep, etc. That is, lowest life cycle costs. And, he has many to choose from.

If this in itself calls for a fresh look at Indian products and services and their manufacture and supply, the changing world-wide scenario of greater quality consciousness and the acceptance of ISO 9000 series of International Standards for Quality and Quality Management Systems, make the review most urgent and critical. Many countries are clustering into regional groups to meet the challenges of competition. From January 1993, all manufacturers, whether selling nationally or internationally, are expected by their customers to produce evidence that they operate to ISO 9000 Standards. This Standard provides for controls to ensure quality of production and delivery; reduction of wastes, down-time and labour inefficiencies; as well as elimination of technical barriers to global trade. Such harmonising of production standards throughout the world enjoins Indian industries to urgently do a preliminary audit of their organisations in terms of quality control and formal production and management systems. They have to re-think and re-orient their approach to quality and quality management systems from one of almost conformity, an "it will do" attitude, inspection catching defects, following up with correctives and cure. Involved are a clear definition of objectives, commitment, written procedural instructions for every step or action, a system of monitoring, measurement and appraisal, documentation, traceability to know who did what, when and where, and eventual accreditation. The need of the hour is for a crash technique to achieve this transformation in a matter of months, what it took advanced countries abroad years to accomplish. That could very well be VALUE ENGINEERING, for the following reasons:

1. Quality is value. Proof of which is in the variety and range of characteristics that define value, illustrated in Fig. 1, page 17.

2. Value means performance, quality and esteem. Therefore, when you engineer for value, you also engineer for quality as needed for the item.

3. There is a definite relationship between value and quality as illustrated by Richard J. Park CVS, in the FAST diagram he had developed for an article in Value World. An adapted version of the diagram is given in Fig. 22.

4. The heart of Value Engineering is the concept of FUNCTION. Function Analysis focuses on improvement, integrating input resources of people, information, materials, energy, etc. to guarantee performance, quality, cost and delivery. It identifies all aspects of quality demanded by the customer in terms of functions and enables goal-oriented quality control.

5. On line customer participation in the development process can increase responsiveness and perceived quality of the result. The Value Engineering Job Plan enforces a team approach, involving the customer, the user, besides technical personnel concerned, and a consensus, in decision-making. It makes it easier for defining quality, securing fidelity to make the items to conform to such designated quality, and catering to customer needs with the right quality needed for the purpose.

6. Quality characteristics comprise materials, machinery to produce, processing, tolerances, finishes, skills of men, etc. In Value Engineering the search is to find that combination of all these, which will cost the least and yet ensure performance efficiently, effectively and well. So, through Value Engineering, the needs of the job are met with the ideal: just right, nothing more, nor less.

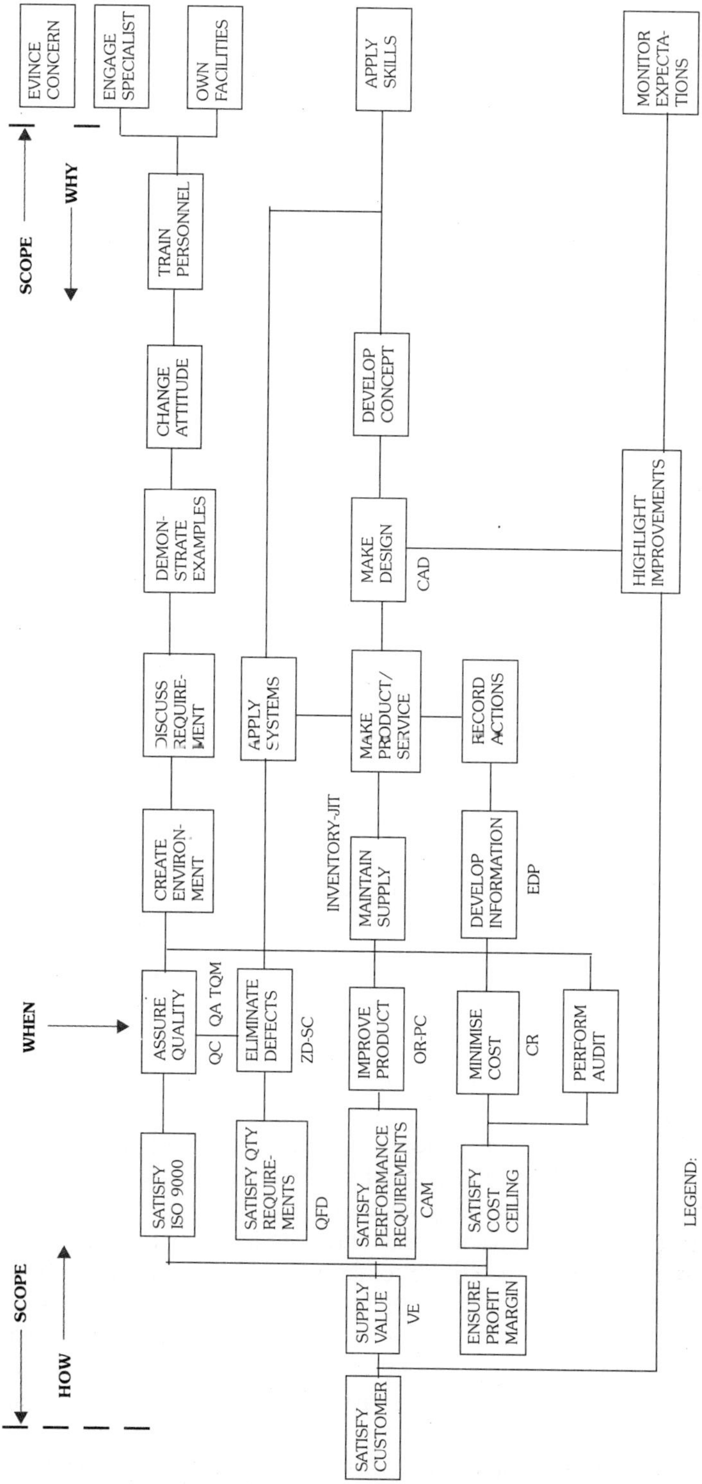

LEGEND:

VE : VALUE ENGINEERING
QFD : QUALITY FUNCTION DEPLOYMENT
CAM : COMPUTER ASSISTED MANUFACTURING
QC : QUALITY CONTROL
QA : QUALITY ASSURANCE
TQM : TOTAL QUALITY MANAGEMENT
ZD : ZERO DEFECTS
SQC : STATISTICAL QUALITY CONTROL
OR : OPERATIONS RESEARCH
PC : PRODUCTION CONTROL
CR : COST REDUCTION
JIT : JUST-IN-TIME
EDP : ELECTRONIC DATA PROCESSING
CAD : COMPUTER ASSISTED DESIGNING

Adapted from VALUE WORLD July-Sept. 1991

Fig. 22

7. Quality should be aimed at not only the present needs of the customer, but also, the future needs. Quality characteristics that the customer desires would vary, but the basic function for which he needs the item remains unaltered. In Value Engineering, the basic function is provided reliably, effectively and well and the target level of cost cutting is derived through working on the support and secondary function. Even here, equivalents at lower costs are found.

8. Value Engineering teams are in effect Quality Circles in management. Quality Circles have been proven as powerful sources to solve problems in quality and productivity at the operational level and within departments. Imagine the idea extended to include Managers and Specialists, multi-disciplined, over an extended jurisdiction, for making economic decisions. Value Engineering is more in-depth and far-reaching, thus broadening the spectrum of available alternative solutions.

9. Because they all meet standards — open, national, and international — products are reaching an equality of quality at similarly high levels of performance. Defect-free products are becoming the rule and not an exception. As a result, quality is virtually disappearing as a competitive advantage. It will no longer differentiate suppliers in any meaningful way. In many cases, quality at the near-perfect levels would exceed most customer requirements — good enough for the use intended. Superior quality beyond this point of sufficient return to the customer will represent unnecessary and often unrecoverable cost. The winner would be the one who delivers not the highest quality product, but the highest quantity of customer value.

10. Superior quality is a reality when there is a definite plan of attack and when that plan is followed through to implementation. Mere accreditation to ISO 9000 Quality Standards will not by itself bring about an overall improvement in the quality. There are lots of levels of quality and there are a couple of things that will automatically dictate where it will wind up: the approach taken, the methods used, and the implementation. The critical question would be whether all these would get the company and the product or service to the level where it should be. Training, development of a culture supportive of the operating discipline are vital. Value Engineering Job Plan offers a structured approach to match the total need: where we are now (how bad it is), where we are headed (how good it can get), what has to be done to get there, and makes it a collective commitment to meet the most exacting customer quality standards in everything done. It comprises a team approach, identification of the problem, analysis, creative ideation of solutions, evaluation of the ideas, framing action plan, documentation, taking action, follow up, recording, monitoring,

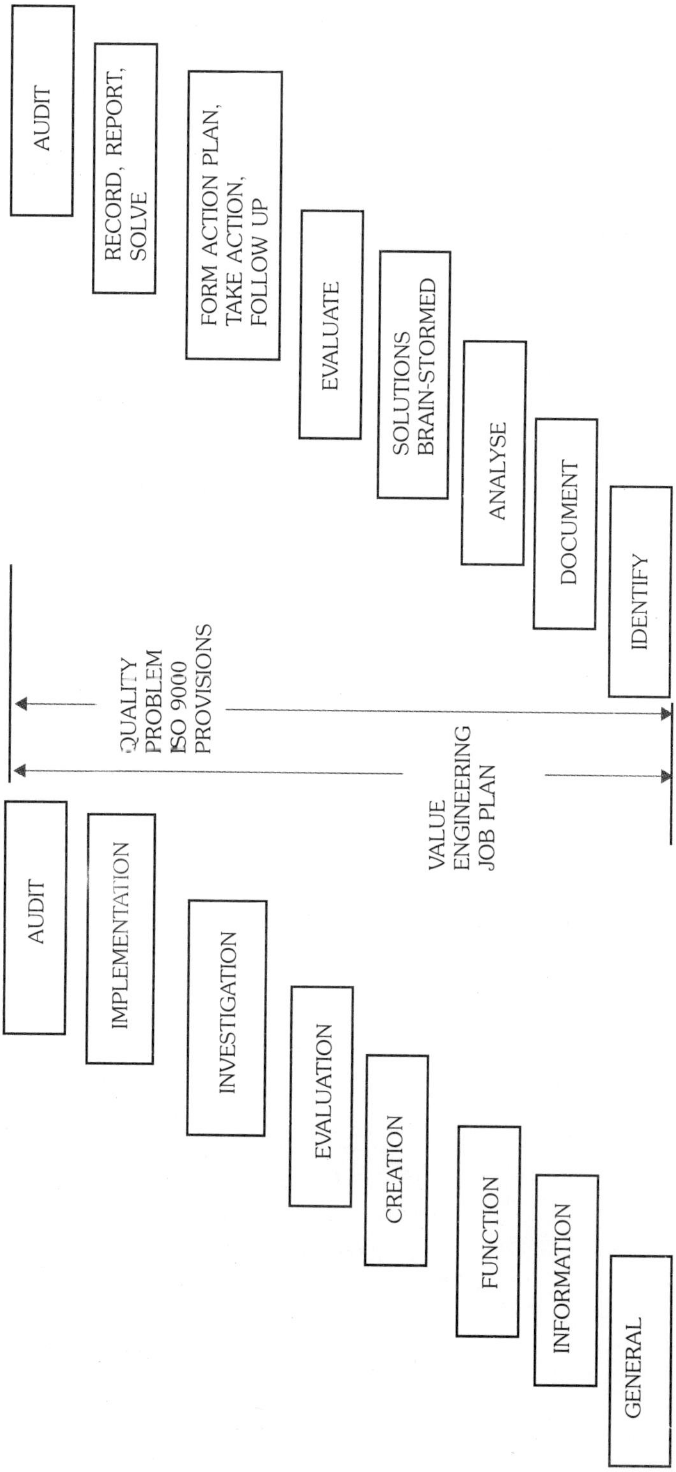
GENERAL
INFORMATION
FUNCTION
CREATION
EVALUATION
INVESTIGATION
IMPLEMENTATION
AUDIT
VALUE ENGINEERING JOB PLAN
QUALITY PROBLEM ISO 9000 PROVISIONS
IDENTIFY
DOCUMENT
ANALYSE
SOLUTIONS BRAIN-STORMED
EVALUATE
FORM ACTION PLAN, TAKE ACTION, FOLLOW UP
RECORD, REPORT, SOLVE
AUDIT

Fig. 23.

reporting, auditing, etc. Figure 23 shows a comparison of Value Engineering Job Plan with the ISO 9000 Standard requirement to solve quality problems.

Cost effective delivered quality and performance through Value Engineering Job Plan compliments the concepts pioneered by Deming, Juran, Feigenbaum, as well as the approaches of Ishikawa, Taguchi and others. It adds value by assuring quality. Hence, assuredly, Value Engineering is the crash technique that Indian managements are searching for in today's context.

Benefits

When the first Value Engineering study was made in the late 1940s, no one imagined that the savings would be so enormous and that the concept of Value Engineering would spread so very rapidly. For its first several years, the value programme was confined to the General Electric Company, USA., and manufacturing, where a saving in a product would be magnified by the number of times the product was produced. It is a tribute to the success of the technique that it steadily evolved since then into a proven management technique for universal application: in Government activities, Department of Defence, Construction industry, and so on.

General Electric, USA, where Value Analysis took birth, in the first 17 years of its application, enabled savings estimated at more than $ 200 million for purchases of GE products, from toasters to turbines.

Value Engineering is mandatory for any US Department of Defence contract. Former Secretary of Defence, Robert McNamara, staked his all behind the Value Engineering technique for Defence budget savings. Reported savings in DOD amount to some $ 9 billions through Value Engineering. In fiscal year 1986 alone the savings totaled $ 2.5 billion, for an investment of $ 100 million in Value Engineering effort. US Army Corps of Engineers claim a savings of $ 600 million in 13 years of Value Engineering effort, involving 200-man years.

In a recent survey made by the Society of American Value Engineers on 26 Value Engineering programmes, the following facts emerged:

1. The annual expenditure for the programmes ranged from $ 32,000 to $ 11,000,000. The average was $ 364,000.

2. The annual savings ranged from $ 243,000 to $ 43,000,000. The average was $ 9,872,000.

3. This works out to $ 27 saved for every dollar spent.

Value Engineering is now being used by over half the FORTUNE 500 Corporations. Phillips Industries, which ranked 451 in the rating years ago, saved some $ 62 million in 9 years and at the same time improved and simplified its products, to rise to the 79th position.

Joy Manufacturing Company, USA, uses Value Engineering since 1963. They report on their world-wide operations that the returns range from 3:1 in the first few years of application, to current levels of 24:1. Their savings equal more than 5% of net sales. Percentage cost improvement per item range from a low of 5% to a high of 73.8%.

In an year, Matsushita Electric Works Ltd. Japan, set a goal of savings at 5.2 billion yen and got 5.6 billion yen with Value Engineering efforts. This represents 1.6% of their sales. Hitachi, similarly set its target for an year at 6.8 billion yen, or 5.5% to sale and surpassed it with their Value Engineering effor

Some forward looking companies in India are using Value Engineering. But, sufficient documentation is not available to indicate their experience in detail. A typical case is that of Tata Steel. To Tata Steel should go the credit for spreading the message of value efforts in India in the late 1960s. Initial efforts were mainly for training executives of the company for using the Value Engineering technique, and off and on, for taking up adhoc projects. Side by side, attempts were made also to spread the message to other subsidiary and associated companies in the area. Although the scope of Value Engineering work was expanded in the years that followed, only in 1988, did a formal Value Engineering group get established. Since the beginning, they have conducted many workshops, trained nearly 2,000 of their officers and reaped substantial benefits. During the 12 year period, 1987-88 to 1998-99, over 562 projects were identified and taken for study. The bulk of these have been implemented and cost audited. The cumulative total savings is estimated at Rs. 5,600 million. The projects include yield improvement, reduction in losses, quality improvement, reduction in mill stoppages, reduction in maintenance effort while simultaneously improving the life of components, etc.

Other Indian industries using Value Engineering include TELCO, other Tata industries in and around Jamshedpur, ESCORTS, BHEL, ITI, MICO, L & T, SAIL, PREMIER AUTOMOBILES, WALCHANDNAGAR INDUSTRIES, W.S. INDUSTRIES, ENFIELD, and so on. Very recently, the Indian Railways have done one round of Value Engineering Workshops for their officers all over the country.

A rule of thumb is that savings of 2% to 5% of gross sales can be achieved through a Value Engineering programme. Returns of 20:1 are usual. Much higher returns have been possible. A minimum average of 10:1 can be guaranted.

PART II

VALUE ENGINEERING JOB PLAN

STEP-BY-STEP APPLICATION

Selection of Project

Before a value study can be made, a project must be selected for the study. It is true that any item can be subject to value study and at any point of time in its life cycle and that it will yield an average minimum of 10% return on investment. However, wisdom dictates that any such effort should be directed towards getting the maximum return, considering the limitations in Value Engineering resources available. Therefore, projects have to be screened and probable items, chosen.

There are many ways to choose the probable items for value effort. Some managements choose the items that they want examined. Where there is a Value Engineering group in the company, the Value Engineering personnel may decide what to evaluate. In still others, the employees are given the opportunity to suggest items from which selection is made.

Generally, high cost items, highly competitive items, products manufactured in bulk, items with stringent quality conditions, products and services posing vexatious problems for manufacturing, marketing, warranties, and vendor supplies, capital projects, product/process of high degree of complexity and involving large manpower requirements, old products and imported items are good candidates for value studies. Similarly, persistent production bottleneck, breakdowns, heavy rejections, scrap and re-work, customer complaints, monopoly supplier items, and the like indicate the need for efforts to find solutions. Such items of current interest for the organisation are also good candidates for value studies. Short-term considerations suggest current high turn-over items; and long-term approach, items at concept/design stage.

Some of the methods used for selection of items for value study are:

1. Felt need.
2. Reviews by Standing Committees.
3. Suggestion schemes.
4. Seminars.
5. Relative ranking.

6. Preliminary assessment of VALUE INDEX, VALUE GAP, VALUE MIS-MATCH, INDEX of COST SAVINGS POTENTIAL.
7. Brainstorming sessions in own training programmes.
8. A combination of two or more methods.

1. FELT NEED

During normal operation of an enterprise, from time to time, instances in obvious need for improvements and/or cost reductions would manifest itself. Similarly, customer feed-backs, changes in user needs or application of the item, advances in technology, or comparisons with competition will also bring to light the need for changes or modifications. More expensive products or components or critical manufacturing operations which have greatest potential for savings may become evident. Employees facing specific problems on their jobs may want something to be done to remove the deficiency or correct the situation, when they would suggest items for study or attention. The felt needs may be *"personal or company-motivated, problem or profit-stimulated or a combination of these."** All such information should be listed and maintained up-dated. Projects for value study could be selected from the list.

2. REVIEWS BY STANDING COMMITTEES

Various Standing Committees in the organisation would suggest items or areas for attention, as part of their routine work. Examples are Design Reviews, Review of Planning documents, New Product introduction, Quality Management Reports, etc. A list of such items could form the basis for selection.

3. SUGGESTION SCHEMES

Almost all progressive organisations have some suggestion scheme or the other in operation, nowadays. Only, such schemes are normally used to invite suggestions from their employees with the ultimate objective of using or implementing those that are approved by the Committee set up to oversee these schemes. For spotting a project for value studies, ALL the suggestions may be scrutinised from the angle of WHAT out of the lot of suggestions received CAN BE MADE TO WORK. Those that satisfy this test can be ranked for priorities and studied in their turn.

* Mudge, p. 143

4. SEMINARS

Calling a meeting of all the officers of the organisation, giving them an overview of Value Engineering, illustrating the potential benefits with a few cases and inviting them to suggest items, areas and problems that may be subject to value improvement efforts, would generate a fairly comprehensive list of prospective items for value effort. The management could then short-list the items and/or attach priorities as they deem fit.

5. RELATIVE RANKING

Estimated costs of the items, parts or sub-systems are ranked from the highest to the lowest in terms of money value per unit of the product and total amount for the ultimate product. Generally, potential value improvement is the greatest on those items ranked with the highest total costs.

Similarly, relative ranking can be used to list high energy use, low profit margin, highly competitive, most problematic items.

PARETO'S LAW

Ranking can be done by applying Pareto's Law. Table 3 shows the components of an assembly, quantities per assembly, cost of component and cost per assembly. From this tabulation, a relative ranking tabulation, Table 4, can be generated to highlight that the components offering the most promise for cost improvement are Valve body, Screw spindle, Hand wheel, and, possibly, Nuts. A graph can also be drawn as shown in Fig. 24.

Table 3: Brass Wheel Valve — Parts and Costs

Part	Quantity per assy.	Cost per part (Rs.)	Cost per assembly (Rs.)	Percentage assembly
Fiber Washer	1	1.00	1.00	1
Check Nut	1	4.00	4.00	4
Valve Body	1	35.00	35.00	35
Hollow Nut	1	10.00	10.00	10
Small Washer	1	0.50	0.50	0.5
Nuts	2	1.25	2.50	2.5
Screw Spindle	1	27.00	27.00	27
Large Washer	1	0.50	0.50	0.5
Hand Wheel	1	16.00	16.00	16
Floating Piece	1	3.50	3.50	3.5
Total cost of assembly			100.00	100

Table 4: Relative Cost Ranking

Part	*Percentages*	
	In descending order	*Cumulative*
Valve Body	35.0	35.0
Screw Spindle	27.0	62.0
Hand Wheel	16.0	78.0
Hollow Nut	10.0	88.0
Check Nut	4.0	92.0
Floating Piece	3.5	95.5
Nuts	2.5	98.0
Fiber Washer	1.0	99.0
Large Washer	0.5	99.5
Small Washer	0.5	100.0

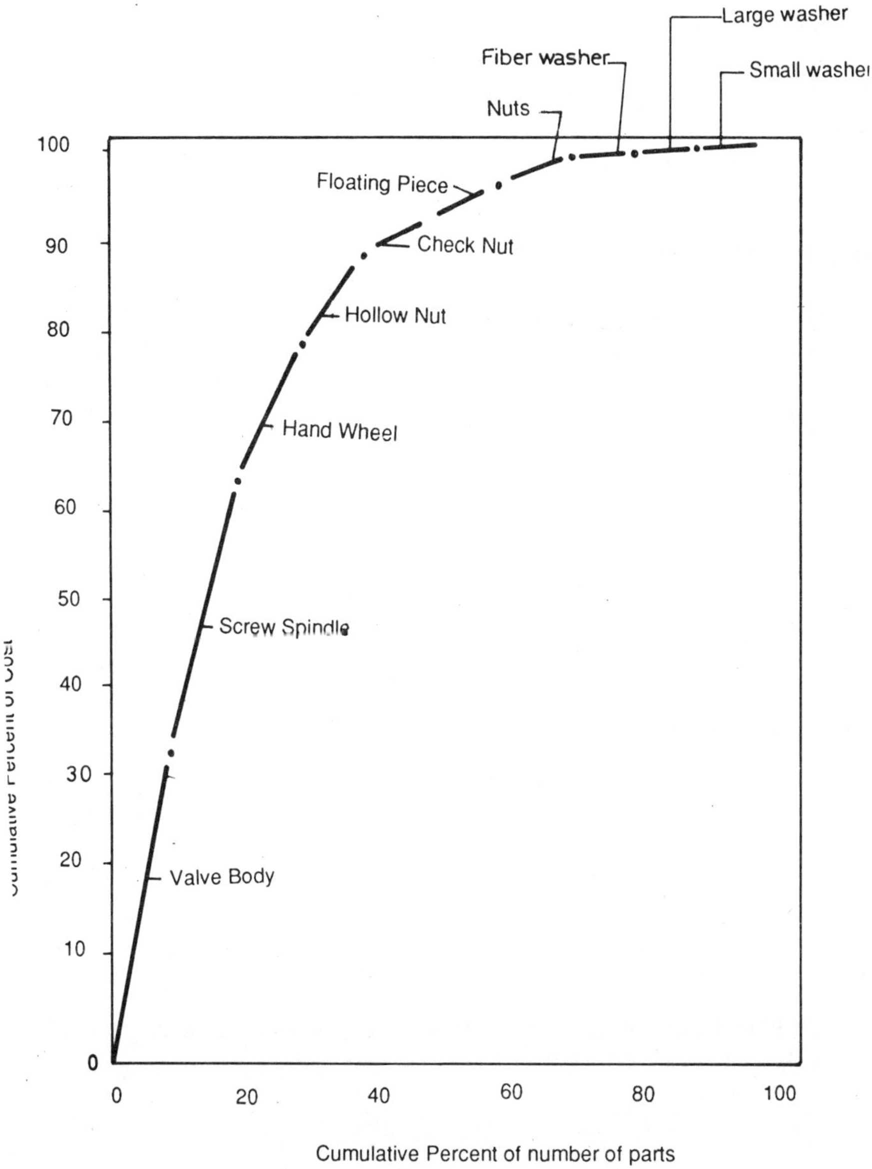

Fig. 24. Cumulative Cost Distribution Curve

ABC Analysis

This is an extension of the relative ranking technique. Listing every item, the unit costs, multiplying unit cost by annual usage, and arranging in descending order of magnitude, will enable categorising the high expenditure items or "A" items (20% in number, and 80% in cost), the low expenditure items, or "C" items (70% in number, and 10% in costs), and the rest, middle group, or "B" items. Cost concentrations of items become visible, making selection easy.

Modified ABC Analysis

Considerations of other factors than costs, like excessive scrap, re-work, test, inspection time, etc. can improve the selection process.

6. PRELIMINARY ASSESSMENT

Value Index

$$\text{Value Index} = \frac{\text{WORTH}}{\text{COST}}$$

By definition, Worth is the least cost for performing the function.

The worth of all secondary functions is ZERO for value engineering purposes. And, worth is associated with the necessary function(s) and not with the present design of the item.

Experience has shown that low value indices (or COST to WORTH ratios greater than 2) will usually indicate good potential for value efforts. (see examples in Fig 25).

Value Gap

By definition, Value Gap = COST – WORTH

A high figure shows good potential for value improvements (refer Fig. 26).

ITEM	BASIC FUNCTION	COST C	LOWEST COST ALTERNATIVE TO ACCOMPLISH BASIC FUNCTION	COST OF THE ALTER-NATIVE WORTH W	RATIO C/W
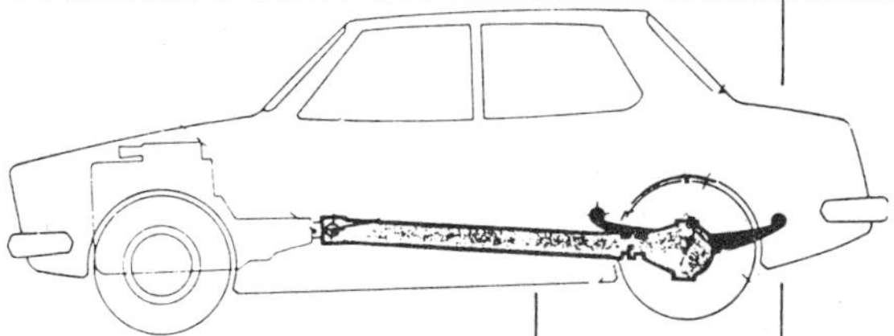 PROPELLER SHAFT	TRANSMIT TORQUE	18,000	LEATHER BELTING	1,100	18:1
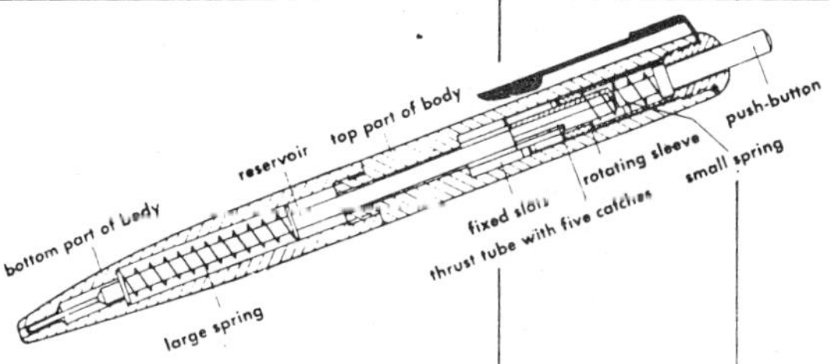 JOTTER	MAKE MARKS	7	INK POT CROW QUILL	1	7:1
 MUG	HOLD LIQUID	10	KULLAD (Throw-away CLAY cup)	0.20	50:1

Fig. 25

SELECTION OF PROJECT

ITEM	BASIC FUNCTION	COST (RS) "C"	LOWEST COST ALTERNATIVE TO ACCOMPLISH THE BASIC FUNCTION	COST OF THE ALTERNATIVE (RS) "W"	VALUE GAP C – W
AUTOMOBILE HOSE PIPE 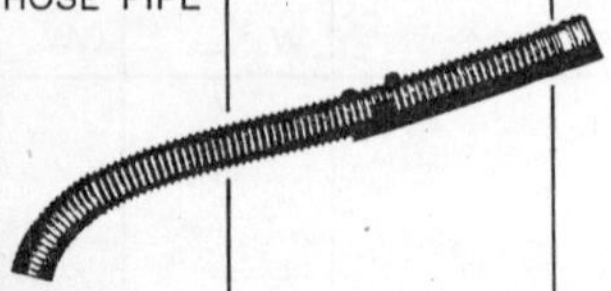	CONVEY OIL	60/=	PLASTIC TUBE	6/=	54
RAILWAY COACH BERTH READING LIGHT 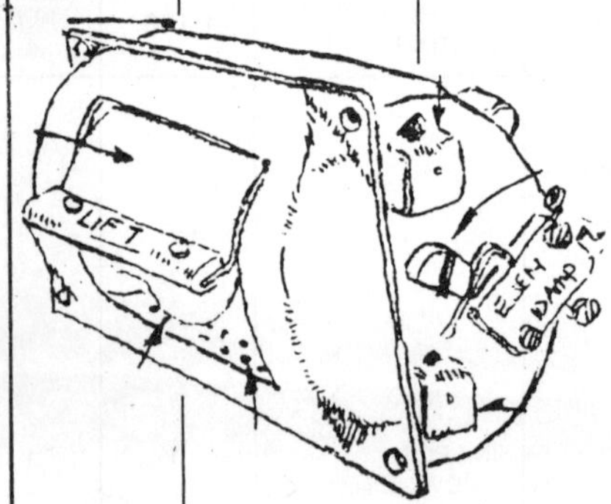	DIRECT BEAM	75/=	WALL FITTING (BULB, HOLDER, WIRE, SWITCH.)	18/=	57
JOTTER 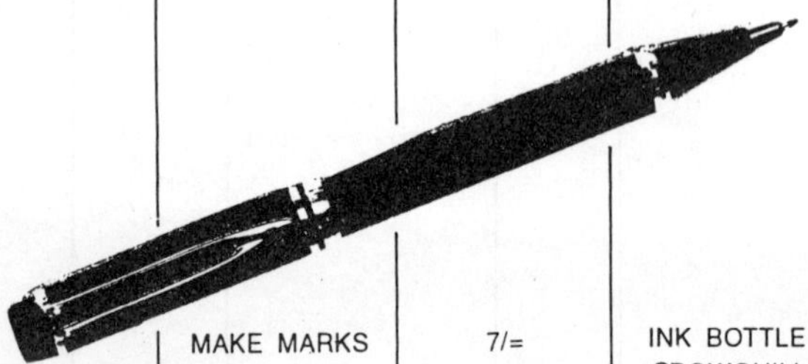	MAKE MARKS	7/=	INK BOTTLE & CROWQUILL	1/=	6

Fig. 26

Index of Savings Potential*

$$\text{Index of Cost Savings potential} = \frac{\text{Estimated study savings}}{\text{Estimated costs of study}} \times \text{Probability of Implementation}$$

where:

Estimated Savings	=	*Present Cost (before VE) – Estimated Cost (after VE)*
Present Cost (before VE)	=	*Quantity × Present Cost Per unit.*
Estimated Cost (after VE)	=	*Quantity × Estimated Cost of proposed, per unit.*
Estimated Cost of study	=	*Estimate of Cost of VE Study + Estimate of Cost of Implementation*
Probability of Implementation	=	*0.0 for no chance of implementation. 1.0 for certainty, with no chance for not being implemented. Interpolate for the range.*

The item with highest index should be considered for the value study, first.

7. BRAINSTORMING IN TRAINING COURSES

If the company runs its own training programmes, (as many major organisations do at present for their key personnel as a regular feature) — especially in Value Engineering — the participants could be put through a brainstorming session during every programme and a list of probable items for study can be prepared. These can then be short-listed by the top management and prioritised.

NOTE: When an organisation commences a Value Engineering programme, and when a team attempts their maiden studies, it would be advisable to select comparatively easier projects, problems and simple items. Otherwise, if the measure of success in the first few items happens to be low, the managements and the team members are likely to become despondent and show reluctance to continue the value work.

* Tufty, p. 25

TYPE OF PROJECTS

A typical listing of the type of projects follows:

Facilities	Buildings.
	Land.
	Heating.
	Lighting.
	Power.
	Fuel.
	Material Handling.
	Layout.
Hardware Projects	Complete Product.
	Assembly.
	Sub-assembly.
	Component part.
	Packaging.
	Forms.
	Materials.
	Production Equipment.
	Tools.
	Jigs and Fixtures.
	Transportation.
	Sequence of Operations.
	Job time.

Software Projects

Design

Systems.

Processes.

Procedures.

Plans.

Methods.

Product planning.

Production planning.

Marketing plan.

Order handling.

Shop scheduling.

Machine loading.

Distribution program.

Billing.

Accounts receivable.

SELECTING TEAM MEMBERS

A successful Value Engineering study requires a knowledge and expertise in the technical field of study and a solid background in the principles of Value Engineering. For the latter, the participants should have taken a 40-hour Value Engineering MOD I Training Course as a minimum requirement.

A diversity of talents and expertise are needed — as diverse as possible. To mould the team into a productive group, it should include ideamen, communicators, developers and organisers; integrators, producers and processors. In every organisation, there will be individuals with these characteristics, traits and styles. An effective organisation uses their strengths to make the functioning whole.

Larry Miles had identified eight essential qualifications for value effort as*:

1. *Knowledge.*
2. *Imagination.*
3. *High degree of initiative.*
4. *Self-organisation.*
5. *Personality.*
6. *Cooperative attitude.*
7. *Experience.*
8. *Belief in the importance of value.*

Larry Zimmerman and Glen Hart add *diplomacy and salesmanship*** to this list. I would like to add CONSTRUCTIVE DISCONTENT and HUMILITY as two other essential traits.

Selection of the team members must be appropriate to the specific requirements for the project under study. A team studying Iron and Steel Plant items will include a Metallurgist. A Water Treatment Plant study team

---

* Miles, p. 268, 269

** Zimmerman and Hart, p. 126

would include a Sanitary Engineer; a team for a Bridge, a Foundation Engineer; that for a Hotel, an Architect; and so on.

In a manufacturing concern, there would be representatives from among Design, Purchase, Production, Industrial Engineering, Quality Assurance, Marketing and Cost. Other people would be invited to the meetings as necessary at appropriate time for consultation, if they will have some contribution to make.

It is beneficial to utilise the services of a qualified Value Specialist for the study, as a team member. His expertise in the field of Value Engineering, proper application of the Value Engineering methodology, and references to past projects will produce effective results in quick time. This is particularly true with early efforts at value work, when the skills are being learnt.

The intention is to place every member in the team at equal footing when starting the value study. However, one of them would be the leader and one, a facilitator.

The selection is subject to management approval and support. Sometimes members are selected who occupy high heirarchical positions in the organisation to ensure certainty of implementation. Another way is to name the official who has the problem as the leader. Sometimes the team includes a person who does not know anything about the item under study: who is ignorant enough not to know that "it cannot be done." For that matter, a Secretary, a Clerk or a Worker. They ask innocent questions that shatters assumptions and open minds to exciting new ways. The axiom is that, if they can be convinced that the solution proposed is the best, it certainly will be.

A subtle point in team selection is the relations between the members. It is not always good policy to select members on the basis of their getting on well with others. For, mutual conflict produces ideas. It may also produce results in ways that amity cannot.

If possible, the same people are not selected over and over again for the teams, on the basis that they have experience in making value studies. This breeds laxness and sterility of ideas, which are to be prevented. By the same token, the team should not include the Designer who originally designed the item.

WHY TEAM WORK IS IMPORTANT

What is so powerful about team work ? They work. They have passed the test of time. In fact, one of the best ways of injecting change is the use of teams.

The pace of change in business today is awesome. The only viable approach to deal with this pace is to unleash the power of people by implementing the process of team based continuous improvement. Hence, teams have become the basic units of management structure of many successful companies. They have learnt that there is no longer any such thing as a single function Manager in any capacity. They have also realized that if they cannot solve problems as teams, they will not last very long, and their future success would depend on their ability to tap the collective wisdom — that is the accumulated judgments, perceptions, experiences, intuition, and intelligence — of all the employees. Employees are generally pragmatic. They look for new and better ways of doing their jobs. And, people who know best how the job should be done, are the ones doing it. Work teams have delivered too much success that the idea is stretching beyond corporate boundaries as alliances — as strategic partnerships, vendor – supplier teams, and other customer – involvement activities.

The 1991 Industry Week Survey of 340 US companies cites improved team work as one of the most important tools they were using to solve major issues: like customer service, cost reduction and product quality. A 1992 study by the University of North Carolina cites growth of people and team work as the most rewarding change in managing a company. General Electric Co., Motorola Inc., and General Motors Corp., use team work as a matter of course. Boeing has as many as 240 Design – Build teams on the job at one time. Like pieces in a jigsaw puzzle, Design, Engineering, Supply and Production from locations in USA and Europe are working in teams to build Ford's world car, managing across boundaries. Combination of computers and communications, voice mail and e-mail, and affordable desk top video conferencing make possible collaboration in real time, 24 hours a day. No matter what any company called its drive for competitiveness during the last decade — re-engineering, re-structuring, flattening the organisational hierarchy — the end result had a common theme: turning loose functionally diverse teams of creative professionals with a mandate to come up with world class ideas.

Teams do jobs that can't be done otherwise. They are designed for results, not longevity. Teams can form, do their jobs and then disappear. For instance, Iridium International Satellite Communication network (SATCOM), is rooted on teams forming, disbanding, and reforming around new tasks as needed. Texas Instruments has similar reconfigurable teams that form and reshape themselves depending on the operation.

The table overleaf compares traditional task force approach and team approach.

	Task Forces	*Teams*
Composition	• Departmental or experienced members.	• Work related members.
Characteristics	• Take directions. • Demand more resources. • React to emergencies.	• Take initiative. • Work with what they have. • Take steps to prevent emergencies.
Attitudes	• Compete. • Spend more money to improve quality.	• Cooperate. • Save money by improving quality.
Solution urgency	• Moderate. • Stop at present goals.	• High. • Continually improve.
Focus	• Focus on blame/excuses.	• Concentrate on results/ solutions.
Scope of activity	• Tackle Departmental problems.	• Solve complex and cross departmental problems.
Management Direction	• Moderate to high	• Moderate.
Rewards	• Seek individual rewards.	• Focus on team contributions.

Investigations show that the result of team work is considerably better than the sum of all results brought about by the same people working alone. Done right, they deliver spectacular results. Fortune reports that the use of cross-functional teams had reduced new product introduction time by 50% to 70%. General Electric admits reduction in assembly labor by 40%. Ingersoll Rand cut production time for a new power tool by 75%. General Mills, in their cereal plant, raised productivity by 40%. 3 M turned a failing division by tripling their output. Once sagging Rolls Royce was reshaped using multi-functional team principles for everything from new product development programs to changes on the manufacturing floor at Crewe, England — making the company profitable. Harvard Business Review reports cut in failure rates by 84%. Zebra Technologies Corp., using team approach, pioneered an industry-first use of the structural plastic ABS/polycarbonate to combine parts, reduce overall weight, facilitate easier manufacture and repetitive assembly, cut down direct labor content by 50% and market the product in less than 20% to 25% less time.

Increased complexity in almost everything organisations do demands greater coordination and communication among persons in different functions and/or geographic area. Whether it is product development, process improvement, customer satisfaction, or vehicle for fixing the organisation, like re-engineering, de-layering, or re-structuring, the one common vital element today is teams.

Quick completion of the work, simultaneous consideration of the expertise of all specialists involved, fewer check backs, less correspondence, more ideas and combination of ideas, etc., are vital to find a better solution. A team is set up to play a bigger than a person role. Team work is sharing power, involving others, and organizing people around the work that is important to the organisation's customers. To wit, team work in Toyota Motor Co. means involvement of all employees in the plant (4,000 in one plant), generation of 40,000 ideas annually about material savings, general quality, and labour savings, and implementing 20,000. This global giant produces quality products, saves time and makes tons of money.

Developing faster design/manufacturing cycles has become top priority today. Critical to the speeding up process are team work and composition of the team. For example, Designers want a new level of product performance. So, they want the item to be rugged, strong and with a high factor of safety, so that it does not fail under both normal working conditions and an occasional over-load. Naturally, it tends to become more expensive. Manufacturing wants low cost and high quality, which are seemingly contradictory. Sales promise early deliveries and discounts to fill their order books; but in the process impose problems for manufacture and supply. Similarly, each specialist thinks of his discipline and concentrates on doing his best for his subgoal, in turn causing problems for the others. Rarely do each functional specialist have self-contained tasks. In most cases, others possess critical information and expertise. For example, the Designer may propose the size, shape, material and characteristics of the product; not its producibility, nor its maintainability. The Production Manager would know the problems of making it as designed and the Maintenance Engineer, in keeping it working. The Materials Manager would know the specifications; but the Vendor, making similar items for many years and many users, would better know which of the several items that conform to the specifications is the best; or which specification hurts the performance or utility of the item. Thus, there is a high degree of interdependence between functional specialists, if their combined efforts are to result in excellence. Assistance from others is often required to implement decisions and programmes (Refer to Fig. 5, page 23).

US Automobile industry typically takes 4 to 5 years and billions of dollars to bring a new car to market. Auto makers used to design cars in a sequence of decisions. Stylists would determine what the car would look like and then hand off the design to the Engineers. Engineers would try to reconcile the mechanical demands of the car with its appearance, and hand off the result to manufacturing specialists. These latter would then try to figure out a way to build the car. But, Chrysler's LH Cars, the product of a reorganized engineering team working on the total car, (and not simply its components such as body, chassis, power train, and electricals), was created in just 3 years. The NEON was then developed in only 31 months and at a cost of $ 1.3 billion. The combined use of team approach and technology, involving everybody in one platform, including styling, engineering, manufacturing, purchasing, and proving out concepts in pilot facility and mini assembly plant, enabled this optimization. Land Rover DISCOVERY program went from concept to manufacture in slightly more than 2 years and to market launch in less than 3 years.

To get the best solution, optimising for the company as a whole, the functional specialists must cross the functional barriers and work as one integrated unit, owing allegiance to the organisation goal and its objective of the best product or service to the user. Changing of allegiance is a tricky job; but in it lies success. Only a team approach ensures this. The Designer should design to affordable cost, producibility and maintainability considerations, using manufacturing, maintenance and user expertise and information. Manufacturing should similarly use maintenance, inspection and user expertise and information to make the product work, sell and serve. Materials Manager should use the expertise of all Vendors to advantage, and not only the strength of the registered suppliers. The Vendor, an expert in his line, may have a better item to give than what is specified, with equivalent or better performance and same or lower costs.

In this age of specialization, when no one manufacturer will have all the core competence to produce all the right components, out-sourcing will have to proliferate; and in such a situation, it will be in the better self interest to take advantage of this vast resource. Removing departmental optimization syndrome is not easy. It involves far more than simply re-drawing the lines of authority and job rotation. Though a tricky job, in it lies success. Only a team approach ensures this.

Team builds that same common focus and collective effort — here, VALUE. The members working towards this common goal would act in compatible ways, despite strong individual differences. Individual differences are but natural in contemporary organisations, because diverse talents are recruited to deal with changing, complex needs. Heterogenity in background, experience and knowledge cannot be avoided.

Taking care of all the members in a way that values them as individuals and for the special contributions that they make, encourages achievement of common orientation, coordinated behaviour, dedicated involvement and full contribution.

The need for continuous improvement has triggered numerous work design changes: like more self-management, expanded job boundaries, more flexible work assignments, etc. Jobs evolve from narrow and task-oriented bias to multi-dimensional units that naturally gel together to complete a whole piece of work. More work is done now in teams, and value adding work. Employees have more responsibility and greater variety of task. They spend more time doing real work. Work becomes more satisfying, since they achieve a greater sense of completion and accomplishment from their jobs.

Ten years ago, it was not uncommon for an employee to receive a skeptical look from his or her boss when a request to work from home-even part time – was raised. The issue has now come a full circle. Not only have work at home and other forms of work place flexibility become more accepted, but companies are beginning to abandon traditional status-symbol offices for environments that better reflect the way that work is done by teams and with customers, suppliers and partners, helping people do their jobs more effectively. This trend is escalating upwards.

Team ensures fuller use of the resources of the members and increases their competence. Joint responsibility increases individual challenge. It leads to greater commitment, motivation and better performance. A cohesive team increases the range of skills and knowledge available. In a rapidly changing world, constantly requiring new knowledge and skills. Each one can no longer be expected always to have all the necessary expertise. On a complex problem, different people with different information can contribute to make a better decision than otherwise.

Teams are not easy to start. They require careful planning, a structure to start and a problem that cannot be better addressed by other means. Teams are not an extension of the traditional organization. They are never fully self directed, or completely independent. Teams need chartering, direction, monitoring and feed back from management. But as they gel, they set up their own roles, rules and relationships: and produce results. The chemical manufacturer Rohn & Haas Co., has successfully redesigned its Louisville work place to a self regulated teamwork environment, helping people to do their work easier and with increasing proficiency. The St. Peters facility of MEMC Electronic Materials, silicon wafer makers to the booming semi conductor industry, has 100% employee participation in empowered work teams throughout the plant, besides supplier improvement teams, cross functional work teams, corrective action teams and total machine performance teams.

(Self directed work teams are led by the natural leader of the group — and not the Foreman or Supervisor. They decide how best to go about doing whatever they have to do. Management only defines what work has to be done; but leaves how to do it best to the people who are doing it, as such deciding is best done by them).

With team work, not only does one learn and get help from one another, not only does one gain speed and directness in solving problems, but also become charged with great dynamism, enthusiasm and exhiliration. This is most conducive, fertile atmosphere and climate to generate new and better ideas, new and better products, and new and better ways of doing things.

To succeed, teams need time, patience and tender nurturing. Famous auto designer Donald Peterson of Ford says that the team approach to design and work started in Ford in the early, 70s is still in its infancy.

TEAM LEADER

To maintain the study on course and on schedule, one member is named the Leader. Usually the person who has the problem or who is most concerned with it would be named the Leader. It has the added advantage that once the Value Engineering Change Proposal is finalised, he would himself take action to implement it. The selling of the proposal would be facile.

Team performance and effectiveness depends more on the Leader, his skills and his actions than on anything else. Half his job, the easy half, is working with his team. The other half is giving the team a powerful purpose, coordinating interdependent work, obtaining support resources and negotiating for time and availability of team members. It takes a superb leader to build that kind of team where people work together and adjust and take their cues from others and move ahead as a cohesive unit. That is not easy. That takes time, skill, nerve and a missionary zeal. Peter Drucker quotes a retired senior executive of Toyota saying this about their Design Team: "it doesn't perform yet." The team began work in 1950.

The team Leader must be CREATIVE; i.e.,

Create trust and win-win relationship amongst members.

Resourceful — using group processes.*

Expand team capabilities.

Aware of the VE Methodology.

Technically skilled, but not over-applying them.

Imaginative, inspiring, innovative, illuminating.

Versatile, delegating and letting go.

Empathetic.*

(*such as coaching, problem solving, role negotiation, etc.)

Note the acrostic.

Good team Leaders do not push the members. They use team goals and mission to pull them into high performers. The most successful team leaders set high expectations with each person. A team Leader does not actually "lead," but "builds," "develops," and "supports." He guards against group decisions being gained by compromise. In Value Engineering, there is no compromise. What is required is positively provided. The team Leader ensures that the group is not misled by any flashy member who expresses himself well. In addition, he also helps the one with the best idea to organize himself and express well his or her thoughts.

TEAM MEMBERS

Team members may come from all relevant functions: like, marketing, design, product development, manufacturing, materials management, engineering, quality assurance, etc. They may also include representation from the legal sector, safety, product liability and customer base. The qualifications suggested for the member are also akin to that for the team Leader. A group of five to seven members is considered the best size for a team.

TEAM COORDINATOR

To arrange for the logistics and the set up for the actual study sessions, to schedule the meetings, to collect and keep the vast amount of information and data required for the study, to record the ideas gathered during the creative session, to prepare the recommendations and reports, etc., to follow up at every stage of the study, one individual is designated Value Engineering Team Coordinator, Facilitator or Value Engineer. If the studies are few and far between, he can be one of the members of the Team. But, if there is a large quantum of work, a member of the permanent organisational set up of the company may be vested this responsibility.

TEAM FACILITATOR

Some use a team facilitator to coordinate and arrange for the necessary logistics for the value study. He is chosen for the knowledge of the system, his ability to teach or mentor the needed techniques to perform each step of the value study, his understanding of the usable creativity techniques, road blocks, wrong beliefs and identifies ways of strengthening the mix of individual skills. He coaches, manages relationships, provides encouragement, locates potential obstacles and works to remove them. He treats differences as strengths and seeks a win-win solution that can be supported.

General Phase

The General Phase lays the foundation for value efforts. Project selection and forming the team for Value Engineering studies form part of this phase, if not completed earlier. The team consists of 5 to 7 members depending on the size of the project, and work to 6 ground rules.

Value Engineering is team work. Success in team work depends more on good human relations, i.e., working with people, rather than use of techniques. Use of good human relations would mean cooperation, assistance, moulding into a dynamic and creative group of all the people who will be contributing to the study, etc. This is **Rule No. 1.**

A true team is a group of associates, all *"subordinating personal prominence to the efficiency of the whole."** It is important to preach, practice and demonstrate team spirit all through the study. So also, finding and using *"the best means of working successfully with all people in relationships which bring out the best in everyone."** This is **Rule No. 2.**

Getting off on the right foot on a Value Engineering study is like starting a new job. So, laying out the responsibilities of each member of the team will lead to a well coordinated effort. In this phase, the entire Value Engineering process, the project in hand and individual responsibilities are outlined. **Rule No. 3** will be work on specifics, divided and allocated to each member.

Resistance to change and progress are human — almost instinctive. Identifying and overcoming road blocks — *"those imposed on us by others and those imposed on us by ourselves,"* * will be **Rule No. 4.**

Rule No. 5, is to apply good business judgement; have an open mind; curb your overenthusiasm to please and to force your personal opinions on others.

Rule No. 6. Profess and practice better relations.

Art Mudge recommends the following ten-step guide* to better

---

* Mudge p. 38, 40, 44

relations:

1. *Be a good listener.*
2. *Determine the other fellow's incentives.*
3. *Put yourself in his position.*
4. *Discuss everything with an open mind.*
5. *Explain your objectives.*
6. *Base all decisions on facts.*
7. *Don't act as the infalliable judge.*
8. *Learn from the experience of others.*
9. *Work on a give-and-take basis.*
10. *Stress the greater rewards available through team work.*

INFORMATION PHASE

Lack of full information and use of inadequate information and misinformation are the major causes of poor degree of value. Therefore, the search for pertinent and accurate information from the right sources is imperative in Value Engineering. The more exhaustive and diligent the search is, the better the information will be and, so, better the value attained in the final solution.

Traditional connections to customers are no longer sufficient. Companies should no longer develop new products on information gathered from traditional tools. On the other hand, they should cull all information that the focus groups, market research, consumer surveys, for probing the consumer wants and needs. Besides, they should involve the customer as a partner in development and production.

Collecting, collating, verifying, testing, updating, processing and selecting information is the first step. The important consideration is to get ALL THE FACTS and to get them from the BEST SOURCES. All information are important, regardless of how unrelated they seem, or how much disorganised they are when collected. After all the facts have been gathered, they can be organised.

It is suggested to begin with delineation of the overall problem, product, project, process or procedure. A sample of the item is obtained, if possible and convenient. Specifications, drawings, sketches relevant to the item, are procured — the assembly, sub-assembly, part or process are covered and the quantities of each, recorded. Requirements established by the manufacturers, the users, the maintenance and the service are noted. Details of operating experience, maintenance, servicing, and report of concerned personnel are secured. Through consultations, as needed, full information is obtained on application, marketing, engineering, product history, performance needs, production problems, procurement, scrap, reject and rework, quality management, warranty and so on. The nature and type of equipment used, methods, sequence of operations, tools, dies, moulds, jigs and fixtures needed, the tolerances, fits and allowances applied, finishes and treatment given, are areas to be covered.

The next step is to determine the costs. *"Good costs provide a tool* *for measuring the facts that have been secured."** They also *"provide a means to determine the amount of effort that can be economically spent"** in any area of the project under study. Cost figures normally developed in industries are for use in profit accounting, to make tax returns, and to fulfil mandatory obligations. From them, meaningful costs have to be developed for the purpose of making correct value decisions. Starting out with the best costs that exist, understanding them, knowing their structure, necessary modifications are made to convert them into meaningful costs. It helps if costs are transferred to the drawing, specification, etc.

Specifications and requirements determine the nature, type, size, shape, properties, characteristics, etc. of the final product, process or procedure. Naturally, these also influence the cost of the final product. The costs of each specification and requirement are calculated. They are then analysed to determine which of these are imposed on the producer by the user and which, by himself. This analysis will be handy when, in the later phases, screening out of the imaginary from the real specification or requirement is done.

The knowledge, information and data secured in this phase will be directly used in the next, Function Analysis phase, to break down, into specific details, exactly what the item does; is supposed to do and must do; where, in what order and in what sequence; how and why. Hence the need for accuracy and completeness.

* Mudge, p. 52

Function Phase

It is the Function Analysis and approach that distinguishes and differentiates the Value Engineering technique from all other cost reduction and cost management programmes.

In the Function Analysis Phase, the team defines the Function(s) of the item under study, classifies them and evaluates the functional relationships. When this analysis is complete, necessary and un-necessary functions will become visible.

FUNCTION DEFINITION

Value Engineering defines FUNCTION as that which makes a product work or sell. Miles defines it as *"a want to satisfy a requirement."** Function is certainly the end result or action desired by the customer. It is the requirement, the goal, or the objective that one desires to accomplish. It is what one pays for.

The customer wants a function to be achieved reliably, efficiently and well by the product or service that the customer buys. In other words, the customer wants:

something performed,
something carried,
something stopped,
something rotated,
something joined,
something protected,
something opened,
something closed,
something covered,
something insulated,
something exposed,
and so on.

---

* Miles, p. 25

It may be under free or open conditions. Or, it may have to be achieved under specified conditions, within certain set limits and against some restrictions; like:

supported in narrow confines,
carried forward and backward,
moved over rough terrain,
stopped intermittently,
rotated by manual means or remote control,
joined without overlap,
cooled rapidly,
heated slowly,
and so on.

Or, the customer may want a size, contour, an appearance, a smell, a tint, a texture, a finish, a glaze, etc. And, these may be to bring operational ease, comfort, facility, and/or satisfaction to self or to others he or she wishes to please. The key to Value Engineering is the identification of what exactly the user or customer wants from a product, service, system, organisation, component, etc. i.e., the FUNCTION. In this context it is important to remember that the customer really buys the FUNCTION, or the satisfaction derived from the use of the item. This is his concern. He is least interested in how it is accomplished — so long as it is accomplished effectively, reliably and well, and at reasonable costs.

Using the information gathered in the Information Phase the function is described, asking such questions as:

1. What is the item ?
2. What does it do ?
3. Is that what the customer wants it to do ?
4. Is that what the customer cares about ?
5. Is that what the customer believes he is paying for ?
6. What must it do ?

The product may comprise a number of assemblies, sub-assemblies and components. The service may correspondingly comprise a number of operations. A system may similarly comprise a number of sub-systems. The procedure is to separate them into functional units, and analyse their functions. For example, a refrigerator is seen as made up of a cooling system, an insulating system, a container system, a control system and aesthetics to please. A transport vehicle is seen as carrying people, manoevering, controlling.

Another method will be to strip the item to the last component or element, and analyse their functions. For example, a knife switch may be broken down into its parts — insulating base, switch blade, contacts, bolt and nut. A transport vehicle may be divided into body, chassis, transmission, engine. For each the component parts are listed, and the function of all parts analysed/identified.

The mechanical and electrical functions may be easily spotted. But, in other cases, it may not be easily discerned.

From the details secured in the Information Phase, a detailed description is first made and then a precis. Such brief, but succinct, description will enable function identification (See Example: Connector). Improve and clarify, until the description says what the function really is.

RULE 1: states that the function must be defined in TWO WORDS — a VERB and a NOUN. Verbalising is not permitted. Experience shows that the number of words it takes to describe a function is inversely proportional to the understanding of what the function is.

Example: CONNECTOR

Its description may read thus

Drawing No. x x x shows a CONNECTOR, a part of a commercial electrical equipment assembly, called a Voltage Regulator. The Voltage Regulator is used in power-line systems to **provide** voltage **regulation** to those lines.

Five of these connectors are used per voltage regulator to connect high and low voltage bushings to the core and coil. Each connector is mounted in a 1/2 in. hole in the insulating board. The connectors are required for simple field maintenance, ie. ability to **readily disconnect** and replace the porcelain bushings when they are damaged in final manufacture, shipment or operation. It must be possible to do this when the unit is on the ground, as well as when it is mounted on the power pole.

Original connector was designed 5 years ago when, as a rush job, the insulating board had to be added to mount other required and newly designed equipment. It comprises 11 parts, some standard and others, special.

It is designed to **carry** a maximum of 30 amp. **current** with minimum losses. This is made possible by **connecting** the **terminal** wire from the insulating bushing on the cover of the tank between two 3/8 in. brass nuts. The connecting to the **core and coil** is accomplished by crimping the core and coil lead into a copper tube at the lower end of the connector and **fastening** into the assembly **tight** by a hollow brass nut. Both these connections must be **readily disconnectable**. And, at the same time, they are able to **withstand** normal shipping and operational **vibration, without opening out.**

Current sale is 1,750 units per year. Forecast future demand is 3,000 to 5,000 units per year for the next 5 years, if cost and price were reduced.

Field failures reported are nil. Marketing complains breakages during shipping, warehousing.

Manufacturing problems were on two parts — stud and copper tube.

On the stud, when it was re-chucked to drill, bottom drill, cut relief and thread, either the threads got damaged, or the part tended to be unstable in the chuck. Copper tube was splitting when head was formed, causing high scrap rate. Hence productivity is low, and cost high.

The insulating board is required to mount new equipment. There is air in the upper chamber, above the insulating board and air and transformer oil in the lower chamber, below the board. During operation, heat generated induces a pressure of 7 psi above the atmospheric pressure, in the lower chamber. It is therefore important that the assembly does not move and that it **seals the opening** in the insulating board through which the connector passes.

This description may be precied. For this example, however, if the text is considered as the precis itself, it could be screened to cull relevant verbs and nouns, and refined through discussions as below to improve and clarify, until the combination of verb and noun say exactly what the function really is.

VERBS AND NOUNS CULLED FROM DESCRIPTION

VERBATIM	**REFINED THROUGH DISCUSSION**
Provide Regulation	Not, relevant, as input current = output current, 30 amps.
Readily Disconnect	FACILITATE DISCONNECTION
Carry Current	CONDUCT CURRENT
Connecting Terminal **Connecting Core and Coil**	ESTABLISH CONNECTION
Fastening Tight	APPLY PRESSURE
Withstand Vibration **Without Opening Out**	INDUCE FRICTION
Seals Opening	CREATE SEAL

RULE 2: To provide precision in thinking and understanding, work

functions are expressed as ACTION VERBS and MEASURABLE NOUNS, which establish quantitative statements and sell functions, in PASSIVE VERBS and NON-MEASURABLE NOUNS, which establish qualitative statements. Some typical verbs and nouns used commonly for defining functions are listed in the following:

Work Functions*

Verbs

Support	Change
Transmit	Interrupt
Create	Establish
Hold	Shield
Enclose	Modulate
Collect	Control
Conduct	Transmit
Insulate	Emit
Protect	Repel
Prevent	Filter
Reduce	Impede
Amplify	Induce
Rectify	Provide
Apply	

Nouns

Measurable		Non-Measurable	
Weight	Oxidation	Component	Device
Light	Flow	Part	Article
Heat	Current	Table	Wire
Radiation	Insulation		
Friction	Density		
Voltage	Energy		
Force	Circuit		
Damage	Repair		
Protection	Liquid		
Fluid			

---

* Mudge p. 62

Sell Functions*

Verbs	Nouns	
Increase	Beauty	Symmetry
Decrease	Appearance	Effect
Improve	Convenience	Exchange
	Style	Features
	Prestige	Form

RULE 3: Keep function definition SIMPLE, and choose VERBS as BROAD as possible. Using the same words as in the item description restricts the ways in which the function can be accomplished.

The following examples will illustrate:

(a) Approaching from the point of view of USE: (Fig. 27-A and 27-B)

Function definition

SUPPORT WEIGHT

PROVIDE COMFORT

ENHANCE APPEARANC

CHAIR

MAKE CIRCUIT

BREAK CIRCUIT

ELECTRICAL SWITCH

Fig. 27-A

* Mudge p. 62

Function definition

REFLECTOR ON BICYCLE

INDICATE PRESENCE

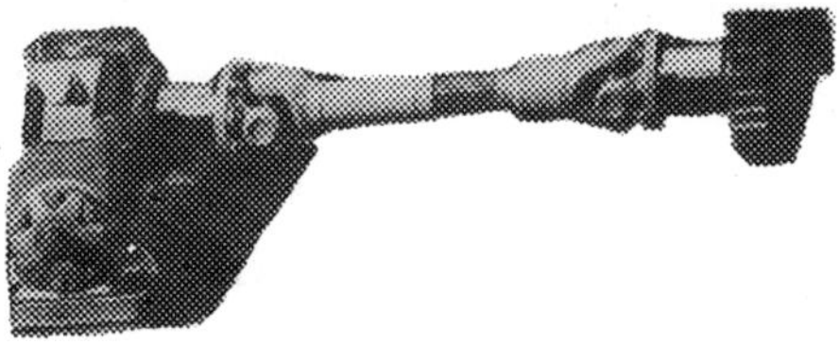

SHAFT

TRANSMIT TORQUE

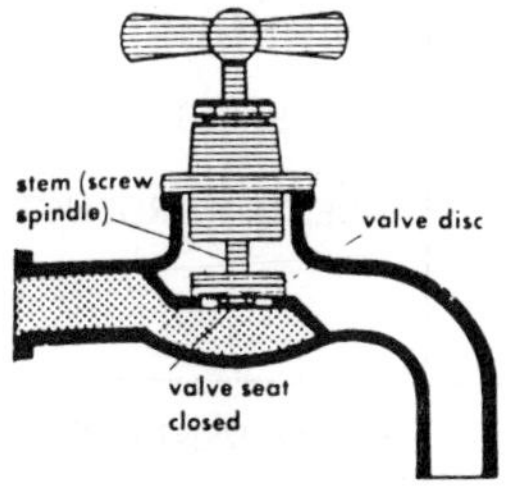

WATER TAP HANDLE

INCREASE MECHANICAL
ADVANTAGE

Fig. 27-B

(b) Analysing on the basis of PARTS: (Fig. 27-C)

ITEM	FUNCTIONAL UNIT	FUNCTION DEFINITION
 CIGARETTE LIGHTER	SPARK IGNITION UNIT	PRODUCE HEAT
	LID	PREVENT EVAPORATION
	INNER CONTAINER	HOLD FLUID
	OUTER CONTAINER	HOLD PARTS ENHANCE BEAUTY IDENTIFY OWNER
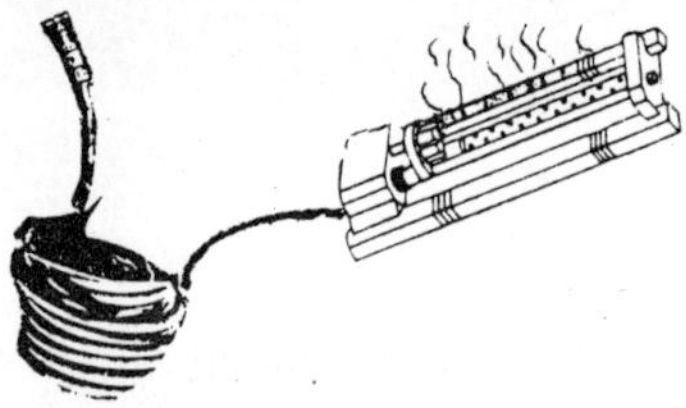 LAWN SPRINKLER SYSTEM	PIPES AND FITTINGS	CARRY FLUID
	VALVES	CONTROL FLOW
	NOZZLES	SPREAD FLUID
	WATER	SUSTAIN GROWTH
 PENCIL	WOOD	PROJECT GRAPHITE CARRY ITEMS (PAINT, PRINTING)
	GRAPHITE	MAKE MARKS
	PAINTING	HELP SALES
	PRINTING	INDENTIFY PRODUCT
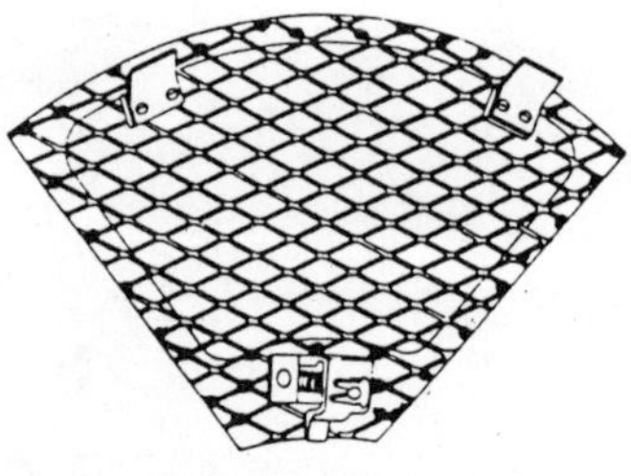 SCREEN FOR LARGE MOTOR	EXPANDED METAL	ALLOW VENTILATION EXCLUDE PARTICLES
	METAL FRAME	STRENGTHEN PART CARRY PART
	LOCKING	FACILITATE MAINTENANCE
	SHAPE	IMPROVE APPEARANCE
	PAINTING	PROTECT SUFRACE

Fig. 27-C

(c) Defining on the basis of CHARACTERISTICS: (Fig. 27-D)

The functions of the Railway Wheel Tyre would be:

PART:	Wheel Tyre	= Lengthens life of wheel
SHAPE:	Flange	= Prevents derailment Hugs rail
	Tread	= Transmits load
RAW MATERIAL: Steel		= Resists compression
PHYSICAL PROPERTY:		
	Tensile Strength	= Resists stress
CHEMICAL COMPOSITION:		
	Low percentage of Sulphur	= Maintains hardness
	Correct percentage of Chromium, Nickel, Molybdenum	= Resists corrosion, Toughens steel Withstands high temperature
TREATMENT:	Hardening tread	= Restructures molecules/grains.
MACHINING:		= Removes metal

Fig. 27-D

FUNCTION CLASSIFICATION

RULE 4: Divide all functions into two levels of importance — BASIC and SECONDARY. Basic function denotes *"the Primary Purpose for a product or service."** Secondary functions are those for *"other purposes, not directly accomplishing the primary purpose, but supporting it, or result from a specific design approach."**

Normally, an item has only one basic function. Rarely, if any, there will emerge two basic functions. Even there, in most cases, the functions involved would turn out to be re-statements of each other, or a combination of two distinct items into one. Secondary functions are either dependent or supporting some other action.

Ideally, the best value item will have only the basic function in it. Practically, however, the basic function will have one or more support functions to complete the product or service. Therefore, the target in Value Engineering is to accomplish the basic function in the best way, and to support it with minimum number of secondary functions; hence the importance of classifying the functions.

Functions can be classified by a number of methods.

1. FAMILY TREE

The difference between the input and the output indicates what the basic function of the item being studied is (Fig. 28).

10 amps. ⟶ [Fuse] ⟶ 10 amps.

Input - 10 amps.
Output - 10 amps.
Basic Function - PROVIDE CONTINUITY

Fig. 28. Fuse

A functional family tree of the system, sub-system, assembly, or the item is developed, placing the functions in order of priority arranging. Every function may have several auxiliary functions in the second generation. In turn, these auxiliary functions of the second generation may have their own auxiliary functions in the third generation, and so on. The clarity of representation of such family trees determines which functions are first in line for improved solutions (Fig. 29 & 30).

---

* Mudge, p. 61

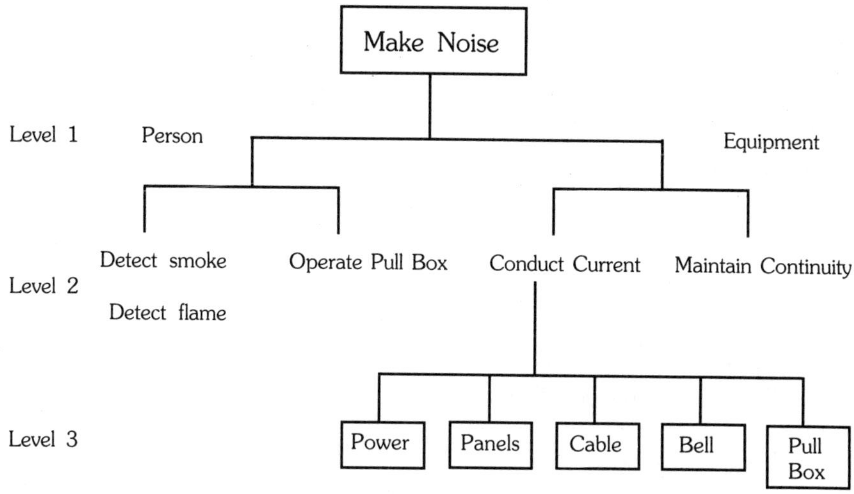

Fig. 29. Semi Automatic Fire Alarm

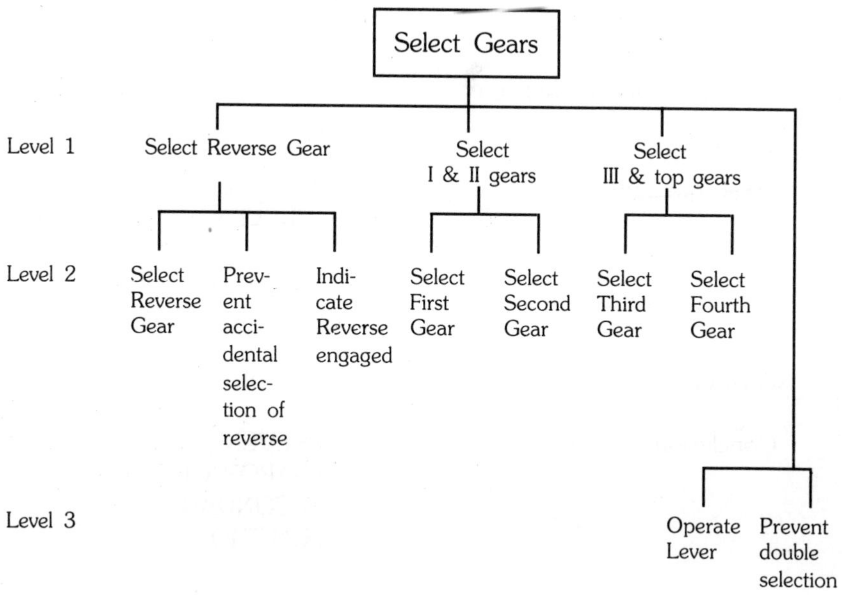

Fig. 30. Automobile Gear Box

2. LOGIC QUESTION

The logic question asked is:

IF THE FUNCTION THAT YOU ARE CONSIDERING IS NOT ACCOMPLISHED, WILL THE PRODUCT SATISFY THE PURPOSE FOR WHICH IT WAS MADE?

If the answer is "NO", then the function is BASIC.

Example:

CIGARETTE LIGHTER

(i)	Function being considered	-	PRODUCE HEAT
	Logic question	-	IF we eliminate "PRODUCE HEAT" will it satisfy the purpose for which it was made ?
	Answer	-	NO.
	Conclusion	-	PRODUCE HEAT is BASIC FUNCTION
(ii)	Function being considered	-	PREVENT EVAPORATION
	Logic question	-	If we eliminate "PREVENT EVAPORATION", will it do the job for which it was made?
	Answer	-	YES, it could.
	Conclusion	-	PREVENT EVAPORATION is SECONDARY FUNCTION

3. NUMERICAL EVALUATION

The following procedure is used: Using Function Definition Form No. 6, determine the functions of each part and then check in the basic function. Transfer all the basic functions to Function Classification Form No. 7, Avoid repetition. Codify, ie denote by a key letter each basic function. Then make a paired comparison, using a simple 3 point scale -

(1) for MINOR difference in importance,

(2) for MEDIUM difference, and

(3) for MAJOR difference.

Determine the weighted importance for each function relative to every other function. Add the weights of each.

That function which gets the highest total weight factor is the basic function. The descending order of importance of the secondary functions are as per descending value of the weight factor against each.

An example is given in the following.

Figure 31 shows a wooden packing case, used to crate and despatch a machinery, with a flat base, but irregular sides and top faces. The Figure also gives the bill of materials.

Figure 32 shows the defined functions in the upper table and the numerical evaluation of the function relationships in the lower table. Basic function of the packing case is seen as corresponding to key letter A, which has weighted total of 13 points, the maximum; i.e., PROTECT PART.

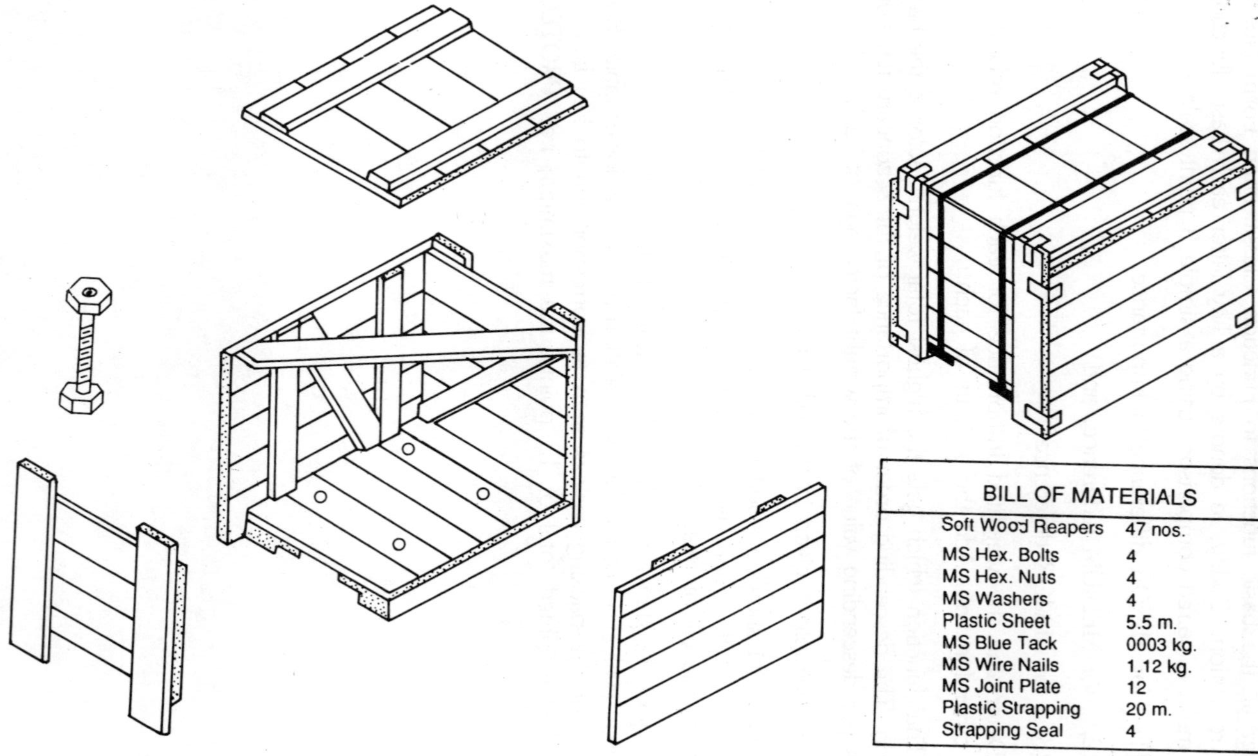

BILL OF MATERIALS	
Soft Wood Reapers	47 nos.
MS Hex. Bolts	4
MS Hex. Nuts	4
MS Washers	4
Plastic Sheet	5.5 m.
MS Blue Tack	0003 kg.
MS Wire Nails	1.12 kg.
MS Joint Plate	12
Plastic Strapping	20 m.
Strapping Seal	4

Fig. 31.

FUNCTION WORKSHEET

Part	Function	Key Letter
Wood Reapers	Protect part (being shipped) Facilitate transport Facilitate stacking Carry part (being shipped)	A B C D
Bolt, Nut and Washer	Locate part (being shipped)	E
Plastic sheet	Protect part (from dust/dirt)	
Blue Tack	Fasten part (Plastic Sheet)	F
Wire Nail	Fasten part (reapers)	
Joint Plate	Fasten part (of crate)	
Strapping	Restrain loosening (of crate)	G
Strapping seal	Restrain loosening (strap)	

	B	C	D	E	F	G	TOTAL
A	A2	A2	A2	A1	A3	A3	13
	B	B1	B1	B2	B3	B3	10
		C	C1	C1	C2	C2	5
			D	D1	D2	D2	6
				E	E1	E1	2
					F	F1	1

Scale:

Major - 3
Medium - 2
Minor - 1

Fig. 32.

4. FAST DIAGRAMMING

Function Analysis System Technique (FAST) is a diagramming technique which reveals the relationships and inter-relationships of all known functions. It will display in logical sequence all the functions and show their dependency and priorities.

A simple part may have one or more functions. It is not unusual to find some of them having 20 or 30 functions. A complex product, project or system may have hundreds of functions.

Procedure

Using Function Relationship Form No. 8 place all the functions identified in the centre column, under FUNCTION. Then, with each function, ask, HOW is (the function) to be accomplished ? Place the answer (function) in the column, HOW, on the right. The answers to the question WHY is (the function) necessary ? is placed in the column, WHY on the left. Continue the process with each function, until completed, An example is given in Fig. 33.

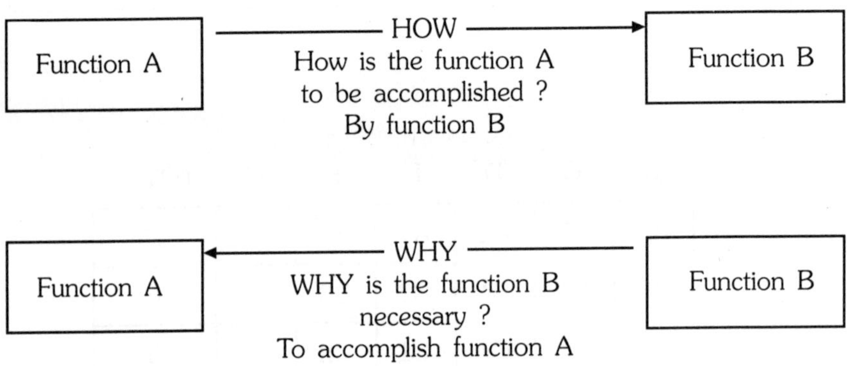

Fig. 33

Some functions under the HOW and WHY columns will also indicate NEEDED FUNCTIONS. A summary can be made in Form No. 9.

Build the FAST model for the existing plan, product, process, procedure, programme, project or design along the lines indicated in Fig. 34, Basic FAST Model and the ground rules given in it.

The function to the immediate right of the left scope line is the BASIC FUNCTION. Any function on the How or Why line is a critical path function. If the line enters through the basic function, it is a major critical path. Otherwise, it will conclude in an independent (supporting) function and be a minor critical path. Supporting functions are usually secondary. An example is given in Fig. 35.

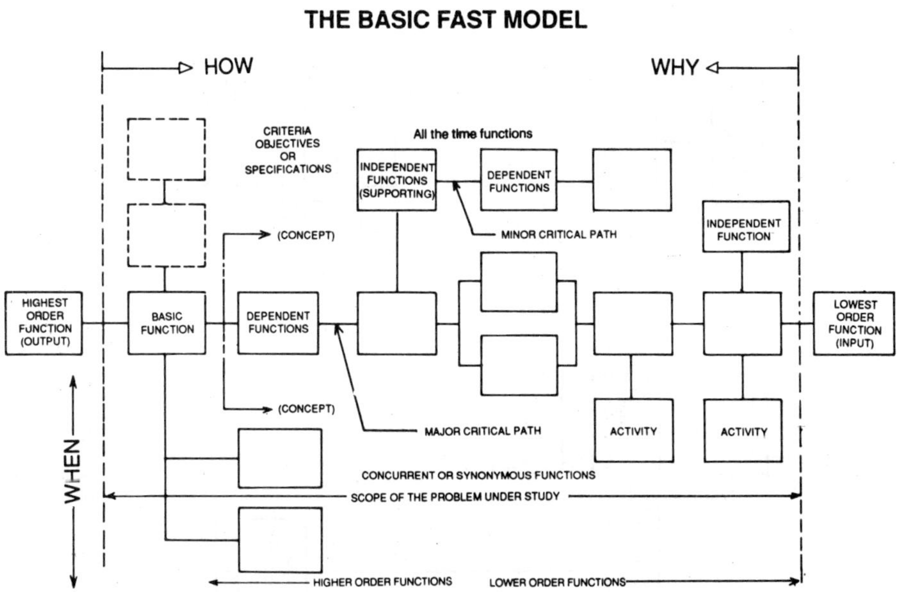

Fig. 34.

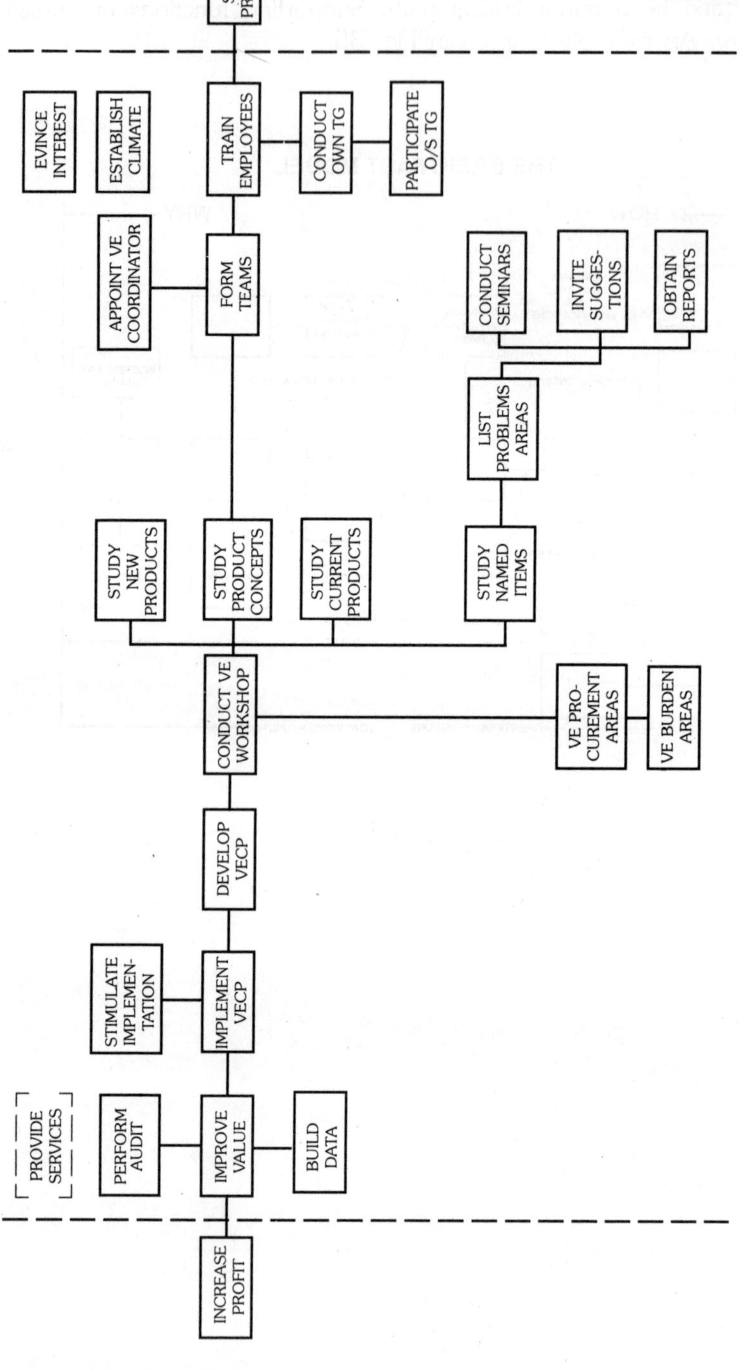
INCREASE PROFIT
IMPROVE VALUE
PERFORM AUDIT
PROVIDE SERVICES
BUILD DATA
IMPLEMENT VECP
STIMULATE IMPLEMEN-TATION
DEVELOP VECP
CONDUCT VE WORKSHOP
VE PRO-CUREMENT AREAS
VE BURDEN AREAS
STUDY NEW PRODUCTS
STUDY PRODUCT CONCEPTS
STUDY CURRENT PRODUCTS
STUDY NAMED ITEMS
LIST PROBLEMS AREAS
CONDUCT SEMINARS
INVITE SUGGES-TIONS
OBTAIN REPORTS
FORM TEAMS
APPOINT VE COORDINATOR
TRAIN EMPLOYEES
CONDUCT OWN TG
PARTICIPATE O/S TG
EVINCE INTEREST
ESTABLISH CLIMATE
START VE PROGRAMME

Fig. 35.

SOME DIAGRAMMING TIPS

1. Only two types of FAST diagrams may be needed for the study: One which represents existing plan, product, project, etc., and the other which shows the proposed concept or change.

2. Being used to conventional practice of thinking of solutions, when making the diagram, the tendency will be to go off at a tangent and include alternatives or choices that do not exist in the item under study. Eschew this tendency.

3. When making the proposed FAST model, restrict yourself to a specific concept, at a time. This may cause several functions to come into existence and an equally large number of FAST diagrams. Integrate all of them into one composite FAST model.

4. Keep in mind the objective (the highest order function) to be accomplished.

5. Make templates of the functions and try to arrange them on the table in logical sequence. This will facilitate comparing various alternatives and possibilities. Once a decision on the final shape is made, draw the diagram on paper.

6. Involve every member in the discussions. Stating, re-stating the functions, creatively proposing ideas, hitch-hiking on other's ideas, role playing, etc. will help to produce good proposals.

FUNCTION — COST ANALYSIS

After defining the functions and classifying them, the next step in Value Engineering is to determine the cost of each of the functions so defined.

Placing a cost to each function reveals areas of bad value. By compiling a function cost matrix, it will be possible to establish which are the high cost functions and whether or not any anomalies of cost exist.

Function cost is the cost of the method chosen to perform the function under consideration. This is easy in the case of simple parts, each performing only one function. Where an item serves one function, the cost of the item is the cost of the function. But, where it serves more than one function, the item and its cost should be prorated to each function.

The simplest method to determine the function cost is by comparison with each other. However, this is not always possible.

Based on the experience and informed judgement of the team members, a consensus could be evolved through discussion.

Estimate of function costs can also be made by synthetic costing based on theoretical considerations of quality and quantity of material necessary to perform the required function, the most appropriate form and dimension, the most economical processing, machining, procedure, etc.

Yet another approach is to determine what part or parts perform the basic function and then place a cost on them. Worth is assigned only to those components having basic function. Those items performing secondary functions have no worth. Then the cost to worth ratio is calculated. Or, Cost — Worth, i.e., the Value Gap, is calculated.

Examples are illustrated in Fig. 36.

GROUNDING LEAD
Cost Rs. 25

SHAPE looks like a AUTO BATTERY CABLE
Cost Rs. 14
WORTH Rs. 14

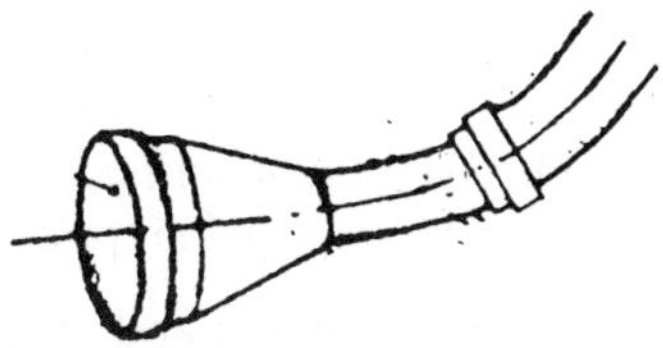

OIL FILLER RECEIVER
Cost Rs. 18

SHAPE looks like a PLASTIC FUNNEL
Cost Rs. 2
WORTH Rs. 2

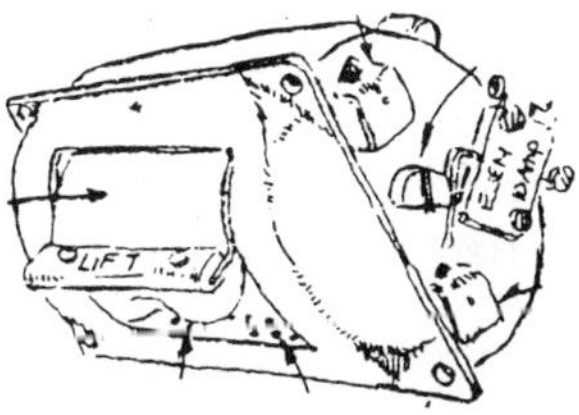

RAILWAY COACH BERTH READING LIGHT
Cost Rs. 75

SHAPE looks like a WALL-LIGHT FITTING
Cost Rs. 18
WORTH Rs. 18

PENCIL, Cost Rs. 1.50

Primary Function	- MAKE MARKS
What material in it makes marks ?	- GRAPHITE
Cost of Graphite	- Rs. 0.60
WORTH of Pencil	- Rs. 0.60

PENCIL, SHARPENER, Cost Rs. 1.00

Primary Function	- REMOVE WOOD
What in the sharpener removes wood ?	- BLADE
Cost of Blade	- Rs. 0.30
WORTH of Pencil Sharpener	- Rs. 0.30

Fig. 36.

WORTH IS THE MEASURE

WORTH is defined as the *"lowest cost required to perform the function."* It is used as the measure of the value in the performance of a particular function.

True Worth, in terms of use and esteem value, is usually evident after the product is in the customers' or consumers' hands. It will then be learnt — rather late — that we have built in more supposed worth and incurred more cost than the customer or consumer needs or can use, or that we have cut cost in the product or service and delivered less worth than the customer or consumer expected or needed. In both cases, the customer or the consumer would consider the item over-priced. Value Engineering helps to give the customer or the consumer the true worth and at fair price.

After the function is fully understood, described, compared and evaluated, the lowest cost that seems likely to accomplish all of the USE and AESTHETIC functions that are necessary (or required by the customer), emerges as the worth. Intense search, analysis and creative thinking are needed to establish this measure. Using the knowledge, imagination and creativity, compare the existing design, product, process or material with suitable combinations of simplest, most reliable alternatives established for effectively accomplishing the total function at the cost approximating as much as possible to the WORTH of the item. Then a decision is made.

TIPS TO DECIDE WORTH

Ask the following questions:

1. What is the cost of achieving the basic function in the existing design ?

2. Do you consider this cost for that function right ?

3. If not, what would be your estimate of a reasonable cost to perform that function ? This could be estimated worth. Assume at this point that the function is needed.

4. What is the cost of achieving this function if some other known item is used ? That could be the worth.

5. Is this a common, easily performed function, or one that is rare and difficult to achieve ?

6. What is the cost of some other item that will almost, but not quite, perform the function ?

7. Can it be used ? If so, can its cost be taken as a reasonable cost to perform the function under consideration ? That could be taken as the probable worth. Hereagain, it is assumed that the function is needed.

8. Is the function necessary ? If not, what other function can be substituted for it ? What is the cost of that alternative function ? That could be the worth.

If two items doing same function are compared and one is more costly than the other, the lower cost item will indicate ways to improve the value of the higher cost item. This principle is used to assess the worth of any function. Comparison is by shape, size, look, similarities, geometry, etc.

Function can be evaluated by comparison. Evaluation may be done in a number of ways, as under, says a world authority in Value Engineering.

1. Compare with a standard that performs a similar function.

2. Compare with a product that has similar shape or appearance.

3. Compare with a product with similar properties.

4. Compare with a product requiring similar process to produce.

5. Breakdown into functional areas simple enough to compare with common commercial products performing similar functions.

6. Compare with a Cadillac.

7. Determine the cost of just that quantity of material required to perform the function.

8. Do creative thinking and establish.

USE OF FUNCTION-COST MATRIX

Often, the part itself would be performing more than one function. It may perform one basic function and a number of secondary or support functions. Then the cost allocation has to be done on some basis. This is where the team's professional experience, technical know-how, training for skill building in value studies, common sense and data collection of the Information Phase will combine and contribute to produce a consensus on the pattern and details of allocation.

The following methods are commonly adopted to construct a function — cost matrix:

1. Co-relating cost of components (or estimated parts thereof) contributing to perform the function. For example;

   (a) In a pencil, the basic function MAKE MARKS is performed by the graphite; and so, all cost of graphite is allocated to this function.

   (b) In a match stick, the function PROVIDE SAFETY to the user of the match stick is performed by the chemical coating on the stick and half the length of the stick itself. Both costs are added and allocated to this function.

2. Determining the contribution of each part to the required performance of the function, as illustrated in Fig. 37, Matrix for the functions of an Oil Pump.

3. Determining cost per period of time, per unit weight, per dimension, etc., and synthesising.

4. Preparing cost models.

OIL PUMP*

Functions

DIRECT OIL
TRANSFER OIL
EXPEL OIL
FACILITATE ASSEMBLY
PROVIDE LOCATION (to Crank Case)
PROVIDE ATTACHMENT (to Crank Case)

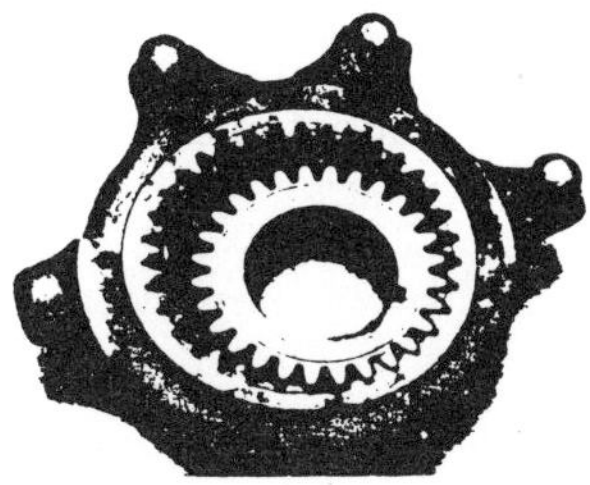

Oil pump gears and housing

Oil pump, assembled

Oil pump cover and elbows

COMPONENTS	COST Rs.	FUNCTIONS: DIRECT OIL Rs.	TRANSFER OIL Rs.	EXPEL OIL Rs.	FACILITATE ASSEMBLY Rs.	PROVIDE LOCATION Rs.	PROVIDE ATTACHMENT Rs.
Delivery elbow	30.00	16.00			14.00		
Suction elbow	30.00	16.00			14.00		
Oil pump gear housing	94.80		40.80	20.80		11.20	22.00
Oil pump cover	94.00	34.40	32.00	3.60	24.00		
Driving collar	26.40		26.40				
Driving gear	47.60		47.60				
Driven gear	45.60		45.60				
Elbow gaskets (2)	0.40				0.40		
Bolts and washers	2.80				2.80		
Bolts to casing	4.40		4.40				
Bolts to crankcase	3.60						3.60
Assembly	20.40	5.20	5.20		5.20		4.80
Total	400.00	71.60	202.00	24.40	60.40	11.20	30.40

* Adapted from Raven, p. 204

Fig. 37.

COST VISIBILITY

Our accounting system, as it is organised at present, cannot make cost visible, such FEATURES as:

shape,
various quality aspects of the material,
the intricacies of the manufacturing process, etc.

Large number of components, fasteners, joints, holes, supports, machining surfaces, materials, shapes, finishes, fits, tolerances, allowances, safety factors, special processes, are some of the cost drivers, with relentless capacity to push up costs, without making it visible on.

The cost of making a hole, would, traditionally be the summation of direct and indirect expenses on equipment, labour, methods, etc. for all holes made in a day prorated on the number. Say, Rs. 0.75 per hole. The interesting point is what do we do with these holes ? Can they be left open ? The answer is, NO. They have to be filled with fastener or dummies. The cost of a fastener may average Rs. 1.50 each. Which will make the meaningful cost of a hole as Rs. 0.75 + Rs. 1.50 = Rs. 2.25 each.

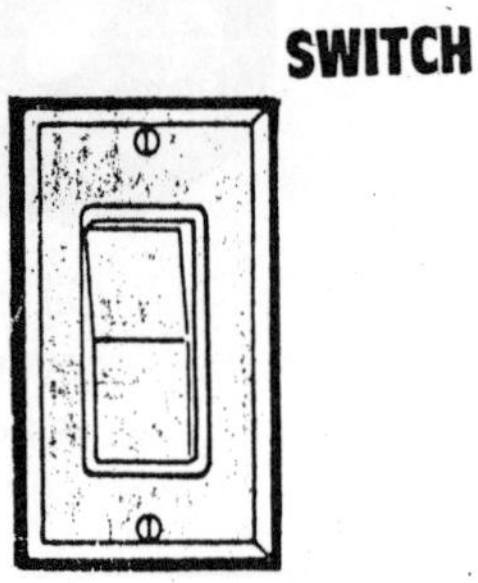

Fig. 38.

Hot forged gear shafts are used in automobile gear box. These are

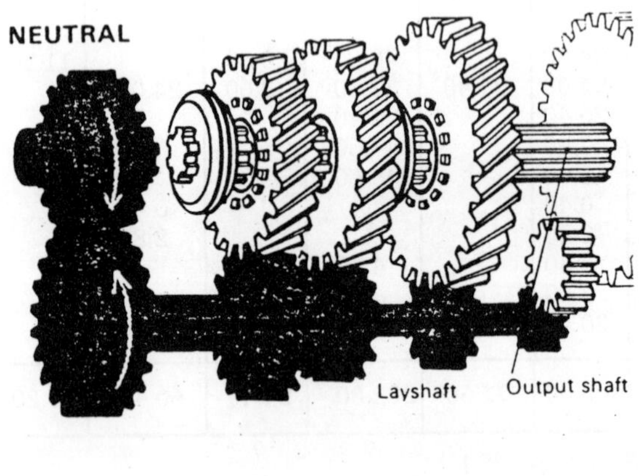

Fig. 39

machined to finished sizes, when approximately 50 to 60% of the steel is removed. The gap between two gears shown is provided to permit the cutter for the smaller gears to run clear, i.e., to facilitate machining. At first sight the cost of this would amount to the cost of removing the metal between the two gears. But, what is not immediately visible is that the presence of the length of metal in the gap has ramifications throughout the whole gear box, increasing the size of all components above it by that gap.

The ultimate selection of the design in any item is not based purely on technical and engineering issues alone. Intangibles like aesthetics, quality, architectural content and other similar non-technical and non-engineering issues in fact over-ride. Therefore, the examination of Cost Vs: Function is not computation of quantifiable INITIAL COST and OPERATING COST alone.

MEANINGFUL COSTS

Meaningful costs have to be developed for the purpose of making correct value decisions. Where activity-based costing is practiced, it will be very helpful to ascertain meaningful costs.

Many companies are now giving activity-based costing and activity-based budgeting a try. Instead of concentrating on traditional items like salaries, supplies and insurance, activity-based budgeting focuses on the process integral to a business. It gives a qualitative measurement, and identifies cost drivers — the factors that determine the final cost of an operation. Activity-based costing breaks down and calculates the cost of each step in any job, making it possible to define the difference between value-added and non value-added steps. Then follows elimination or reduction in activities that are non value-adding wastes, targeting of improvements, prioritizing, etc. Activity-based costing helps sharpen the decision-making. US auto makers are using this approach.

Activity-based costing data helps gathering process-driver data and reveals startling process weaknesses.

Creation Phase

The dictionary meaning of creativity is *"power or ability to create, originate, or to produce."* In common usage, it implies inventiveness, innovativeness and productive thinking. A creative person is said to be one who comes up with new and different ideas, designs, theories and works of art in ways that are not amenable to explanation. Creativity is also viewed as what Edison called inspiration, when he said that *"invention is 5% inspiration and 95% perspiration."*

Innovation and creativity are the life-blood of any organisation. Without them, we are all doomed to react, to scamble defensively in a world that is changing fast. With them, change becomes opportunity — new markets, new technologies, new ways of looking at old problems.

The essence of creativity is not to come up with something totally new. Creativity works through a new combination of things you already know, a fresh look at elements with which you are already familiar.

Harvard's Theodre Levitt defines creativity as thinking new things; and innovation, doing new things. It is thinking and doing new things that enables us to effectively meet the challenges of change.

Great importance is attached to creativity these days. For, creativity is seen as a special human power that will solve difficult problems, generate ideas and products, and transform organisation into lively, growing and prosperous ones.

These days, our fascination with this all important capability borders on an obsession. Unshackling our workers to allow their creative juices to flow has been the ultimate objective of just about everything from Quality Circles to Re-engineering.

Unlike what is generally believed that creativity is a special gift, endowed to few by God, everyone is creative. All people have potential to be creative. Only some are demonstrably more creative than others; and in some activity. Some people are good at seeing details, but they never see things in an unfamiliar way. So, they are not very creative. Other people are very good at going often on divergent thinking and free association. They see the big picture. But they can't pay attention to details.

So, they do not get anything done. The few, most creative people and organisations, are able to see the big picture, to be divergent and free associating and pay attention to details and analysis. They are imaginative, inductive in thinking and with a touch of craziness. They abandon the familiar and seek the outrageous.

Continous improvement depends on the ability of Managers and employees to engage in creative and innovative problem solving. Innovation and creativity are not confined to the laboratories. They are the ideas, big and small, that people have anywhere in the organisation — anywhere in the world — about what they are doing and how to do it better. Anybody can think up new things, anybody can do new things — provided they are encouraged to do so, that they feel free to experiment. For innovation and creativity to bloom, companies must develop an atmosphere of openness and respect, creating a management approach that rewards risk-taking and eliminates the fear of mistake-making.

Creativity can be learned and developed if one overcomes the blocks to one's creativity through training. Even apparently uncreative persons have developed potentials for creative output. Creativity is the soul of Value Engineering. In the Creation Phase of the Job Plan, the Team members are made to think creatively in terms of focussed objectives — how to accomplish the functions. Here past experience is combined and re-combined (frequently with some changes) to form a new combination which will satisfy some need and produce suitable usable ideas (not just ideas).

All functions defined, classified and sorted out as NECESSARY and UNNECESSARY are covered in this phase. The search is for innumerable solutions for accomplishing the NECESSARY function. The two word definition of a function is considered a complete problem in itself. For each, the Team generates ideas to solve. All known creativity techniques can be used; but, usually, the BRAINSTORMING technique is favoured. It produces good results. It is appealingly simple, fun, therapeutic and it works. When properly practiced, with a disciplined attention to the principle of deferred judgement, brainstorming can produce highly original, often ingenious, solutions. It is found to be specially effective in groups where individual energies combine synergically and the diversity of knowledge and experience within the group stimulates connection making.

Osborn (1963) reported that a Denver Post Master and eleven of his staff brainstormed the problem, "what can be done to reduce man-hour usage ?" and generated 121 ideas. Some of them led to a saving of 12,666 man-hours in the following nine weeks. A Pittsburgh departmental store, stuck with some non-moving chair covering material, brainstormed "other uses" for the fabric, leading to the sale of the entire stock in a week. A group in Heinz Foods spent just one hour on the problem, "how can we help increase the sale of products made at this factory ?" and generated more and better ideas than a Special Committee had produced in ten conferences. Sylvania Electric's highly successful "flash cube" was born in a brainstorming session.

Four simple ground rules are applied:

1. Criticism is ruled out (Defer judgement).
2. Free wheeling is desired.
3. Quantity is wanted.
4. Combination and improvement are sought.

The two word function definition is the starting point.

A large quantity of ideas are generated. For, the more solutions you devise, the less chance there is for settling for something less than the best available solution. Every idea is listed — whether it is good, bad or indifferent. And, every member of the Team is made to contribute ideas. The Team has a free discussion, with the Team Leader only questioning and guiding and occasionally supplying problem related information. Examples to stretch the Team's mental muscles are given, to make them look at things differently. The use of a flip chart and felt pens is recommended. The filled sheets can be displayed along the side walls of the room, so that the listed items are constantly in view. Otherwise, small cards are used to write the ideas and these are pinned to bulletin boards. The strategy of Value Engineering is to usefully combine the knowledge, experience and talents of the Team members, to secure usable ideas in great numbers. Sessions are generally restricted to 30 minutes to an hour.

Other creative thinking techniques used are Mind Mapping, Free Association technique, Gordon's Synetics technique using anologies, Checklist technique, Morphological Analysis technique, Crawford's Attribute Listing technique, Evaluation Comparison technique, Phillips 66 Buzz Session technique, Reversing technique, etc.

The types of talent or skill that a person must have to participate effectively in the creative process are:

1. An ability to transfer or apply knowledge or technology already in existence to the solution of more than one problem.
2. An ability to associate ideas which are at first sight appearing to have no relationship at all and thus gain a new perspective on an old problem.
3. An ability to redefine an old problem in a different way in order to see new approaches or dimensions for further analysis and eventual solutions.

4. An ability to fantasise or engage in unconstrained thinking and thus go beyond conventional thought patterns to the unorthodox where many a novel solution may lie.

5. An ability to keep and use the curiosity of a child that you once were.

A researcher and consultant of Harvard Business School suggests that there are three basic components necessary for creativity in an individual:

(a) Skill in the domain of endeavour, such as special training, education or talent.

(b) Creativity-relevant thinking skills, such as brainstorming or metaphor and analogy techniques that allow the individual to come up with new ideas and new perspectives.

(c) Motivation, indicating an inner drive or impulse to meet the challenge. Interest, enjoyment, satisfaction, sense of freedom or autonomy and (not external pressures) add motivation.

Environmental stimulants to creativity include:

i. being part of a team where people have diversity of skills, are cooperative and supportive of people's ideas, yet at the same time challenge each other's ideas,

ii. fostering communication and collaboration,

iii. absence of surveillance,

iv. management support toward innovation, risk-taking and rewarding and recognizing creative work,

v. a problem perceived as important, with a sense of urgency not only to them but to others as well, and something difficult that perhaps nobody else has been able to solve, and something where they feel their skills are being stretched.

At in-house Value Engineering Workshops teams generated in 10 minutes time 355 ideas for ATTRACT ATTENTION and 424 ideas for REDUCE CONSUMPTION.

WAYS TO BECOME MORE CREATIVE

1. Practice creativity everyday, everywhere. Try your imaginative powers on little things.

2. Take notes. Record your ideas, problems, etc.
3. Observe with application. Develop a greater curiosity for ideas and things. Ask, "in what other ways can I use this?"
4. Learn to listen, with your eyes as well as your ears.
5. Build idea sources: trade magazines, friends, past jobs, newspapers, helpful hint columns, observations, experiences, etc. Search out and collect.
6. Understand first, then judge. Be specific. Avoid generalities. Beware of semantics.
7. Keep your mind open.
8. Build big ideas from small ones. Every idea has some merit in it. Look for it.
9. Use creative questioning: WHO, WHAT, WHEN, WHERE, WHY, WHICH, HOW and IF. And, IN WHAT WAYS ?
10. Expect the best of yourself.
11. Adapt and improve.
12. Be constructively discontent.
13. Form a habit of creative thinking: Make creative thinking a way of life.
14. Be a non-conformist in ideas and work, both intellectually and personally. Do not adapt to any pattern.
15. Fantasize. It is no waste of time.
16. Use the creativity Rules (Rule of 24, 25 and 26).

SIXTEEN WAYS TO SOLVE PROBLEMS CREATIVELY

Here are some guidelines to solve problems creatively, based on recent research:

1. INVOLVE YOURSELF in the problem, Read, review, examine and analyse all material you can find on the problem. Look at the problem

from every side and angle. Constructively question to understand.

2. THINK IN TERMS OF AN ANOLOGY. How can the way something else was done be applied to what you are now considering?

   Radar was the outcome of studying the uses of reflected sound waves among bats. Airplane cargo doors were designed from the analogous opening of a clam shell. The cigarette packages incorporated the design for opening the cellophane covering along the lines of the pea pod seam weakness.

3. CONSIDER THE GAPS IN KNOWLEDGE. Look for the missing element. Make a list of things that bother you, the things you need, the things that are wrong with the product or the method, etc.

4. LOOK FOR THE PARADOX. The seemingly contradictory relationship that exists. You have made some cost controls, but it does not show up in net results; or some costs have gone down, but others have gone up.

5. THINK OF ALL POSSIBILITIES. Keep on asking "What if ?" and "In what other way ?" Do not let an accepted fact or solution keep you from thinking of alternatives. Try out different assumptions. Imagine that one of the assumptions affecting the problem is removed; then see where the problem leads to now.

6. THINK OF WAYS YOU COULD CHANGE THINGS. Practice by looking at a picture or an advertisement and listing questions that cannot be answered by looking at it. Think of how you would change it. Mentally shift the positions of various parts, change order of events, change the situation and see.

   Think of how you would change something by making it longer, shorter, larger, smaller, by adding, taking away, multiplying, dividing, substituting, combining, reversing, etc. Be flexible in asking questions as you are in finding answers.

7. THINK IN TERMS OF FUNCTIONS. Take things apart in terms of their functions, attributes, properties and characteristics. List them and think about new uses for them. Can you think of different uses for the parts of such common items as a lead pencil, ball point pen, a coil in the fan regulator, etc.

8. THINK OF YOUR ENVIRONMENT AS IN PROGRESS, NOT STATIC. Ask "Why is that not changed ?" or "Why is that not made differently ?" Think of helping to channel changes.

9. SHARPEN AND EXPAND YOUR WAYS OF SEARCHING FOR INFORMATION. Find out how others did it, or solved something. Compare and contrast several methods. Use trial-and-error thinking, experiment, draw conclusions, find implications.

10. LEARN FROM MISTAKES. Don't forget them. Study them. They may lead you to a better way of doing something or making an improvement on something current.

11. FOLLOW THE PATH OF CREATIVE PEOPLE. Study the case histories and lives of innovators and creative people. Emulate their perseverance.

12. READ FOR IDEAS AND IDEA STIMULATION.

13. LISTEN FOR IDEAS. Does the person talking have an unusual slant on something ? Could you use it on something else ?

14. SUSPEND JUDGEMENT. Do not draw early conclusions. Avoid settling for an early partial or total solution; but stay open.

15. TRY PROBLEM ON OUTSIDERS. When you discuss the problem with others, you will see it differently, because you have to put it into terms intelligible to them. Their answers may be less important, but their unexpected questions may bring new areas of your brain into play.

16. WHEN STUCK, TAKE A BREAK. Go on to something else. Give your sub-conscious a chance to work. Do not force it. Creative ideation is a ripening process.

IDEAS

Ideas always start small and insignificant. However, if it is with potential and capacity for producing results in a going, working and productive business, it is made effective through business action in the hands of an entrepreneur. Look at these examples:

1. The world's first departmental store was started in Tokyo in 1650. The idea was that the merchant is the principal of economic life, not merely a middle man. This meant fixed prices to customers, the organisation buying on account, standardisation of merchandise, etc. More customers, more profits. Japanese House of Mitsui capitalised on the idea to become the most powerful business in history, employing over a million people throughout the world by 1945.

2. The rise of the discount houses began in late 1940s with the application of an idea developed by Sears, Roebuck & Co almost 20 years earlier. Sears became leading appliance seller by demonstrating a sample of each appliance on the store floor and delivering the order straight from the warehouses: saving in costs of shipping to store, uncrating, recrating for delivery, etc.

3. Sears also had the idea that the poor man's money could be made to have the same purchasing power as the rich man's. Same dependable quality goods were delivered against mail orders in suburbs.

4. Bata capitalised on the idea that the peasent in Europe went barefoot, not because he was poor, but because there were no inexpensive, standardised, well designed and durable shoes in the market. Bata used mass production methods of Henry Ford to solve this problem.

OTHER TECHNIQUES

As will have been noted form page 62, Value Engineering uses all techniques – some old and some new – in its approach to solve a problem. While many examples could be cited to prove this, it is suggested that no effort should be spared to take advantage of the benefits of doing so.

Pratt & Whitney, Canada, have successfully integrated into their product development and project management function performance specification, quality function development, paired comparison, direct value measurement and risk assessment. With the result, they are reaping advantages in product value creation and project management effectiveness.

Ingersoll Rand uses design failure effects analysis and process failure mode effects analysis as routine.

Target costing was introduced in Toyota in 1959, based on value that the customers are willing to pay for in functions. Target costs are the difference between price and anticipated profit margin. If the required profits will not be obtained from manufacture in house or by suppliers, then the target costs will not be applied.

Kaizen has been applied successfully to support development of competitive excellence.

EVALUATION PHASE

In the Evaluation Phase, the quantity of ideas generated in the Creative Phase are judged or appraised, refined and combined as needed, to determine how each of these ideas can be utilised to accomplish the needed function and fulfil its governing parameters, or criteria. The dynamic continuation of creative thought process with creative judgement added enables determination of how the ideas from many functions can be used or melded together within the total problem solution.

DEVELOPMENT

For easy and constant reference, the goals, objectives and criteria of the value study and the governing parameters defined in the Information Phase are reviewed and used as bench marks for development work. Inherent in the philosophy of Value Engineering is full retention for the customer of all the necessary and required features of the item. Alternatives have to be developed without reducing in the slightest degree the quality, safety, life, reliability, dependability and the attractiveness that the customer needs. If at all, these could be improved, which often happens when accomplishing the needed use and aesthetic functions.

"What else would do the job ?" is the penetrating question to be answered in the course of development of ideas. The fuller the answers found, the more effective the grade of value effort done. Too often, too many feel that previous means, methods and costs are about the optimum. They, being accustomed to making decisions in their own fields on conventional basis, and not used to seeing materials or processes used differently, feel that the approach to build value alternatives on the basis of function definition and creative ideation, is wrong. Hence, they would be hesitant in suggesting or agreeing to this approach of preparing value alternatives. It is natural; however, it has to be overcome.

The search is to find out specific alternative ways of meeting the goals and objectives. It requires creative thinking by the Team and statement of many possibilities, like:

1. If the function performed by the item is necessary — and therefore,

the item itself is necessary. Only after determining that the function must remain should one look for alternative ways of performing the same function at the lowest conceivable cost.

2. If the function can be accomplished by another means, working on a different principle, but without sacrificing any of the required criteria. Simple comparison with other items which are similar in at least one characteristic; functional comparison; and scientific search of new disciplines, will help answer this question and find the alternatives.

3. If the part itself can be simplified, without endangering the required performance, quality, reliability, feasibility, producability, operability, maintainability, serviceability, economy, etc. The search would be for combinations of actions, changes in sequences, place, time, etc. of actions, substitution, and so on.

The item under study is challenged with the questioning attitude: challenged with the question WHY? In this context, Kiplings poem is quite appropriate:

"I have six honest serving men
They taught me all I know
Their names are WHY, WHAT, WHEN,
WHERE, HOW and WHO."

A seventh serving man, Can, would make a more expanded list.

WHY ? and WHY NOT ? are questions that will demand convincing answers. WHAT IF ? will help to forge viable alternatives. All these questions are used to make the idea work.

A CAUSE AND EFFECT (Fishbone) type of analysis would show up, where and how unnecessary actions have crept in, or what work is being done over again (Fig. 40). The effect or problem is recorded on the right side of the chart and the major causes, on the left side. For every effect, there are likely to be several groups of causes: like, people, machine, methods, materials, policies, procedures, plant, etc. These are placed in logical sequence. The key is to push the causes as far back as practically possible. Then, to look for cures to the causes — and not the symptoms of the problem. Brainstorming and use of check sheets will help to generate the diagram. A well detailed Cause and Effect Diagram will take the shape of fish bone; hence the name.

A WHY-WHY Analysis helps to determine the specific steps that should be taken to implement a solution (Fig. 41).

A HOW-HOW Diagram uncovers possible improvements (Fig. 42).

A FORCE FIELD Analysis illustrates the relative pros and cons of a solution, helps to aid thinking and develops a strategy to amend the solution to take care of these forces (Fig. 43). The driving forces move a situation towards change. The restraining forces block the movement. When these opposing forces are equal, there is no movement — and so, no change occurs. Also, when the restraining forces are too strong to allow a movement, the desired change will not happen. Change can be approached from the perspective of strengthening the driving forces, or reducing the restraining forces. Strengthening the positive, often, has the unexpected result of reinforcing the negative. Hence, the more effective tactic will be to diminish or eliminate a restraining force.

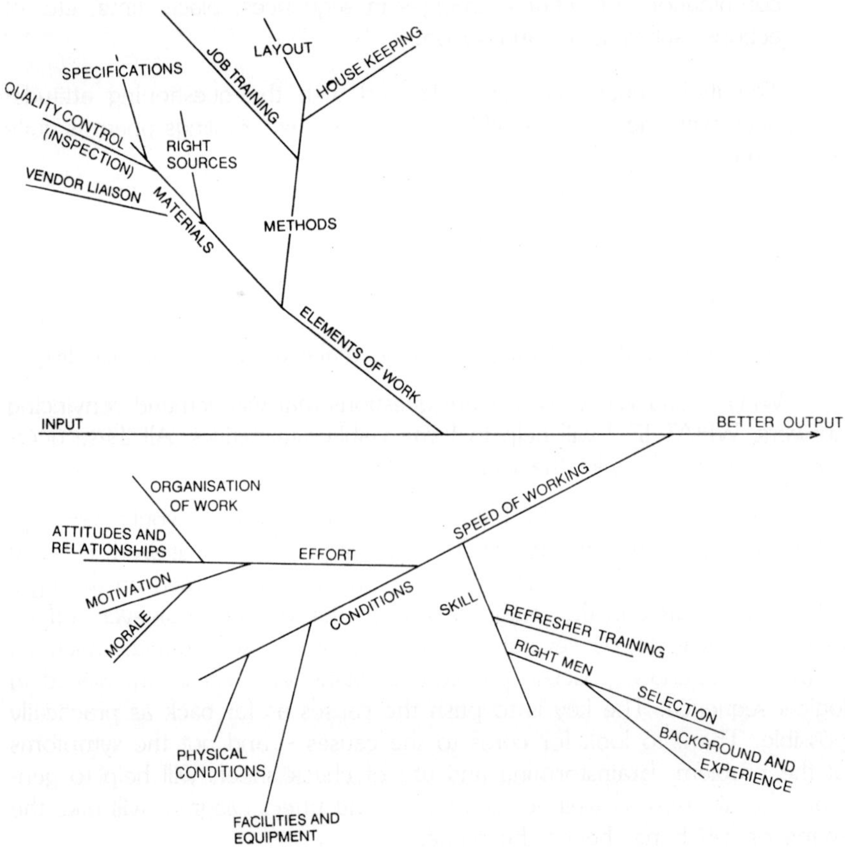

Fig. 40. Cause and Effect Analysis

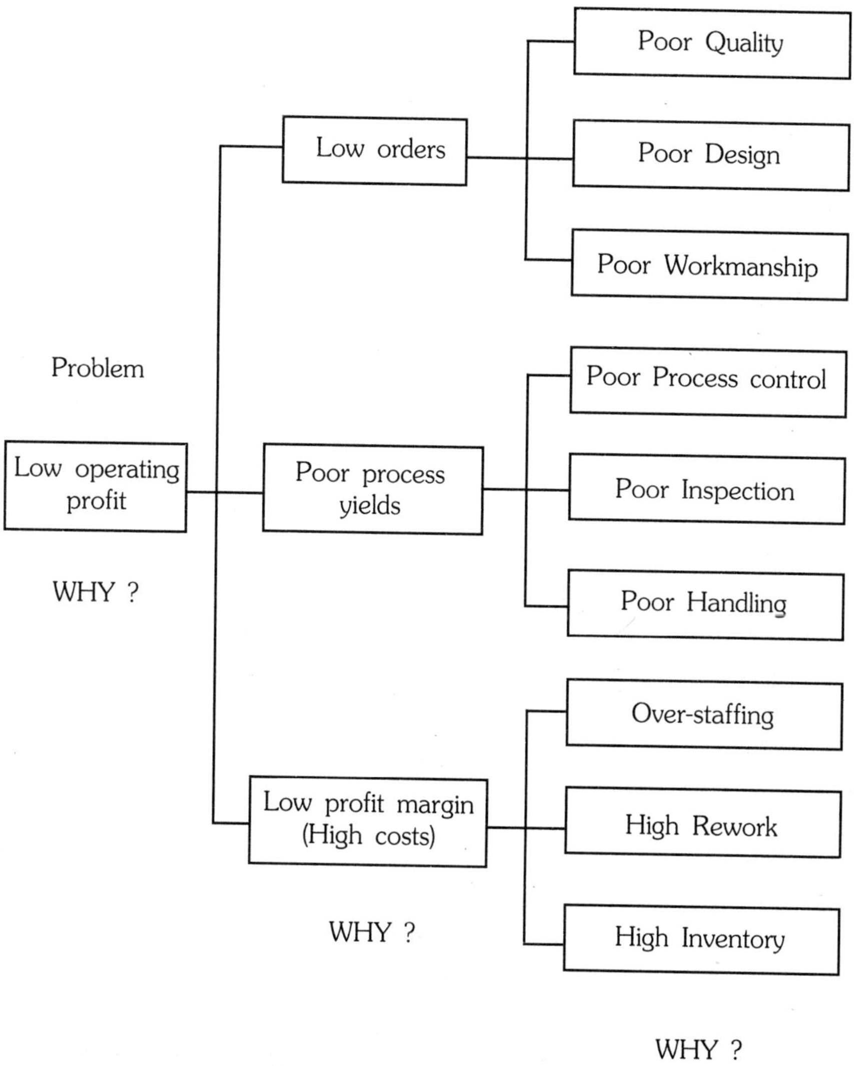

Fig. 41. Why-Why Analysis — A Steel Mill

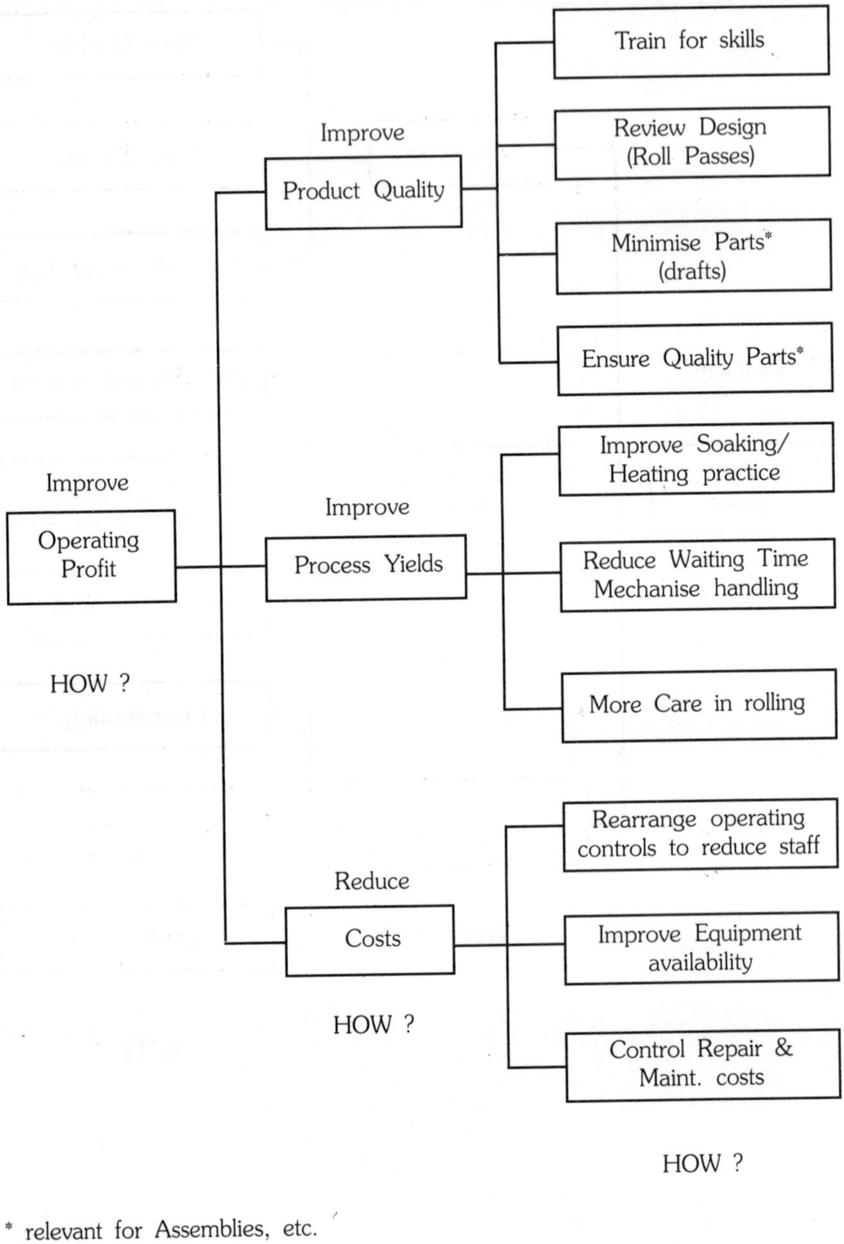

Fig. 42. How-How Analysis Steel Mill Rolling

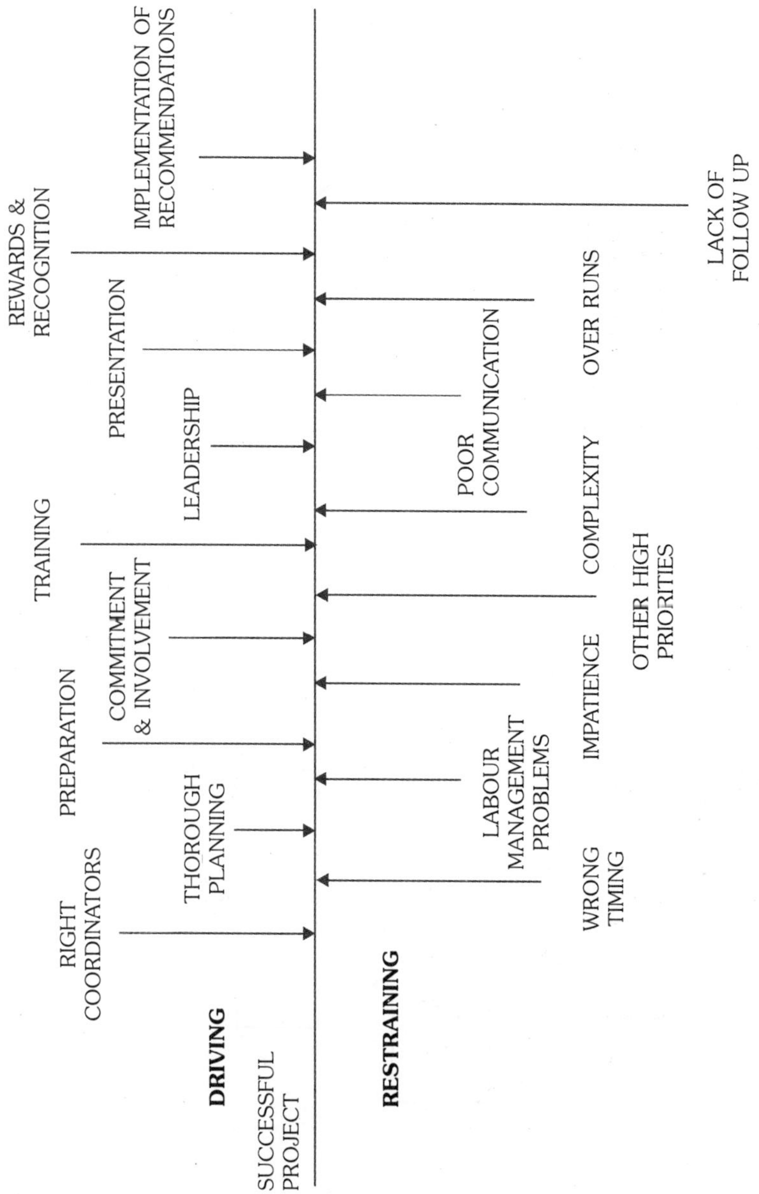

Fig. 43. Force Field Analysis - A Project

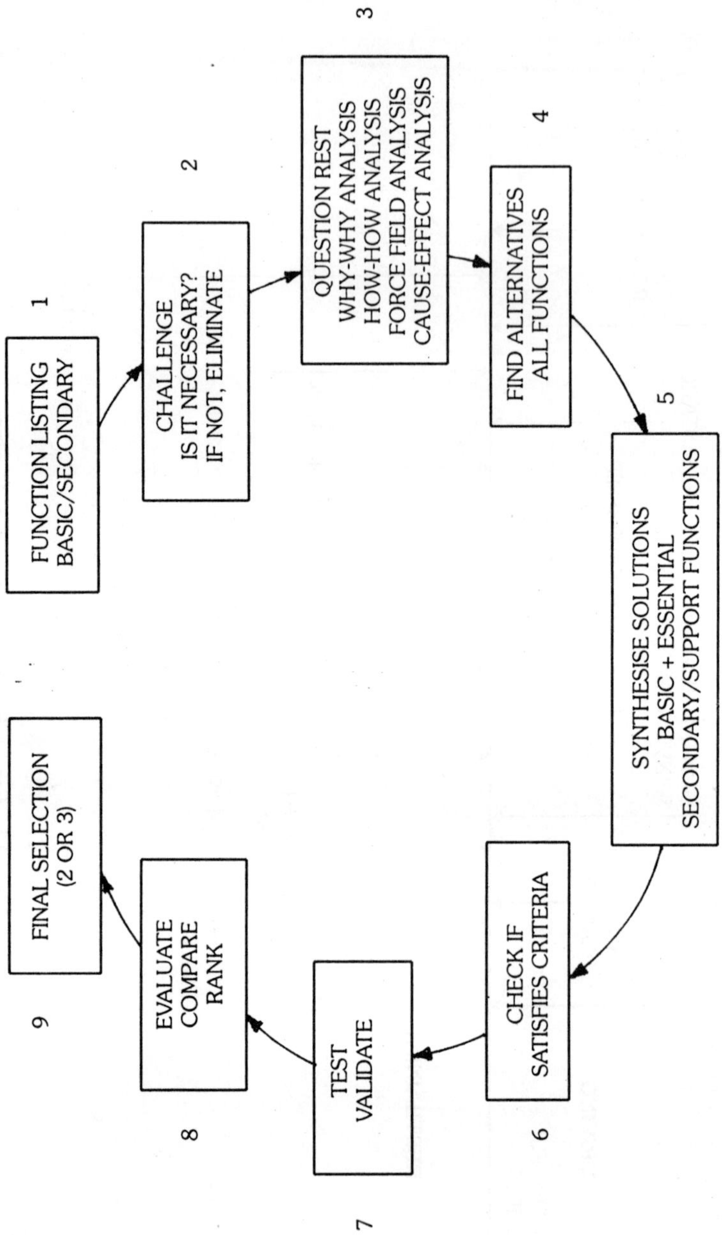

Fig. 44. Creative Ideation Steps

A nine-step Creative Ideation Process (shown in Fig. 44) provides an easy to use method that includes the suggested techniques dovetailed with the key creative thought process — divergent, convergent, or both — for each step. Divergent thinking is the generation of a large number of creative ideas. It is a branching out process, un-inhibited by restrictions. Brainstorming and Cause and Effect Analysis are two examples of divergent thinking that the Team uses in cause identification, solution and idea finding. Convergent thinking is complementary thought process of selecting the best idea from the many that result from the divergent thinking techniques; it is logical and analytical.

The FAST diagram would have identified the REQUIRED FUNCTIONS to be performed and the SUPPORTING FUNCTIONS. These are analysed with the objective of simplifying the design, the operation, the process, the procedure, the methods and the means. Each is evaluated as to its effectiveness or usefulness, with the hope of eliminating, modifying, combining or reducing functions. Greater attention to the supporting functions (which generally account for up to 60% of the total cost) yield good solutions.

It is generally believed that there are at least eight ways of doing practically anything. People intent on expressing their creative ability are never satisfied with the ONLY WAY. Some ideas may stand out above the others. These will find favour automatically. On some others, additional data would be required. These are not discarded, but kept for the future time when proper data will have been collected, to make them usable. A new way of performing a basic function may improve the performance without reducing the cost. It may substitute for some necessary secondary function performed in the original item and thus eliminate some parts or production steps. It may, on the other hand, make necessary a new set of secondary functions and so, corresponding parts. It will have its cost impact as well. But, in all cases, the proposed solution is worth development and must be developed. Every attempt must be made to depart from the ordinary patterns, typical solutions and habitual methods. Experience shows that it is often the new, fresh and radically different approach that uncovers the best value solutions. These are tailored in various permutations and combinations until finally the total function is achieved.

The pros and cons (advantages and disadvantages) of each idea are listed. During development, the disadvantages are sought to be overcome by additional creative thought. Also, the good points of many ideas are combined.

Rich dividends are secured from looking for development of the item from such angles as:

1. MINIMISING THE NUMBER OF PARTS. It will mean less materials, less handling, less inventory, less inspection, less re-work.

2. MINIMISING THE SURFACES OR SIDES to which components are assembled. This helps to reduce the jigs and eliminate wasted assembly time.
3. PROVIDING CLEAR ACCESS AND VIEW of the assembly. This enables manual assembly and upgrading to mechanisation, automation and robotics. It also helps cost reduction.
4. MAXIMISING PART MATING, SYMMETRY, RIGID PARTS. It enables easier handling, orienting, self-locking, elimination of screws, etc.
5. USING MODULAR DESIGNS. It eases assembly, inspection, replacement.
6. EASE OF MANUFACTURE. As the number of parts drop, complexity of those remaining increases. The lowest cost method of manufacture is usually the best. For example, a housing may have been cast. It could be made easily and less expensively by designing it as a weldment. Or, one that has been combined with a few brackets and other fixtures might be made from sheet metal. Each has a range of features — tolerances, allowances, chamfers, ribs, or threaded holes, that integrate to make up its cost.
7. SERVICING AND MAINTENANCE ISSUES. Oft forgotten, these important issues are better considered and adequately provided for at the very earliest stages of design.
8. USING OFF-THE-SHELF COMPONENTS. There would be no need to design every piece from scratch and incur correspondingly high expenditure.
9. OUTSOURCING TO THE MAXIMUM EXTENT POSSIBLE. Outsourcing is not a dirty word when it is a true partnership. Today, being good at too many things is neither practical nor profitable. The successful companies of the future will have to react with incredible speed and flexibility by shifting their shape to create and deliver value better than their competitors, by being very highly good at what they do. The cornerstone of shape shifting will be alliances with highly competent and closely linked partners.
10. SOURCE REDUCTION AND INVENTORY REDUCTION. Inventory, buffers, and other assets are there due to surplus stock, to cope with uncertainty. At every step a margin or factor of safety or buffer is added for JIC — just in case. Working without an inventory safety net and large supplier base would mean careful section of suppliers, working much more closely with them, good understanding and

partnerships, as well as use of reliable technology and information systems that can play the role of safety nets. But, the end results will far outweigh the time, effort and expense.

11. INVOLVING AS FEW PEOPLE AS POSSIBLE. It is best to involve as few people as possible in the performance of a process.

12. SHARING THE KNOWLEDGE, EXPERTISE AND FULL DATA WITH SELECT SUPPLIER. It secures a win-win alliance with him, which will reflect in product improvement, reliability, quality-reliability and cost savings.

13. REMAINING ENVIRONMENT FRIENDLY. Avoid use of potentially harmful or hard to dispose off materials. Look for ways to turn trash into products and to re-cycle scrap — the key being REDUCE, RE-USE and RE-CYCLE. Set sights far beyond — to the long term issue of source depletion, more important than earth-friendly designs, low impact processing and waste minimization.

14. Many of the data in the procurement process is duplicated in the supplier's order fulfillment process, where a large number of activities are the same. Apart form little coordination, inconsistencies, errors and misunderstandings it may lead to wasted work. Stream lining cross company processes could be the next possible avenue for boosting efficiencies.

Having accomplished the function development of an alternative, encompassing the basic function, the required or specified secondary functions and their defined criteria and specifications, a cross check is made to be sure that all parameters have been accounted for, in some manner or the other. The alternative proposed should meet all technical, quality and safety requirements. Then, it is followed through with the development of the specific design, sketches, etc.

Costs are established for all the ideas/solutions and listed in descending order of magnitude. In the functional development of alternatives, the lowest cost idea is first used, and then worked upwards, until the lowest cost method or methods of accomplishing the complete functional requirements are attained. The quest is to find that alternative which will cost the lowest, satisfy all the functional requirements and will work; then the higher cost alternative and so on.

METHODS OF EVALUATION

The workable solutions as developed are then evaluated, ranking the feasible, i.e., the acceptable solutions according to the criteria and goals established (ref. Information Phase, and bench marks).

Evaluation is a tree-pruning, converging and elimination process. Advantages, disadvantages, contrasts, similarities and differences are rated against objectives and criteria determined already. The best two or three ideas are then selected for investigation and further development.

RANKING is the simplest form of evaluation. Here, it is decided that X is better than Y; and Y is better than Z. On this basis the list of alternatives or priorities are set out in the order of importance.

Another common approach is to select one criterion as the dominant one and treat the others as constraints. The ranking is done then. For example, the criteria may be capital cost, running cost, spares availability, etc. If it is decided that capital cost would be the dominant criterion, the selection may be made on the lowest capital cost idea or item, but which meets an acceptable level of running cost, spares availability, etc.

SIMPLIFIED IDEA RATING/RANKING SYSTEM is a quick and effective means to boil down the many ideas that are generated during the Creation Phase to a more manageable few in number for further development. Scoring categories are decided by the Team. Basically two inputs are chosen, each with a 5 point spread. The process takes approximately 2 hours to evaluate 100 ideas.

WEIGHTING is a step further than ranking. It is done by assigning relative weights to each criterion and then deriving an overall measure of effectiveness. It can be done using a five point scale and making paired comparison of all five point ideas, then all four point ideas, and so on.

Table 5

			Candidate A		*Candidate B*		*Candidate C*	
Criteria	*Weight*	*Factor Weight*	*Raw Score*	*Weighted Score*	*Raw Score*	*Weighted Score*	*Raw Score*	*Weighted Score*
Capacity	10	0.333	6	2.000	9	3.000	4	1.332
Life	7	0.233	7	1.631	5	1.165	7	1.631
Capital cost	6	0.200	7	1.400	5	1.000	10	2.000
Running cost	4	0.133	9	1.200	8	1.065	10	1.330
Availability of spares	3	0.100	8	0.800	10	1.000	6	0.600
Total	30	1.000	37	7.031	37	7.230	37	6.893

Ideas are also rated based on appropriate criteria and weighting. As a variation, a set of criteria composed of objectives can also be used. To make the evaluation work still simpler, a three point scale is used.

A simple example is given in Table 5. To choose a machine on the basis of five factors: capacity, life, capital cost, running cost, availability of spares. We decide that capacity of the machine is most important, and give it 10 points. Then, life of the equipment is important, but less important than capacity to perform the job, and so we give it 7 points. On similar considerations, capital cost is given 6 points; running cost, 4; and availability of spares, 3.

Machine B, with the highest weighted score, is selected.

Two more examples are given in the following Fig. 45 and Fig. 46.

DIFFERENT IDEAS FOR PACKING

KEY	GOALS, CRITERIA, FEATURES	WEIGHT
A	COST	7
B	DURABILITY	5
C	AVAILABILITY	1
D	APPEARANCE	0
E	PROTECTION (MOISTURE, ATMOSPHERE)	10
F	PROTECTION (DAMAGE)	8

	B	C	D	E	F	TOTAL
A	A2	A2	A3	E2	F2	7
B		B2	B3	E1	F1	5
C			C1	E2	F2	1
D				E3	F3	0
E					E2	10
F						8

Scale

Major preference 3

Medium preference 2

Minor preference 1

Evaluation Scale

Excellent	5
Very Good	4
Good	3
Fair	2
Poor	1

	Cost (A)	Durability (B)	Protection (E)	Protection (F)	Availability (C)	Total
	7	5	10	8	1	
Present way Put poly sheet and wrap with alk, hessian.	2 / 14	3 / 15	3 / 30	2 / 16	4 / 4	79
Idea 1 Put 1mm thick poly and wrap with plain hessian.	3 / 21	3 / 15	3 / 30	2 / 16	5 / 5	87
Idea 2 Wrap with wax paper	4 / 28	1 / 5	3 / 30	1 / 8	3 / 3	74
Idea 3 Use adhesive tape on circum, after wrapping with poly.	4 / 28	1 / 5	2 / 20	1 / 8	3 / 3	64
Idea 4 Put cardboard on sides and wrap with alk, hessian.	2 / 14	3 / 15	1 / 10	3 / 24	3 / 3	66

Idea 1 is selected

Fig. 45.

CHOICE OF POWER SYSTEMS

KEY	CRITERIA	WEIGHT
A	CAPITAL COST	5
B	RELIABILITY	7
C	ADAPTABILITY	3
D	OPERATING COST	9
E	AVAILABILITY	14
F	ACCEPTABILITY	2

Scale

Excellent	4
Good	3
Fair	2
Poor	1

	B	C	D	E	F	TOTAL
A	A2	C3	D2	E3	A3	5
B		B2	D3	B3	B2	7
C			D2	E4	F2	3
D				E3	D2	9
E					E4	14
F						2

	Capital Cost (A)	Reliability (B)	Adaptability (C)	Operating cost (D)	Availability (E)	Acceptability (F)	Total
	5	7	3	9	14	2	
Oil Hydraulics	3 / 15	4 / 28	2 / 6	2 / 18	4 / 56	2 / 4	127
Water Hydraulics	4 / 20	4 / 28	4 / 12	4 / 36	3 / 42	4 / 8	146
Pneumatic	1 / 5	2 / 14	2 / 6	2 / 18	2 / 28	2 / 4	75
Existing Arrangement	4 / 20	3 / 21	4 / 12	1 / 9	3 / 42	4 / 8	112

Water Hydraulics is selected

Fig. 46.

Investigation Phase

The functionally developed alternatives from the Evaluation Phase, which are workable solutions to the problem or value effort, are, in this phase, refined from semi-finished state to the finished state. That is, the workable solutions are now thoroughly investigated on and made saleable or acceptable to the user.

The process involves in-depth review of the technical, economic and commercial feasibility of the selected alternatives, as well as the probability of successful implementation. The recommended changes are cross-checked for ensuring that the user's needs are fully and satisfactorily met; the proposals are technically adequate; and quality, reliability durability and safety requirements are satisfied.

The aim is to establish a programme of investigation that will provide the latest information on, and the latest capabilities of, each of the approaches that shows promise in the selected alternatives. Assistance is taken from own specialists, other industry specialists with appropriate skills and techniques, consultants, vendors, research and professional bodies and the like.

The alternatives are reviewed for flaws and problem areas. All available data are supplied freely to every individual with whom the discussions take place, so that both parties will be working from a broad base of knowledge and with same facts. The result will be best value solutions. Technical problems are reviewed with knowledgeable persons concerned; operation problems with the production people; maintenance and servicing with engineering; and so on.

All necessary materials are investigated and delivery schedules and lowest price determined with prospective suppliers. It is scrutinised if cost advantages are taken from the use of standard products/processes/materials/treatments, etc., vendors' available functional products, and easily available speciality items of current usage.

In this age of agility, competitive advantage belongs to manufacturing enterprises that respond rapidity to customer-driven market opportunities with high quality products and services. The modern trend in manufacturing is to switch over to MODULAR MANUFACTURING — designing and assembling the product as a series of sub-assemblies or modules; and getting the suppliers to provide them with whole modules, instead of bits and pieces. In this process, the actual manufacturing is pushed on to the favoured/select subcontractors that MASTER the intricacies of just ONE or TWO PARTS of a product and then supply them by thousands to the whole industry — resulting in PRODUCT BETTERMENT, CONSISTENT STANDARDS, QUALITY RELIABILITY and COST REDUCTION.

Current trend in design circles is the built-in simplicity, flexibility, upgradability and serviceability of modularity. Significant is the way Designers increasingly reach for the catalogue instead of the drawing board. To come out with new models every year or two, instead of once a decade, and to survive fierce competition, products are made from off-the-shelf components, choosing the right ones and then melding them into the market winners. Ingenious mixing and matching lead to products offering 90% of the performance of the most carefully hand-crafted versions, but at 50% costs.

Initial parts selection occurs at the Design stage. That initial component is then stuck all the way through the process, because there will be no time to design in a different component. There is also an enormous change of pace in the component market — especially in electronics. Literally hundreds, if not thousands, of products are spewed into the market every month — and even every week. Design Engineers and Buyers are finding it a great test to their mettle to physically track the market changes. Carefully crafted links to reliable suppliers has become the only answer. For, 70% to 80% of the cost of the product is what is bought from the suppliers. The speed of manufacture and supply, the dependability, the reliability, the product/service quality, and the cost all reside to a large extent with the suppliers.

Conventional wisdom had long held that the more suppliers a company has, short of a truly unmanageable number, the better. Advantages of this philosophy are obvious. It provides an opportunity for negotiations regarding price, delivery and other contract terms. Multiple suppliers for a given part of commodity provide recovery options if one supplier defaults or experiences delivery, quality, financial or other problems. Also, a large supplier base provides a great deal of flexibility in the face of sudden increases in production schedules. These advantages, however, are obtained at a high price — large administrative work load, size of work force required to place and track orders, the opportunities for errors, etc. As the company works towards bettering quality, it will have to enforce unprecedented levels of incoming parts quality, which in turn will cause enormous demand on the company's scarce supplier technical support staff, forcing the companies to limit the number of suppliers. Again, today's increasingly high standards of quality will render even heavy use of sampling plans inadequate to ensure defect rates of the order of less than a few parts per million.

Every business book will refer to the 80:20 rule. If 20% of your customers are 80% of your business, so also you are 80% of the supplier's business. It pays to make permanent customers out of the suppliers to get the best quality, the best delivery and the best prices.

Here, therefore, comes the opportunity and motivation to secure supplier integration as a win-win alliance. Limiting the number of suppliers, carefully selecting them and forging strong partnership links with key suppliers in a value-managed relationship, makes the suppliers an extension of your own enterprise.

Instead of pitting suppliers against one another to get the BEST PRICE, working closely with a few select suppliers enable reducing the TOTAL COST OF THE DEAL. Exploiting the expertise of the vendor, cost and quality advantages, shorter lead times and minimal inventories, their strengths, their better designs and better specifications, their expert knowledge and security of a long-term relationship will be yours. The premium that Timken, Faircrest Steel Plant, awards to its suppliers is 20 year agreements, targeting a 10% value improvement every year. Better designs and just right specifications for own designs result.

It would pay hands down to share with the vendor the plans (even the most confidential ones), give know how needed to make the item, show mutual trust and assist exchange of staff between the company and the supplier while seeking supplies. Traditionally, companies focus on manufacturing costs and not on the cost of transactions. The cost of transactions include inventory, technical support, managerial overheads and waste. In optimising transaction costs, buffer inventories virtually disappear in a just-in-time approach. Ultimately, new designs for existing products and new products for the function required would be conceived when the company thinks not just about what it makes, but also about what its customers use it for and how.

Teams that consist of production, quality, purchase, design, as well as partnership alliances with suppliers and dealers, help effective parts management, streamlining procurement and promoting re-use of existing parts. Estimates on the cost to develop, release and carry a part in the inventory vary widely. A survey of Fortune 500 manufacturing companies found that not a single company, nor a division, had an accurate estimate of the life time costs of a part over its life cycle. But, intuitive estimates ranged from \$ 5,000 for a standard part to as high as \$ 60,000 to \$ 100,000 per part for custom parts.

OUTSOURCING

It is also examined if, in the functionally developed alternative, full advantage is taken of outsourcing.

A study of the organisational purchase process made by Penton Research Services, USA, shows that business and government agencies are now buying more goods and services from outside sources than a few years ago (rather than producing them internally). They also expect to outsource more by the year 2000. In the past, companies used to aim for self-sufficiency, in order that their supplies of materials, semis and components remain dependable — for deliveries, quality and costs. With growth in industries and competencies, there is today a proliferation of sources for every one of these items. Hence the unlimited opportunities for outsourcing.

GM, following the old tradition, makes about 70% of the parts and components it uses in car and truck manufacture. Meanwhile, Ford and Chrysler are outsourcing components and parts, and up-front design engineering, to less expensive external suppliers. Toyota claims that they buy the best parts from all the world over. Lear Jet Inc., builds new Lear Jet 45 in Wichita, with assemblies provided by various units — fuselage from the Shorts unit in Belfast, Northern Ireland; wings from the De Havilland organisation in Toronto, Canada.

WIN-WIN ALLIANCES

Back in 1987, the concept of partnership was limited to the suppliers of raw materials and parts, the manufacturers of the product and the retailer. Today, however, warehousing and transportation have been added to the partnerships. Also, the consumer, because his wants, needs and tasks drive the system. Advances in information technology and the availability of real-time data extend the enterprise beyond traditional boundaries, enabling integrated product development and product supply, literally with the customer's name on it.

STANDARDS

It is a well established fact that use of standard items, having been previously developed and proved, lead to many advantages, like better availability, assurance of specific levels of consistency in size, shape, tolerances, finishes, quality and competitive prices. Therefore, all Standards are consulted, used, and exploited to advantage for securing the maximum potential gains possible. It used to be standardization at low cost or flexibility at high cost, but not both. However, today, by melding standardization with flexibility, it ceases to be the either or proposition of the past. It is possible to have both — and at low cost, by using the modular approach. The modules are given the benefits of standardization and the whole process, greater flexibility. Thus, it will be possible to derive the advantage of rapid changes in design and product, rapid response to market demands and low cost of production of "options" or "specials", in fairly small batches.

All calculations and costs are re-checked. Life-cycle costs are calculated. While reduction in cost is an objective of performing Value Engineering, other related factors have also to be investigated before the change proposed becomes a viable proposition. For example, it is easy to overlook the quality problems of the original item and unwittingly reproduce them in the proposed change. Or, with small batch production, it is only after manufacture has commenced that some feature is found to be difficult to inspect. The skill of the person making the prototype is usually much superior to what the production line men has — ingeneous enough to machine and assemble anything if it is humanly possible. So, manufacture on mass production basis may give rise to poor quality and higher scrap rates than estimated from the trial run. Reliability of a component can be affected by material, dimensions and/or assembly. The routine checks, by Stores receiving section may not be adequate to guarantee freedom from close deviations. Changes in the procedure and norms for acceptance to ensure high reliability may make the final cost of the item prohibitively high. Within certain limits, the greater the number of parts the less likelihood there is for the assembly to be perfect. The same reasoning can be applied to the number of suppliers. Make or buy decisions can entail involved discussion on distribution of overheads and contribution analysis.

Recommended changes are all documented. Design, drawing, sketches, part list, bill of materials, specifications, etc., are drawn up. Prototypes are developed and tested, as appropriate.

The proposals are classified into short-term and long-term solutions. For, it is likely that those indicating the largest savings may require major changes; and so, capital investments, time and risk (as success in major changes cannot be predicted with a high degree of certainty).

Some departments may be affected by the changes proposed. There may also be people who will be affected. A prior discussion with them may convert them to be supporters of the change. Even otherwise, this discussion could give enough tips as to how their objections can be met.

Implementation Phase

No idea, no matter how brilliant, is of any value, until it is applied. Value here is measured in terms of attainment.

The fruits of all the efforts in the preceding phases depend on the successful completion of this phase. Therefore, the goal here would be to prepare the Value Engineering Change Proposal, present it for approval and activate action for its implementation.

A Value Engineering Change Proposal should always be made in writing. An oral presentation of the study results could supplement the written report. The proposal should summarise the study, list the advantages, describe before and after details (inclusive of cost data), make recommendations on the specific actions to be taken, suggest an implementation plan as well as acknowledgement of contributions made by others to the study. The action plan would specify the steps to be taken, who should do what, when and where, and the responsibilities of each individual concerned with the implementation of the proposal. In conjunction, there should be an action time table to facilitate follow up.

The Project Workbook with complete working details may be annexed to the proposal.

The proposal should be factual. Direct and indirect benefits would be included. Similarly, any short-comings or disadvantages due to the proposal are not with-held. For, it is better that these are stated by the Team, and not pointed out by an outsider at some later time. Whenever there are such instances, the Team must consider and record alongside the item what ways and means are suggested to solve or overcome these minus points.

It should be remembered that the acceptance and the use of the Value Engineering Change Proposal will be that of the decision-maker. Therefore, his needs are considered well to include all that he needs to make the decision. Objections and road blocks must be anticipated, viewing the proposal from the other person's point of view, to be fore-armed to counter them successfully.

The installation of a new idea and the introduction of any change would present human problems. So, it would be wisdom to be prepared to face discouragement, set-backs and disappointments. By being ready for them, it would afford the choice of making a new approach. By offering a first choice and an alternative (which is possible by developing the lowest cost, best value solution and the next higher cost and lower value solution during the Development Phase), the risk of rejection could be pre-empted. It lets the decision-maker choose which of the two alternatives to implement. Accepting a compromise here is the only exception permitted from the Value Engineering principle of NO COMPROMISE discussed in the earlier chapter.

Successful implementation depends on integrating the necessary actions to be taken into the normal routine of the organisation. The choice of the leader of the Team, if it is on the basis of who has the problem, or who is most concerned with solving it, would make this happen automatically. Reviewing progress periodically and monitoring at set points would expedite completion.

The final and most critical part of the project work is the audit of the benefits and savings realised and verification that the anticipated results have been achieved. Working in close liaison with the audit, lessons can be drawn to enhance the quality of future project work.

AUDIT

In order to validate that the expected results have been achieved, it is essential to perform an audit of the Value Engineering change through an independent authority. Until this is done the project cannot be closed. The audit process is necessary for the continuing success of the organisation's Value Engineering programme.

Management designates the authority or individual responsible for performing the audit work.

PART III

- PROJECT WORK
- WORK SHEETS
- OBJECTIVES
- TECHNIQUES
- GUIDELINES
- CHECK LISTS
- KEY QUESTIONS

PROJECT SELECTION

OBJECTIVE

1. To identify the items for Value Engineering study.
2. To select from them specific projects with maximum potential for improvements, monetary savings, value returns and indirect, intangible benefits.
3. To prioritise the selected items for study.

STEPS

1. Solicit project ideas.
2. Identify high cost, low value areas.
3. Make preliminary evaluation of potential benefits.
4. Rank and present to management for authorisation.
5. Budget and obtain allocation of resources for study.

TECHNIQUES

1. Felt need. List them.
2. Reviews by Standing Committees — Design review, Review of planning documents, New product introduction, etc.
3. Suggestion Schemes. Invite suggestions.
4. Seminars. Hold Seminars with senior officers, giving them an overview of Value Engineering, illustrating the benefits with successful value improvement cases and inviting their suggestions.

5. Relative ranking. ABC analysis, high cost, high energy use, low profit margin, highly competitive, most problematic items.

6. Preliminary assessment of Value Index, Value gap, Value Mismatch, Index of Cost Savings Potential.

7. Use Guidelines. Verify using attributes listed in the Guidelines.

KEY QUESTION

WHY ?

GUIDELINES

Check Design

1. Is the design five or more years old ?

2. Has it been reviewed ? When ?

3. What were the changes made ?

4. Is it a proprietory item ?

Check item attributes

1. Is it a current item or a planned future item ?

2. Is it being researched or developed ?

3. Is the item under development or study in another unit of the organisation ?

4. Are changes likely to be made when recommendations are submitted ?

5. Is the purpose or function of the item definable and understandable ?

6. Is a list of attributes made ?

7. What in it is imposed by customer, and what by the company ?

Check components/actions

1. Does it have 3 or more sub-assemblies or group of actions ?
2. Does it have between 8 and 16 components or actions ?
3. Are they difficult to use, perform, manufacture, or buy ?
4. Do they appear to be larger, more complex or heavier than necessary ?
5. Are they non-standard forms, shapes or sizes ?
6. Is there any item similar to it, being frequently used in whole or part ?
7. Is there any similarity to other company or industrial standards ?
8. Do they appear to be excessively worked on to produce the finished product ?
9. Is the material used expensive ?
10. Do they require high rated, sophisticated and expensive equipment or skill to produce ?
11. Has production/engineering/marketing/maintenance/serving reported any adverse points on their production, maintenance or service ?
12. Does production involve use of excessive or complex jigs, fixture, tools, dies or procedures ?
13. Has production reported using excessive amounts of equipment or manpower to produce the item ?
14. Do they involve close allowances, tolerances, fits, finishes, treatments ?
15. Were there any complaints/reports that the components/parts are weak or requiring excessive maintenance ?

Check Costs

1. Is the item a low profit earner ?
2. If bought out, can it be made in-house at lower cost ?

3. If it is an in-house production, can it be bought out at lower cost ?
4. Are there competitive items that appear to be better or more reliable, and/or lower in costs ?

Check Market Share

1. Is the item having a small share of potential market ?
2. Is any competitor making or selling same or similar item at same or lower cost ?

Check other details

1. Intricate shapes, deep excavations, special weldments, etc.
2. Expensive detours, traffic, maintenance, etc.
3. Intricate piping runs.
4. Long foundation piles.
5. Environmentally controlled processes.
6. Excessive reinforcements.
7. Expensive assembly line machinery.
8. Coffer dam dewatering.
9. Ornamentation.
10. Automation for the sake of automation.
11. Record seeking design.
12. Excessive safety factors.
13. Items with poor service or cost history.
14. Standard plans or specifications in use more than 5 years old and not reviewed since.

15. Will a change benefit in any of these areas:

Noise	Reliability	Aesthetics
Safety	Fire protection	Simplification
Maintenance	Standardisation	Vibration
Time	Performance	Quality
Weight	Employee rate	Employment rate
Energy use	Configuration	Ergonomics

Check timing of the project

1. Patent position.
2. Effect on a large number of people.
3. Avoidance of loss.
4. Savings and/or improved profits.
5. Availability of items.
6. Inclusion with other changes.
7. Annual volume.
8. Anticipated market life.

VALUE ENGINERING PROJECT WORKSHOP FORMS

PROJECT	Ref No............... Date..................
DETAILS OF ITEM TO BE STUDIED	

REMEMBER TO RECORD FACTS AND FACTS ONLY

Form No. 1

Team Selection

OBJECTIVE

1. To ensure that the Team possesses necessary technical expertise appropriate to the requirements of the item under study.

2. To ensure that the individuals possess necessary skill for applying the Value Engineering methodology. (They must have completed a course of Value Engineering Module I training–minimum).

3. To include the diversity of talents needed for the study - i.e., a combination of idea men, communicators, developers, organisers, and a lay person.

TECHNIQUES

1. Train for skill to apply Value Engineering methodology, all key, decision-making personnel through standard Value Engineering Workshops (either in-house, or external).

2. Select members by merit/competence.

3. Rotate members.

4. Name the Leader, Co-ordinator and fix time frame.

5. Force feed.

GUIDELINES

1. Check if individual is Value Engineering-trained ? (If not, arrange for his training)

2. Check qualifications of members chosen against recommended essential qualifications. Verify that the group is representative thereof.

3. Check what technical, functional know how will contribute to the study ? Verify that the group is representative.

4. If too many, ensure constant consultation with those representatives not included in Team.

5. Avoid re-selection of same person as member to the exclusion of others.

PROJECT	Ref No.............. Date..................

TEAM LEADER

NAME	DESIGNATION	TELE. NO.

TEAM MEMBERS

NAME	DESIGNATION	TELE. NO.
OTHERS TO BE CONSULTED		

MAKE TEAM REPRESENTATIVE

Form No. 2

GENERAL PHASE

OBJECTIVE

1. To prepare a strong foundation for the value study.
2. To select the project, if not already done.
3. To form the Team, if not already done.
4. To orient the members with the ground rules for value study.
5. To name the Leader and Coordinator.

TECHNIQUES

1. Use good human relations. Follow the ten steps to better relations.
2. Inspire team work. Divide and sub-divide the task into specific parts.
3. Work on specifics, bringing individual parts of the problem into sharp focus and allocating specific responsibilities to specific members (generally along the lines of their qualifications and experience).
4. Identify, clarify and overcome road blocks.
5. Challenge everything, constructively, to fully understand.
6. Apply good business judgement.

KEY QUESTIONS

1. Are we using the skills of working with people and utilising their skills to the best of our ability ?

2. Are we giving self-respect and generating a sense of mutual responsibility ?
3. Are we readily subordinating our personal prominence to the efficiency of the whole Team ?
4. Are we being over-sensitive ?
5. Are we resisting or assisting ?
6. Is there a good reason for saying...... ?
7. Is this really what is meant ?
8. Is this passing the buck ?
9. Is this avoiding action ?
10. Is this killing the idea ?
11. Is the Team following the ground rules ?

INFORMATION PHASE

OBJECTIVE

1. To secure all and complete information.
2. To gather FACTS and from the best sources.
3. To ensure accuracy of information.
4. To check, re-check, test, update and process all data.

KEY QUESTIONS

1. What is it ?
2. What does it do ?
3. What must it do ?
4. What does it cost ?
5. Ask WHY, WHAT, WHEN, WHERE, HOW and WHO.
6. Ask CAN ?

TECHNIQUES

1. Decide what data are to be gathered.
2. Assign specific tasks to each team member.
3. Record all information secured.
4. Use the key questions to gather information.

5. Seek FACTS, not opinions, views, feelings.
6. Use the best source possible.
7. Determine costs: refine them to meaningful costs.
8. Establish cost relationships: assign costs to specifications, requirements, etc.
9. Use good human relations.
10. Anticipate and overcome road blocks/obstacles/objections.
11. Constructively question everything, understand, then accept the answers.

GUIDELINES

Types of information

Project data

Planning documents.
Drawings.
Specifications.
Sketches.
Materials list.
Cost estimates.

Design data

Information that went into the design.
Rationale used by the Designer.
Assumptions used by the Designer.
Constraints accommodated by the Designer.
Site conditions.
Regulatory/Mandatory constraints.
Design computations.
When designed ?
Changes made in original design, when and why ?

Physical data

Specifications.
Part list.
Shape.
Dimensions, including tolerances.

Weight.
Density.
Colour.
Materials used.
Present process.
Chemical composition.
Physical properties.

Characteristics

Appearance.
Resistance to wear
shock
vibration
fire
weather
skidding
deflection
Sound absorption capability.
Alignment – horizontal
vertical
side-wise

Methods data

How operated ?
How constructed ?
How fabricated ?
How developed ?
How manufactured ?
How installed ?
How maintained ?
How replaced ?
How serviced ?

Production data

Process flow chart.
Man-Machine chart
Equipment used — standard/special.
Tools, dies, moulds, etc.
Jigs and fixtures.

Finishing data

Treatment given.
Surface finishes.
Allowances, tolerances and fits.

Assembly data

Class A and Class B items.

Quantity data

Production per run, or period (hour, day, etc.)
Production rate.
Yield.
Prime production.
Seconds.
Scrap generation.
Rejection and re-work.
Anticipated annual volume in future.
Current usage.
Percentage returns

Performance data

End use.
Life.
Present performance.
Working conditions.

Shipping data

Freight.
Insurance.
Packaging.
Transportation.
Handling.

Marketing data

Share of market.
Anticipated total market requirements.

Bought out items

Present supplier(s).
Other sources of supply.
Cost of item.
Cost of transport.
What extras are paid, if any.
Whether it was bought always, or made at any time.

Requirements data

Desired life.
Desired operability.
Desired reliability.
Desired interchangeability.

Desired dependability.
Desired maintainability.
Desired serviceability.
Desired areas of operation.
Desired performance.
Desired safety.
Desired special features.
Requirements in design.
Desired procedure.

Historical data

Past history.
Competitor's experience.

Experience data

Test results.
Pilot plant results.
User feedback.
Complaints.
Maintenance experience.
Servicing experience.
After-sales experience.
Product recalls.
Warranty claims.

Restrictions

Relating to space
methods
performance
procedures
operations
schedules
cost.

Cost data

Cost of labour, material, overheads.
Cost of elements of physical data, methods data, performance data.
Cost of restrictions as they relate to design, acquisition, operation, maintenance, service, disposal.
Cost for treatments, fits, allowances, tolerances, finishes.

Competition details

Who.
How many.
Where located.

Their prices.
Their share of market.
Their strengths, if identifiable.
Their weakness.

Sources of information

Design drawings.
Assembly drawings.
Part/component drawings.
Bills of material.
Flow charts.
Standard practice sheets.
Job orders.
Shop routing.
Production reports.
Delay reports.
Servicing reports.
Inspection reports.
Scrap and re-work records.
Test reports.
User feed back.
Budgets/financial records.
Cost sheets and exhibits.
Sample of item, assembly, sub assembly or part.
Warranty claims.

Verifying and validating facts

Examine

the basic design with the Designer.
the basic engineering with the Engineer.
the basic manufacturing with the Production Manager.
the after-sales responsibility with the Sales/Service personnel.
the performance with the user, operator and owner.

Consult

the Specialists/Consultants
the contractors.
the vendors.
the distributors.
the retailers.
the people or firms using same or similar process, products or equipment

Refer

Handbooks.
Catalogues.
Operating/Maintenance/Service Manuals.
Technical publications.
Conference proceedings.
Exhibits.
Own company, National and Inter-national Standards.
Government gazettes and publications.
Technical libraries.
Professional organisations.

CHECK LIST

1. Who made the specification/drawing? When ?

2. Was it ever reviewed and revised? If so, when ?

3. What was the revision ?

4. Is it a general specification ? Or, was it prepared specifically for this item (or project) ?

5. Is the specification/drawing intended for strict application? Or, is it only to serve as a guideline ?

6. Is the specification realistic (i.e., are all specified characteristics necessary) ?

7. Who stipulated the physical properties, chemical composition, machining tolerances, surface finishes, etc.? User/Customer/Designer/Others ?

8. Are the specified materials freely available in the market and easy to get ? Or, are they specially made for us ?

9. Whether alternative materials were considered ? If so and rejected, the reasons for their rejection ? Are these reasons still valid today ?

10. When was the material specified ? Have new materials been developed since then, which could be substituted ?

11. How is the item made? Why that way ?

12. Who else makes the item? Or, who else uses a similar item ?

13. Is the item made or bought out ? Was it ever made or bought at any time in the past ?

14. Who supplies the item ? For you and for others ?

15. Is it imported? Is it even now imported ?

16. Are working/operating conditions same today as they were when the item was first designed/specified/installed/made ?

17. When was the item first designed/specified, or installed ?

18. Have new methods, materials, processes, etc. been since developed which provide similar or better performance or service ?

19. Were complaints received regarding the item ? If so, details.

20. Are the costs based on recent estimates ? Or, on latest actuals ?

21. Have life cycle costs been worked out ?

22. How do in-plant rates of costs compare with outside rates for contracts, machining, fabrication, casting, converting, site-work, erection, haulage, servicing, transportation, etc. ?

23. Are there any hidden costs? If so, why ?

24. Where should investigations, changes or improvements be considered to make the item cost less, sell more, perform better, etc. ?

25. Have we consulted everybody who has anything to do with the item ? Even a total outsider ?

<table>
<tr><td>PROJECT</td><td>Ref No...............
Date..................</td></tr>
<tr><td>DESCRIBE THE PROJECT FOR VE EFFORT (What is it ?)</td><td>Present procedure, design, system, performance requirements, criteria.</td></tr>
<tr><td colspan="2"></td></tr>
<tr><td colspan="2">OBJECTIVES OR REQUIRED CRITERIA - NOT TO BE COMPROMISED (What does it do ?)</td></tr>
<tr><td colspan="2"></td></tr>
<tr><td colspan="2">DESIRED CRITERIA OR FEATURES - Subject to trade off and optimisation. DESIRABLE, BUT NOT ESSENTIAL</td></tr>
<tr><td colspan="2"></td></tr>
</table>

BE FACTUAL AND SPECIFIC

Form No. 3

PROJECT		Ref. No.................... Date..........................
INFORMATION PHASE	Industry location, Cost, Quantities, Time, Other indicators.	

SECURE FACTS FROM RELIABLE SOURCES.
Form No. 4

<table>
<tr><td>PROJECT</td><td>Ref. No................
Date.....................</td></tr>
<tr><td colspan="2">LIST OF DOCUMENTS
(List books, periodicals, technical journals, documents, specifications and drawings, etc. used for information, when it is impractical to enumerate or include in the Project Work Book)</td></tr>
<tr><td>Reference/Source</td><td>Abstract of data</td></tr>
<tr><td></td><td></td></tr>
</table>

CHECK FOR COMPLETENESS AND ACCURACY
Form No. 5

Function Phase

OBJECTIVE

1. To identify the function(s).
2. To define the function.
3. To classify the function.
4. To determine the costs — meaningful costs.
5. To analyse the function costs.
6. To determine the worth.

TECHNIQUES

1. Separate into functional units and analyse.
2. Strip to last bolt and nut and analyse.
3. Define function in two words: a VERB and a NOUN.
4. Keep definition simple, and verb, specific.
5. Evaluate by comparison, and by numerical method.
6. Classify functions: **BASIC, SECONDARY, SUPPORT, NECESSARY, UN-NECESSARY.**
7. Make FAST diagrams.
8. Produce cost visibility.
9. Prepare Function-Cost matrix and Function-Cost-Worth matrix.

10. Use good human relations.

KEY QUESTIONS

1. What is the item ?
2. What does it do ?
3. What must it do ?
4. Is that what the customer wants it to do ?
5. Is that what the customer really believes he is paying for ?
6. What does it cost ?
7. What is it WORTH ?
8. Refine the answers asking: How much ?
   How well ?
   For how long ?
   How often ?
   How efficiently ?
   Under what conditions ?

CHECK LIST

1. Is the function at all needed ? Can it be eliminated ?
2. Is some other part also performing the same function ? Can both be combined ?
3. Is the function the result of the design, i.e., due to the present methods and processes being followed ?
4. Is the function performed MORE than actually required ? Should it do so ?
5. What does the item (or project) do unnecessarily ? Is there something that was not originally required ?
6. Does the function seem worth its present cost ? If not, why ?

7. Is the function needed as a result of severe operating conditions ? Limitations like for:
   particular operating conditions,
   ease of operation,
   ease of installation,
   maintenance,
   safety,
   testing,
   any other reason (specify) ?
8. Can these conditions be eliminated ?
9. Are the costs meaningful ?
10. Have costs been attached to all functions ?

<table>
<tr><td colspan="6">PROJECT</td><td colspan="3">Ref No.......................
Date...........................</td></tr>
<tr><td colspan="9">FUNCTION DEFINITION</td></tr>
<tr><td colspan="4">Assembly:</td><td colspan="5" rowspan="2">Basic Function</td></tr>
<tr><td colspan="4">Drawing No:</td></tr>
<tr><td rowspan="2">QUAN-TITY</td><td rowspan="2">PART</td><td colspan="2">FUNCTION(S)</td><td colspan="2">FUNCTIONAL PART</td><td colspan="2">LEVEL ASSEMBLY</td><td>REMARKS</td></tr>
<tr><td>VERB</td><td>NOUN</td><td>BASIC</td><td>SECON-DARY</td><td>BASIC</td><td>SECON-DARY</td><td></td></tr>
<tr><td></td><td></td><td></td><td></td><td></td><td></td><td></td><td></td><td></td></tr>
<tr><td></td><td></td><td></td><td></td><td></td><td></td><td></td><td></td><td></td></tr>
<tr><td></td><td></td><td></td><td></td><td></td><td></td><td></td><td></td><td></td></tr>
<tr><td></td><td></td><td></td><td></td><td></td><td></td><td></td><td></td><td></td></tr>
</table>

FUNCTION IS THE HEART OF VALUE ENGINEERING

Form No. 6

PROJECT	Ref No................... Date........................

FUNCTION CLASSIFICATION

Assembly:

Drawing No:

Key Letter	Functions	Weight
A		
B		
C		
D		
E		
F		
G		
H		
I		
J		
K		
L		

	B	C	D	E	F	G	H	I	J	K	L	Total
A												
B												
C												
D												
E												
F												
G												
H												
I												
J												
K												
L												

Scale:

1. Minimum difference
2. Medium difference
3. Major difference

FUNCTION IS THE HEART OF VALUE ENGINEERING

Form No. 7

PROJECT		Ref No.............. Date..................
FUNCTION RELATIONSHIP		
WHY	FUNCTION	HOW

FUNCTION IS THE HEART OF VALUE ENGINEERING

Form No. 8

PROJECT				Ref No........... Date..............
FUNCTION SUMMARY				
Sl.No.	Basic Functions		Secondary Functions	
	Verb	Noun	Verb	Noun
Higher order functions			Lower order functions	
One time functions			All time functions	

LOOK AT THE FUNCTION - NOT THE ITEM OR PART

Form No. 9

MEANINGFUL COSTS

Start out with the best costs that exist, understand them, know their deficiencies, use them to prepare meaningful costs for the purpose of making correct value decisions.

KEY QUESTIONS

1. What will that cost ?
2. What are the benefits ?
3. How is the product affected by a change in its cost ?
4. How will the sales be affected by a change in its cost ?
5. How will the other products be affected by a change in its cost ?
6. How will the company's future plans be affected by a change in its cost ?

TECHNIQUES

1. Put money value on everything.
2. Evaluate by comparison (where precise costs are not available).
3. Use good business judgement.
4. Use Analysis/Evaluation matrix.
5. Use good human relations.

GUIDELINES

1. Use Standard data.
2. Estimate set-up or fixed costs.
3. Estimate variable costs (based on quantities).
4. Estimate costs of implementing the change.
5. Calculate life-cycle costs.
6. Compare alternatives.
7. Record all benefits, including even, not quantifiable, in money terms.
8. Record also disadvantages, if any; and ways to overcome.

PROJECT				Ref No.............................	
				Date.................................	

COST ANALYSIS

Sl. No.	Operation Process	Cost per unit	Annual Cost	Function secured or desired	Remarks

CHECK AND RE-CHECK TO BE SURE
Form No. 10

PROJECT				Ref No........................ Date............................				
FUNCTION-COST ANALYSIS				**FUNCTIONS**				
Sl. No.	Item or part	Cost per unit	No. used per assembly or project					
Total								

BE OBJECTIVE
Form No. 11

PROJECT	Ref No........................ Date............................

FUNCTION-COST-WORTH ANALYSIS

Sl. No.	Function	Allocated cost `C' Rs.	Function worth `W' Rs.	Basis of Worth	Value gap (C—W)	Value Index (W/C)

COST IS WHAT WE PAY & WORTH IS WHAT WE SHOULD PAY

Form No. 12

Creation Phase

OBJECTIVE

To generate alternative methods for providing the Function and/or the item, through creative thinking, brainstorming and even speculation.

TECHNIQUES

1. Use good human relations.
2. Give free rein to your imagination, innovative talents and creative thinking.
3. Defer judgement. Suppress the judicial part of your mind.
4. Brainstorm. Use all creativity techniques. Blast and create quantity of ideas.
5. Bring new information into the arena.
6. Amplify, simplify, substitute, add, subtract, modify, extend, combine, reduce, eliminate etc.
7. Do not ridicule, criticise or interrupt.
8. Good ideas are hard to come by; so, welcome and foster imaginative thinking.

KEY QUESTION

What else will do the function ?

BASIC RULES

1. Establish positive thinking.

2. Every one must contribute ideas. Do not worry whether they are good, bad or indifferent.

3. Go wild. Produce quantity of ideas. Rebound ideas.

4. Judging, criticising, ridiculing or laughing at ideas not permitted.

5. The wilder the idea, the madder the suggestion, the more welcome it is.

6. Aim for a large quantity of ideas, not quality (at this stage).

CHECK LIST

1. For brainstorming, have the rules, method of approach, and techniques, explained to the team ?
2. Have all the basic functions and needed functions been identified ?
3. Have the Team dismissed from their thinking the present way or hardware accomplishing the function ?
4. Have you removed from sight the item, part, drawing, etc. ?
5. Is there a sheet provided for each function considered ?
6. Have creative thinking techniques been used ?
7. Have the Team created an atmosphere that welcomes and encourages new ideas ?
8. Is there cross inspiration ?
9. Are all members participating ?
10. Are all ideas being recorded ?
11. Has an output goal been set ?
12. Are negative responses being discouraged ?
13. Has the Team generated a large quantity of ideas ?
14. Are the ideas generated without all the constraints of specifications and system requirements ?

15. Have all the basic and required functions been subject to the creation phase ?

16. Are we avoiding action ?

17. Are we killing the idea ?

18. Are we passing the buck ?

PROJECT	Ref No.............. Date..................

CREATION PHASE - IDEA LISTING
FUNCTION .... Verb Noun
REMEMBER — No Criticism! No Road blocks. More QUANTITY - not Quality The WILDER the BETTER!

Sl. No.	Idea	
1 2 3 4 5 6 7 8 9 10		
That is the spirit. You have just warmed up! Keep going!		
11 12 13 14 15 16 17 18 19 20		
Build on other's ideas - add, subtract, amplify, modify, reverse, hike, piggy back, etc.		

THINK ON PURPOSE
Form No. 13A

Sl. No.	
21 22 23 24 25 26 27 28 29 30	
DON'T GIVE UP YET. Consult Check List if you wish and generate more ideas!	
31 32 33 34 35 36 37 38 39 40	
CEATIVITY = IMAGINATION + INSPIRATION + ILLUMINATION So, some more ideas.	
41 42 43 44 45 46 47 48 49 50	

CREATE DELIBERATELY
Form No. 13B

IDEA STIMULATORS

(Use only if, on your own, you have reached a dead end.)

1. Is there anything similar at home or in your office ?
2. How is the function provided by nature ?
3. How is a similar objective provided by nature ?
4. Have you read about something similar some time ?
5. What else is like this ? (Shape, size, colour, look, length, width, thickness, weight, volume, etc.)
6. Is there something which can be adapted ?
7. Can we add something to existing similar parts ?
8. Can we modify other's ideas ?
9. Can it be combined ?
10. Can it be condensed/extended ?
11. Can it be made lighter/heavier ?
12. Can it be made narrower/broader ?
13. Can it be made thinner/thicker ?
14. Can it be made longer/shorter ?
15. Can it be made shallower/denser ?
16. Can it be made portable/fixed ?
17. Can we change the colour ?
18. Can another part also provide this function ?
19. Can we alter the sequence of operations ?
20. Can we change the layout ?

21. Can we change the shape ?
22. Can we change the size ?
23. Is the shape attractive/saleable/feeling right ?
24. Does it operate smoothly/fast enough ?
25. Does it open/shut easily ?
26. Is there an alternative standard product/process available ?
27. Is there a special product ?
28. Can we use scrap or salvage from other plants/processes/shops/ materials ?
29. Is a different power source possible ?
30. Check every centimeter of the product and ask, "why is this necessary ?"
31. What else can we get out of this ?
32. What MORE FUNCTION can be added ?
33. Can we increase frequency ?
34. Can we reduce frequency ?
35. Can we add ingredients or additives ?
36. Can we add costs and get more functions ?
37. Can we change the motions ? (Rotary instead of reciprocating ?)
38. Can we change the direction ? (Up instead of down ?)
39. Can we change the process ? (Forge instead of roll, die-cast, fabricate instead of forge/cast ?)
40. Can we change the medium ? (Pneumatic instead of hydraulic ?)
41. Can we mechanise/automate ?
42. Can we increase/decrease tolerances ?

43. Can we change the allowances ?
44. Can we change the fits ?
45. Can we do the opposite ?
46. Can we change the design ?
47. Can it be vertical instead of horizontal ?
48. Can we use more men ?
49. Can we simplify the process/procedure/method ?
50. Can we consult more specialists ?
51. Can it be made of another (less expensive) material ?
52. Can fluids replace the solid material now used ?
53. Why all this excess material on the product ?
54. Can we use longer/wider/thicker material ?
55. Can we reduce the strength of each and use more number ?
56. Can we substitute material - plastics for metals ?
57. Will use of costlier process reduce rejections ?
58. Can it be hollow, instead of solid ?
59. What will be the simplest example in your experience ?
60. What will be the wildest method to secure this function ?
61. How will a woman look at the problem ? Or, a teenager ? Or, a lay man ? Or, anyone ?
62. Would a primitive man have done it this way ?
63. Is there a parallel in defense or military equipment/systems ?
64. Is there a parallel in biological systems - plant or animal ?
65. Must it be painted ?

66. Must it be weather-proofed ?
67. Must it have the surface finishes indicated ?
68. Why all this packing ? Is it necessary ?
69. Is there a more effective packing ?
70. Can we change the packing material/method ?
71. Can the packing material be usefully utilised ?
72. Will a change in packing material/method lower the cost of handling/ transport/damages in handling/transport ?
73. Why must it be transported so far ?
74. Can we change the means of transport ? (Rail instead of road ?)
75. What do the competitors do ?
76. What is special about our present way of obtaining this function ?
77. Does the competitor use the same product/process/method/ material?
78. How does he make/buy it ?
79. What are the major problems at present ?
80. Are there too many complaints ?
81. Are there any aspects or parts which the users or others dislike and find ways of avoiding them ?
82. Are any of the present parts/hardware lying unused ? Why ?
83. Is any of the parts proprietory ?
84. Is it due to imported technology ?
85. Can we replace it ?
86. Does it suit our conditions ?
87. Are we buying the item/part ?

88. Can we reduce the cost by buying in bulk ?

89. Did we ever make it ? Can we now make it instead of buying ?

90. Is it safe as it should be ?

91. Is the factor of safety too high ?

92. Was there, at any time, too great a stress on safety or whims or fancies of an individual to influence adoption of the present design ?

93. Would you like to own the present equipment and use it/operate it the present way ?

94. Was there lack of full information and therefore were the parameters fixed on the higher side ?

95. Who exactly made the most complaints ? Were they investigated fully ? Should we examine them again now ?

96. Has a search been made of patent literature ? Trade journals ?

97. How much of this is due to custom, tradition, convention, or opinions ?

98. If you were spending your money on this, will you do it this way ?

HOW TO CHALLENGE THE STATUS-QUO

1. Put to other uses ? New ways to use as is ?

2. Adapt ? What else is like this ? What other ideas does this suggest ? Does past offer parallel ? What could be copied ?

3. Modify ? Change meaning, colour, motion, odour, form, shape ? Other changes ?

4. Magnify ? What to add ? More time ? Greater frequency ? Stronger ? Larger ? Thicker ? Extra value ? Plus ingredient ? Duplicate ? Multiply ? Exaggerate ?

5. Minify ? What to substantiate ? Smaller ? Condensed ? Miniature ? Lower ? Shorter ? Lighter ? Omit ? Streamline ? Split up ? Understate ?

6. Substitute ? Who else instead ? What else instead ? Other ingredient ? Other material ? Other process ? Other power ? Other place ? Other approach ?

7. Re-arrange ? Interchange components ? Transpose cause and effect ? Change place ? Change schedule ? Change sequence ?

8. Reverse ? Transpose positive and negative ? How about opposites ? Turn it backward ? Turn it upside down ? Reverse roles ?

9. Combine ? How about a blend, an alloy, an assortment, an ensemble ? Combine units ? Combine purposes ? Combine appeals ? Combine ideas ?

EVALUATION PHASE

OBJECTIVE

1. To judge the ideas generated in the Creation Phase for ability to meet the required criteria.
2. To check how the idea can be made to work.
3. To establish the function cost of each idea.
4. To refine, develop and build up on the ideas feasible function alternatives to attain the required function(s).
5. To select the best two or three alternatives for further development.

TECHNIQUES

1. Use good human relations.
2. Refine, develop and build on all ideas.
3. Filter the ideas carefully: drop only those that will definitely not meet the required criteria after refining, development, etc.
4. Use creative judgement. Forget your biases and prejudices.
5. Consult freely. Use expertise of specialists, vendors, etc.
6. Establish meaningful cost on all ideas.
7. Evaluate by comparison, using matrix, etc.
8. Be objective, as far as practicable.

KEY QUESTIONS

1. Will the idea work ?
2. Can it be made to work ?
3. How might the idea work ?
4. Will each idea perform the basic function ?
5. That which performs the basic function, does it meet all requirements ?
6. Does it meet all user's needs ?
7. If the answers to questions 5 and 6 are in the negative, can the idea be developed to meet them ?
8. What will it cost ?
9. How does its cost compare with its worth ?
10. What are the advantages/dis-advantages ?
11. Can the not so good features be eliminated/minimised ?
12. What will be the additional cost ?
13. Which idea is the least expensive ?
14. How feasible are the selected alternatives ?
15. Will it be easy or difficult to make the change ?
16. What are the requirements for the change over ?
17. What will be the impact of the change ?
18. Will the idea sell ?
19. Will the suggested alternative create additional or new problems ?
20. Is it compatible with the system of which it is a part ?
21. What is the savings potential ?

22. What are the collateral benefits ?
23. What are the intangible/non-quantifiable benefits ?
24. What are the implementation prospects/problems ?

PROCEDURES

1. Use the methods suggested.
2. Choose evaluation criteria carefully.
3. Group similar ideas.
4. Make preliminary screening to separate the best ideas.
5. Select the best two or three alternatives for further development. If necessary, test prototypes made.

SUGGESTED CRITERIA FOR EVALUATION

1. Strength.
2. Dependability.
3. Durability.
4. Accessability.
5. Ease of operation.
6. Ease for maintenance.
7. Ease for servicing.
8. Producability.
9. Reliability.
10. Safety.
11. Availability.
12. Machinability.

13. Insulating property.
14. Bearing strength.
15. Resistance to wear, friction, heat, cold, wind, moisture, corrosion, fire, elements, etc.
16. Dimensions, weight, volume, shape, size, etc.
17. Constraints in handling and movement — risks, damage, etc.
18. Acceptability to user.
19. Acceptability to top management.
20. State of technology.
21. Cost — both on cost and running.
22. Ease of change (implementation)

    (include others as deemed appropriate)

CHECK LIST

1. Check if every idea is considered.
2. Check if all feasible ideas have been retained.
3. Check if all experts/specialists have been consulted.
4. Have evaluation criteria been established ?
5. Check what departments or activities would be affected by the proposed change.
6. Check also who will be affected.
7. Check if their advice or concurrence has been obtained.
8. Check if advice has been taken from production, maintenance etc.
9. Check if users of similar equipment/product/process have been consulted.

10. Check if suppliers of the proposed alternative have been consulted.

11. Check if both advantages and disadvantages have been listed.

12. Check if all functions have been re-evaluated as to their need.

13. Check if any part of the needed function criteria is not fulfilled by the alternative.

14. If so, check if remedial action has been suggested.

15. Check if feasible ideas have been rated according to relative merits regarding cost, performance, aesthetics, advantages/disadvantages, probability of implementation etc.

16. Check if at least three ideas have been selected for further investigation and development.

PROJECT			Ref. No.......... Date.............
IDEA COMPARISON			
IDEA	ADVANTAGES	DISADVANTAGES (Note ways to overcome)	RANK

BE HONEST AND FAIR
Form No. 14

PROJECT							Ref. No............ Date.................
FEASIBILITY RANKING							
	A	B	C	D	E	F	Total
1							
2							
3							
4							
5							
6							
7							
8							
9							
10							
11							
12							
13							
14							
15							
16							
17							
18							
19							
20							

NOW IS THE TIME TO JUDGE

Form No. 15

PROJECT				Ref. No............ Date.................	
IDEA SELECTION					
	weight importance	BEST ALTERNATIVES			
TOTAL WEIGHTED FACTORS					
COST (ESTIMATED)					
WT. FACTOR COST					

BE OBJECTIVE
Form No. 16

Investigation Phase

OBJECTIVE

1. To thoroughly analyse the selected value alternatives for technical, economic, and commercial feasibility.

2. To prepare final cost estimates for the proposals.

3. To consult all concerned.

4. To fully develop the best idea(s), document the details, and recommend to management for approval/implementation.

TECHNIQUES

1. Use search techniques.

2. Refer Standards, — Company, National, Inter-national.

3. Consult — Specialists, Consultants, Users, Vendors.

4. Develop prototypes and test.

5. Use good human relations.

KEY QUESTIONS

1. Does the new solution offer significant improvement over the existing or originally intended item ?

2. Is it workable, practical and acceptable ?

3. Does it meet all the requirements ?

4. What are the costs ?

5. What are the savings ?

6. Who will be affected ?

7. Who has to approve ?

CHECK LIST

1. List of the names of Specialists who have the knowledge needed in the development of the proposals.

2. Similar list of suppliers, servicemen and users.

3. List of reference materials — Standards, Technical Literature, Directories, Handbooks, Journals, Trade Magazines, House publications, Manuals, Catalogues, etc.

4. Have the users' needs been satisfied ?

5. Have the technical points been checked — design, operation, maintenance, service, construction, erection, inspection, testing, etc.

6. Are the safety needs met ?

7. Are all the supporting data collected ?

8. Have the best proposal been properly described and in enough detail ?

9. Have the costs been estimated ? Life-cycle costs ?

10. Have ideas been solicited from specialists and recorded ?

11. Have the alternatives been discussed with people and departments that would be affected by the changes proposed ?

12. Is the plan for implementation drawn up showing steps required to sell the idea, the person suggested for implementing, the time and cost to implement, etc. ?

13. Have you a first choice and an alternative ?

14. Have you enough data/details to present all the facts clearly, concisely and convincingly ?

15. Is the alternative environmentally friendly ? Acceptable ?

PROJECT	Ref No............... Date..................

STUDY SUMMARY

CHANGE PROPOSAL	COMMENTS CRITIQUE	SOLUTIONS

CONSULT, SEEK ADVICE AND ASSISTANCE
Form No. 17

Implementation Phase

OBJECTIVE

1. To prepare the Value Engineering Change Proposal.
2. To suggest an implementation plan.
3. To obtain approval and designate the person to implement the proposal.
4. To monitor progress and expedite completion.
5. To record the benefits and savings.

TECHNIQUES

1. Make written Value Engineering Change Proposal and supplement it with an oral presentation as needed.
2. Consider and cater to the reviewer's needs.
3. Identify and overcome road blocks.
4. Use techniques of report writing and presentation.
5. Have first choice and second alternative ready for the decision-maker to decide.
6. Let independent authority audit and confirm benefits and savings accomplished.
7. Use good human relations.
8. Give credits where due.

KEY QUESTIONS

1. Is the problem defined ?
2. Is the need for the change clearly shown ?
3. Is the Value Engineering Change Proposal concise, complete, factual, and supported by documentation in Project Workbook ?
4. Have you included an implementation/action and time plan ?
5. Have you considered the reviewer's needs and provided for them ?
6. Have you a first choice and an alternative, so that the decision maker may choose, and so decide to accept a proposal ?
7. Have you anticipated all objections and road blocks and prepared solutions or suggestions to overcome them ?
8. Have you given credits where due ?

CHECK LIST

1. Is the problem defined ?
2. Is the need for a change clearly shown ?
3. Is the written proposal:
   simple,
   concise,
   factual,
   precise,
   using familiar and necessary words ?
4. Does it include:
   Before and after details,
   Cost comparisons,
   Advantages and disadvantages, (with suggestions,)
   Direct as well as indirect benefits,
   Intangible benefits,
   Names of Team leader and members,
   Names of others who have contributed to the study,
   Acknowledgements ?
5. Have you included a plan for implementation and a timetable ?

6. Have you made the advantages in accepting the proposal obvious ?
7. Is there enough information to make a decision ?
8. Are the expected results clearly indicated to facilitate the audit ?
9. What was the earlier audit findings on a similar project ?
10. Were lessons drawn from the findings used to guide ?

GUIDELINES FOR WRITING THE VALUE ENGINEERING CHANGE PROPOSAL

1. The proposal must be persuasive to convince the management;
   explanatory to highlight the solution;
   informative to give the general picture; and
   factual.

2. Ask yourself questions like:
   - What is wanted ?
   - What is already known ?
   - Is it purely factual ?
   - Sure of the facts ?
   - What do the facts indicate ?
   - Made comparisons:
     - Within the company ?
     - With other companies ?
     - With past and present records, customs, etc. ?

   - Is there any repetitions ?
   - Are there any contradictions ?
   - Who would be affected ?

   - What would be the future developments ?
   - What financial aspects are involved ?
   - Considered outlay, profits, savings, return on investments, etc. ?

3. Summarise in a single sheet of paper, pin-pointing as simply as possible, the very essence of your findings. Go straight to the point. Use active verbs to give emphasis or force. Avoid negatives, exaggerations, stating the obvious.

4. Decision-making is influenced by the way in which issues are presented, the identification of their significance and the explanations. Therefore, extra care has to be exercised in writing.

5. Record in logical order, under appropriate sub-headings:

   Project title.
   The problem (item),
   Why it was selected for study.
   Facts: Function evaluation, alternatives created, comparisons, cost, etc.
   Value Engineering change Proposal.
   Comparisons: before and after, advantages and disadvantages, (suggestions to deal with them), costs, etc.
   Plan for implementation.
   Acknowledgement. (Do not forget contributions by others).

6. Annex Project Workbook for details.

<table>
<tr><td colspan="2">PROJECT</td><td>Ref No..............
Date.................</td></tr>
<tr><td colspan="3">VALUE ENGINEERING CHANGE PROPOSAL
ITEM:____________
ASSEMBLY:__________ SUB-ASSEMBLY:________ PART:______
QUANTITY PER YEAR: ____________</td></tr>
<tr><td>BASIC FUNCTION</td><td colspan="2">SECONDARY OR SUPPORT FUNCTIONS</td></tr>
<tr><td>PRESENT</td><td colspan="2">PROPOSED</td></tr>
<tr><td colspan="3">FINDINGS & RECOMMENDATIONS</td></tr>
<tr><td colspan="3">SAVINGS</td></tr>
</table>

PROJECT PARTICIPANTS:
DATE:

Form No. 18

PROJECT	Ref No..................... Date........................

FINANCIAL ASPECTS AND EVALUATION OF CHANGE PROPOSED

COST DATA (PER UNIT)	PRE-SENT	PRO-POSED	SAVINGS (Rs.)	PERCENT SAVINGS
MATERIAL COST				
LABOUR COST				
OVERHEAD COST				
OTHER COSTS				
UNIT COST				
ANNUAL REQUIREMENTS				
TOTAL COST PER UNIT				

BE THOROUGH - CHECK CALCULATIONS
Form No. 19

PROJECT			Ref. No .... Date..........................	
LIFE CYCLE COST ANALYSIS (i.e. on Owning and Operating/Maintenance Costs during the Product Life Cycle)				
Sl. No.	Details of Costs per item	Existing Design	Proposal I	Proposal II
1.	Total Initial Cost/per Unit			
2.	Annual Energy Costs of operation per year 1. Power - Watts 2. Fuel, oil - litres 3. Fuel, coal/coke - tonnes 4. Others			
	Total			
3.	Maintenance Cost (annual) 1. Lubrication 2. Replacements 3. Labour 4. Interest on investment (initial cost) 5. Others			
	Total			
4.	1. Scrap Realisation expected 2. Life expected 3. Depreciation per year			
5.	Total Annual Costs (add all Total boxes)			
6.	Comparative savings			
7.	Present worth of total LCC savings			

RECHECK - VALIDATE YOUR ASSUMPTIONS

Form No. 20

PROJECT		Ref No .... Date..................
IMPLEMENTATION PLAN		
1.	HOW SHOULD THE PROPOSAL BE IMPLEMENTED ?	
2.	WHAT SHOULD BE CHANGED ? IN WHAT SEQUENCE ?	
3.	WHO SHOULD DO IT ?	
4.	HOW LONG SHOULD IT TAKE ?	
5.	ANY DEADLINE REQUIRED ?	
6.	IMPLEMENTATION COSTS.	

Form No. 21

GUIDELINES FOR ORAL PRESENTATION

1. The most effective presentation is the BRIEF presentation.

2. Illustrate the points through use of visual aids: slides, sketches, charts, etc. Prepare them in advance.

3. Select resource material:
   What must be said.
   In what detail.
   The best way to say it.
   Keep strictly to the subject.
   Summarise the recommendations

4. Introduce yourself and the Team, describe the project in brief, the benefits from your recommendations, compare original with the recommended, give your plan for implementation, acknowledge contribution by others, conclude with thanks.

5. Use simple words, short, crisp and meaty style. Avoid verbiage, jargons.

6. Express yourself clearly and with ease. Speak with a hard palate and a hard stomach. Open the back of your throat. Relax. Have a pleasant manner of speaking and say things in a likeable way. Make your voice interesting and attractive through phasing, pause, pitch, pace, inflection, stress, emphasis and volume.

7. If you want listeners to have and keep details, give each person a hand-out copy.

8. Listen to questions carefully to answer them completely and well.

   Use the following as appropriate:

Single shot question	Make eye contact. Ask the person.
Time bomb question	Ask audience as a group.
Ricochet question	Redirect to another.
Rebound question	Rephrase and ask the questioner.
Sing along question	For show of hands, or an opinion, or an experience.
Mutiple choice	Give hints to audience, to choose from.
Ask and answer	Ask and answer yourself.

9. Read, refer, rehearse.

People are not computers. They have logical minds. They interpret proposals according to what they are looking for. The answer is to present every proposal first in terms of the effect (benefit or advantage) it has on what they are looking for.

They are not interested in how hard you worked on the proposal, where it came from and other data. What you propose must be in such a form that the executive can assimilate it quickly. Stick to the specifics he can approve, promote or action.

<table>
<tr><td colspan="2">PROJECT</td><td>Ref. No ....
Date..................</td></tr>
<tr><td colspan="3">VALUE ENGINEERING CHANGE PROPOSAL SUMMARY</td></tr>
<tr><td colspan="3">RECOMMENDATIONS</td></tr>
<tr><td>Short term</td><td></td><td></td></tr>
<tr><td>Long term</td><td></td><td></td></tr>
<tr><td>Financial Details

Design
Prototype
Testing & development
Make/Buy
Construction
Tooling
TOTAL</td><td>Short term</td><td>Long term</td></tr>
<tr><td colspan="3">DECISION BY APPROVING AUTHORITY

Received on ______________ Considered on ____________________
Decision APPROVED ☐ NOT APPROVED ☐
TO MODIFY ☐ TO RESTUDY ☐</td></tr>
<tr><td colspan="3">Next review on ________________
Date _____________ Signature ______________________________</td></tr>
</table>

Form No. 22

AUDIT

OBJECTIVE

1. To perform audit.

2. To evaluate results.

3. To validate if expected results have accrued.

4. To review the project to identify any problems that arose and recommend corrective action for the next project.

5. To screen all contributors to the Value Engineering study for possible recognition and rewards and make appropriate recommendations.

KEY QUESTIONS

1. Did the idea work ?

2. Was money saved ?

3. Was design improved ?

4. Could it benefit others ?

5. Should any awards be made ?

6. Has it been publicised ?

PART IV

VALUE ENGINEERING CASES

Value Engineering Raises Production & Productivity

The By-product Coke Ovens in Steel plants (Fig. 47), producing metallurgical coke from crushed coal, consist essentially of rectangular section refractory lined coking chambers, approximately 1200 cm x 50 cm x 425 cm, supported beneath by steel columns and a structural steel base. A battery has 100 ovens. Each oven takes 20t of crushed coal and carbonises it, out of contact with air, indirect heating being provided by the adjacent heating chambers fired with either or both Coke Oven gas and Blast Furnace gas. A charge takes about 18 hours to carbonise.

Fifty two per cent of the cost of energy in integrated Iron and Steel making is contributed by coke to reduce the cost of finished steel. Any saving in the cost of coke would be reflected in the cost of finished steel.

Conventional methods were tried, and with varying degrees of successes to raise production, productivity and reduce cost of coke making: like, improving yields, reducing delays, adopting modular system of maintenance to raise equipment availability and to increase throughput by increasing the capacity of the oven charging hoppers, crushing coal to finer comminution, adding oil spray to reduce the voids between crushed particles, and so on. However, the improvement so gained was not sufficient; A further reduction in cost of coke became imperative. A Value Engineering effort was then made.

Using the Functional Analysis Technique, the oven, the charging equipment, the charging procedure, etc., were studied — what is it ?, what does it do ?, define the Function in two words: a VERB and a NOUN, and so on. In the analysis, out of the several items studied, it was the innocous "LEVELLER", an indirect piece of equipment, that gave the solution, (Fig. 48). When its function was defined as SPREAD COAL, a common sense question was asked why it was skimming some coal out of the oven during its operation cycle (Fig. 49, Before). Even though the material was recycled by the worker engaged for the job, time, energy and money spent to move the crushed coal kilometers over conveyors and heights to bunkers and charging into the oven, had come to no avail. It was discovered that the design was such that to even the peaks in the charge the leveller bar is operated horizontally from the leveller door; if it resulted in some coal being skimmed off, then the oven charge was correct, (Fig. 49, Top). The chain reaction, exploring the possibility of eliminating this necessity, led to reducing the width of the leveller bar without affecting its structural rigidity and totally eliminating the skimming (Fig. 49, After). This increased coal charge per oven by 2.3% and correspondingly reduced the cost of coke produced.

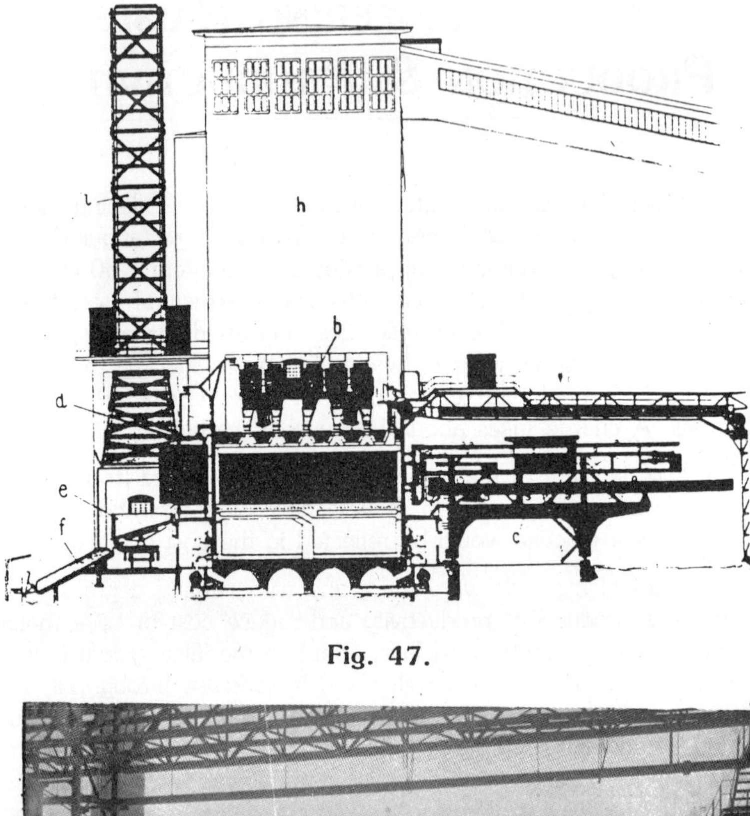

Fig. 47.

Fig. 48.

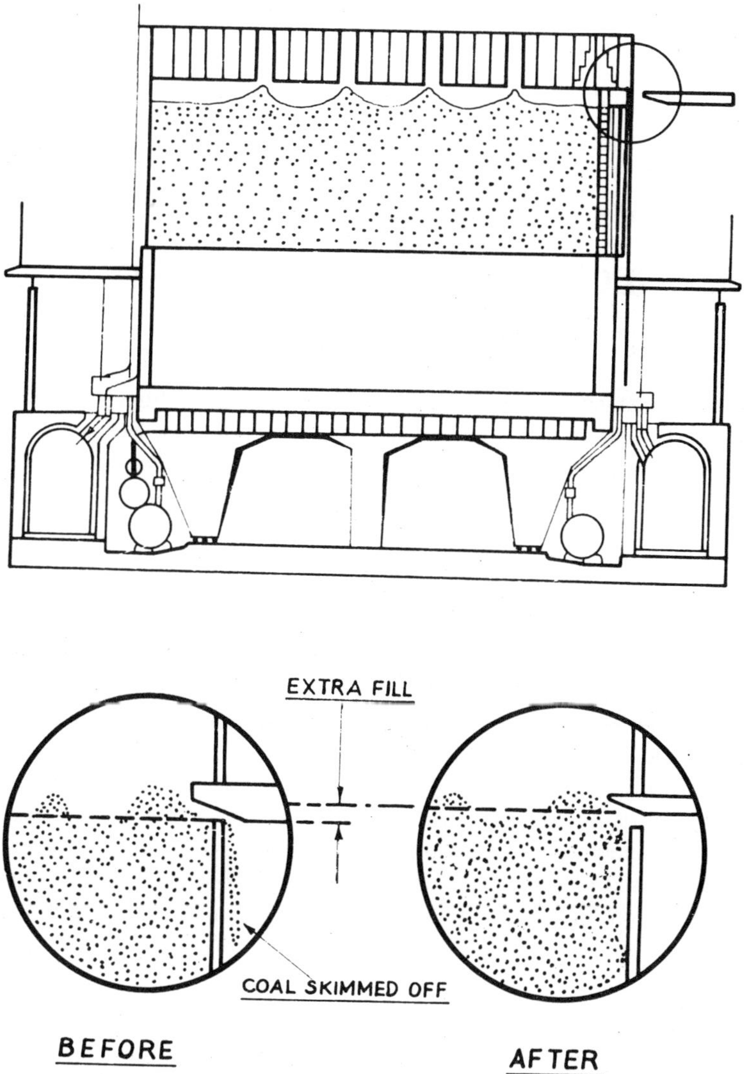

Fig. 49.

VALUE ENGINEERING PREVENTS UNNECESSARY USE OF RESOURCES

The universal spindle in the Blooming mill was a heavy forged piece, machined to size and in one single piece as in Fig. 50. For years this item used to be imported from original suppliers. When the Government imposed import restrictions and foreign exchange controls and the engineering industries began to develop capabilities and capacities for indigenous manufacture of many items of equipment and spares, the item had to be replenished from local sources. However, the huge size of the item and the processing restrictions together made the item prohibitively costly, for reason that special tackles had to be made specially for casting, teeming, handling metal and pressing and forging; as well as unduly long delivery, for reason that the development of these tackles itself would be time consuming. Value study of the design enabled change to a three piece design for the function to be accomplished (Fig. 51). The result: saving in cost, speed of delivery, bringing the item within the capability of more than one indigenous manufacturer, conserving scarce foreign exchange, modification in the specification for material, using high grade alloy steel for the palm ends and lower cost high carbon steel for the stem, and opening out scope for tribological studies to raise the life of the wearing parts.

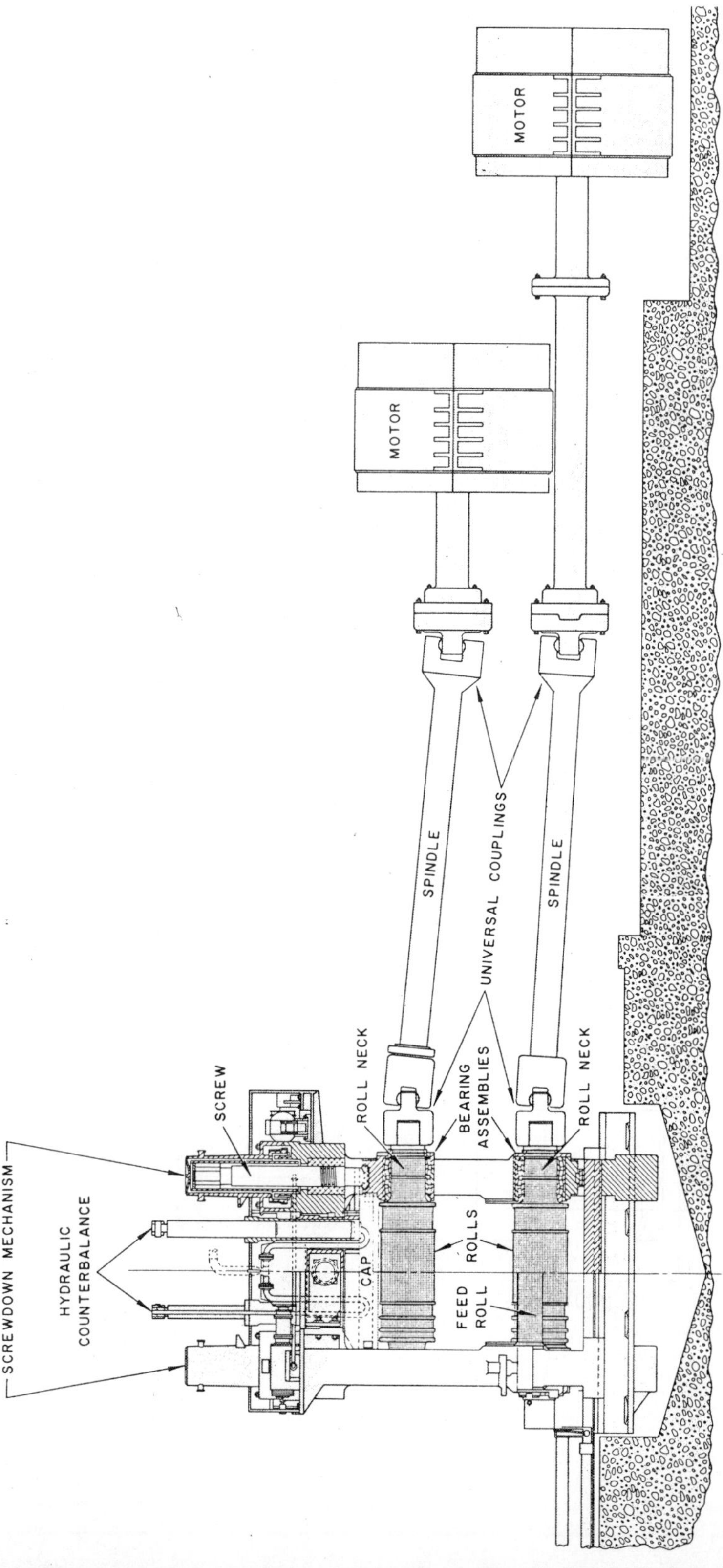
SCREWDOWN MECHANISM
HYDRAULIC COUNTERBALANCE
SCREW
ROLL NECK
BEARING ASSEMBLIES
ROLL NECK
CAP
ROLLS
FEED ROLL
UNIVERSAL COUPLINGS
SPINDLE
SPINDLE
MOTOR
MOTOR

Fig. 50

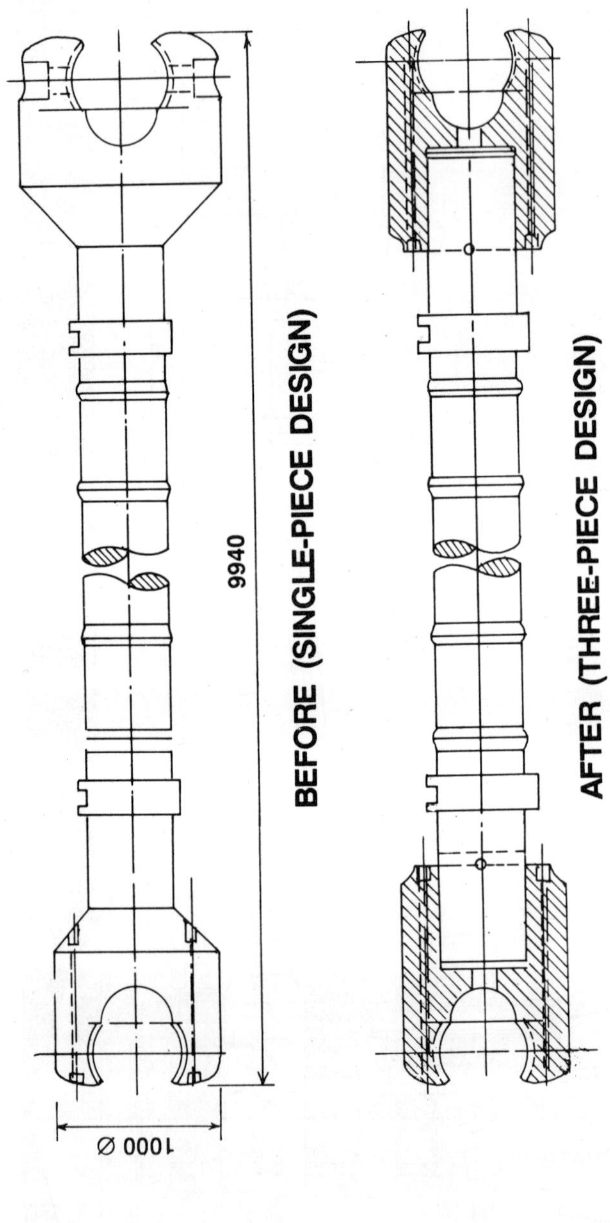
9940
Ø 1000
BEFORE (SINGLE-PIECE DESIGN)
AFTER (THREE-PIECE DESIGN)

Fig. 51

Value Engineering is not mere Cost Reduction

With the advent of the use of oxygen lance to accelerate the rate of production of steel in Basic Open Hearth furnace, basic refractories are widely used for the construction of the roof. The principles of design in a typical furnace are shown in Fig. 52. The range of fuel consumption is from 3,000,000 Btu to 4,000,000 Btu per net tonne of steel when using hot metal and 4,000,000 Btu to 5,300,000 Btu per tonne when the charge is all cold pig. Hence the vital importance of using coolers, particularly for the roof, to minimise cost on rebuild and refractories.

Originally a fabricated design, with two pipe inserts at the ends were used for the coolers (Fig. 53). The product improvement suggested by the Value Engineering study was to change to a casting, with formed pipe coil embedded in the casting (Fig. 54). The additional pipe coil and the change to casting both added to the cost of manufacture of the item (doubled). However, advantage of better heat transfer and cooling of the roof enabled raising the life to the extent of 300%. Net result was a saving due to the change.

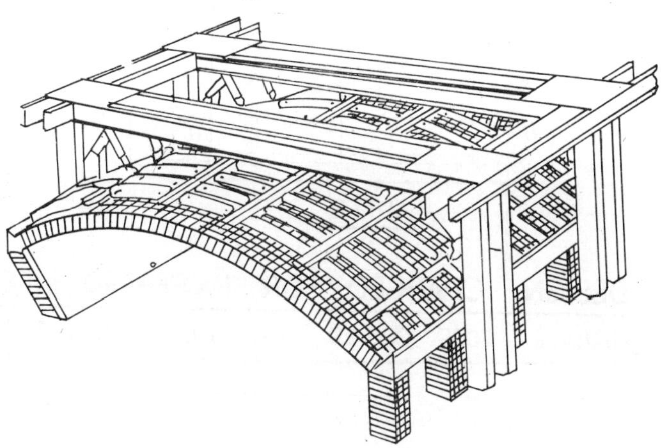

Fig. 52

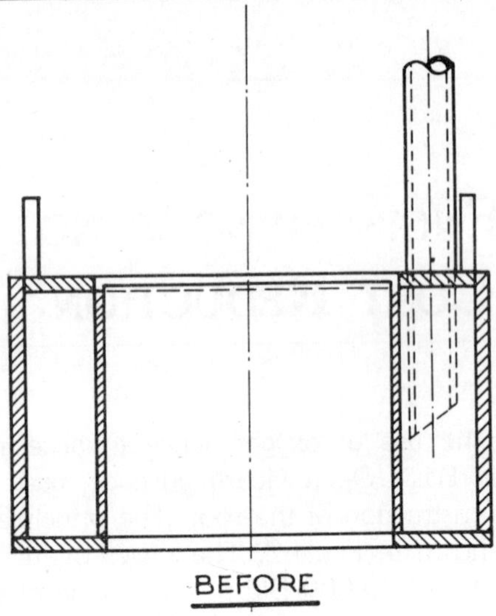

Fig 53.

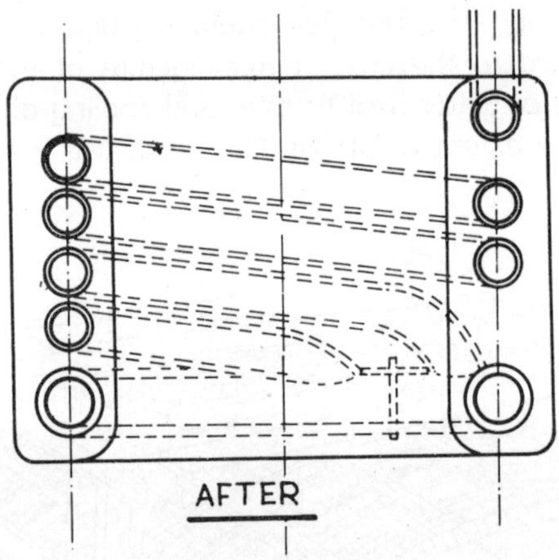

DESIGN CHANGED FOR INCREASED LIFE

(FURNACE ROOF COOLER AT S.M.S. NO. 3)

Fig. 54

Value Engineering means Just Right and Nothing More

As part of a plant wide Safety programme, it was decided to instal SAFETY STOP BLOCKS on the gantries for all the electric overhead travelling cranes. The company being equipped with a large infrastructure of design offices and shops complex, it was easy to make a design, cast the prototype, machine it and try it out in situ, in quick time (Fig. 55A). Simultaneous cost control efforts led to a modification in the design from casting to fabrication and consequent cost saving of 22% (Fig. 55B).

Normally the work would have stopped there. But a Value Engineering study led to a better value solution. The study revealed that except for the portion bearing on the gantry rails (for fixing) and on the wheel of the crane (for surface contact), machining of other areas was unnecessary — gold plating in Value Engineering parlance. Even for these exceptions, rough grinding was found to be adequate. The resultant change (Fig. 55C) not only eliminated quite some machining and replaced the balance by grinding, but also effected a further saving in material margin by gas cutting to rough shape — a saving of additional 25% in cost.

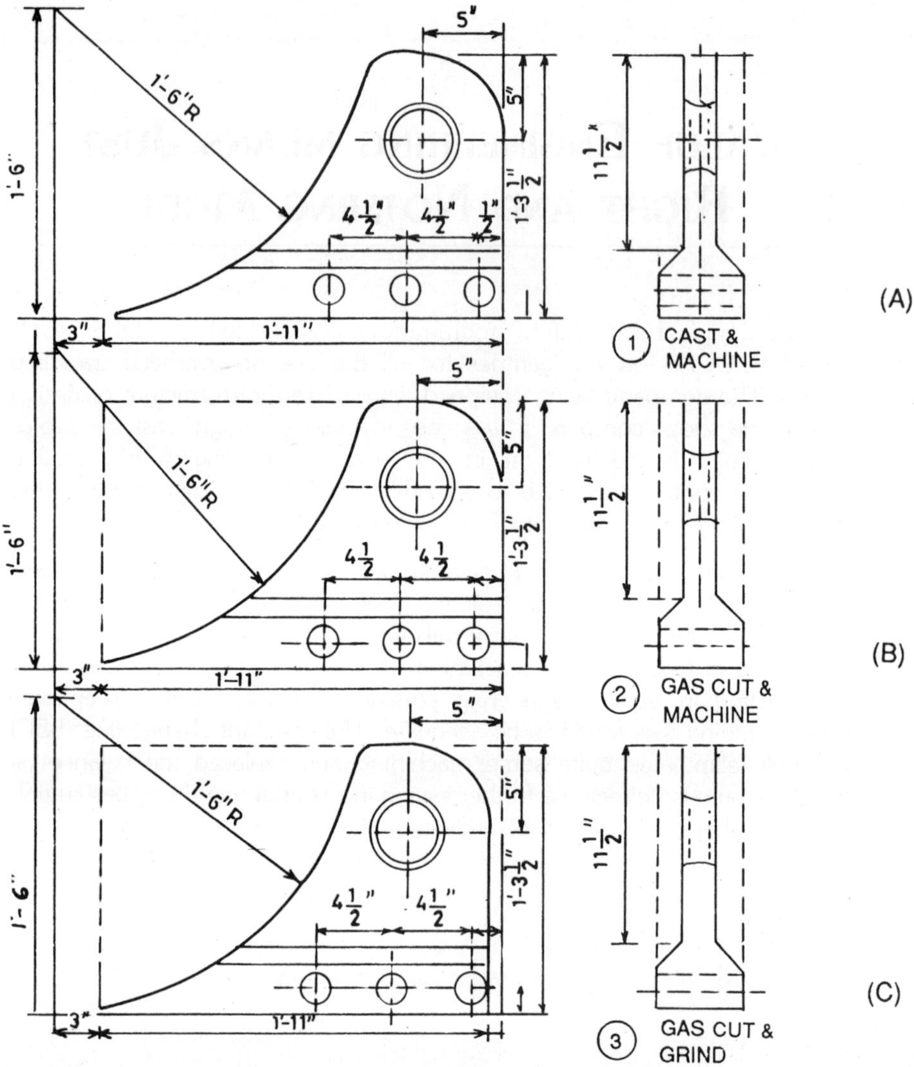

(A)
1 CAST & MACHINE
(B)
2 GAS CUT & MACHINE
(C)
3 GAS CUT & GRIND
1'-6''R
1'-6''
5''
1'-3 1/2''
4 1/2''
1/2''
11 1/2''
3''
1'-11''

Fig. 55.

Value Engineering is Intensive Cost Search

Galvanising is done on the tubes produced to IS-1239. A company uses hot dip method over semi automatic and manual galvanising bath and ancilliaries. The specification calls for a coating of 400 gms of zinc per square metre on commercial basis. The company could produce to an average of 540 gms per sq. mtr. with intense concentration of process control efforts.

The value study brought into sharp focus the potential of saving not being realised in their present operations. For, a saving of 140 gms per sq.mtr. was equivalent to Rs. 1.4 crores per year at current level of production.

In the Information phase, data relating to coating performance, impact of various parameters on the coating, impact of bath composition on the zinc coating, etc., were collected (Fig. 56). Historical data from strip test result was compiled. The behaviour of coating vis-a-vis sizes galvanised, the distribution of outside and inside coating etc., were studied. A herring-bone diagram of cause and effect was prepared (Fig. 57). The search thus led to resolution of the problem into four aspects for brainstorming and creation of ideas to solve, viz:

1. Inside coating.
2. Outside coating.
3. Recoveries from by-products.
4. Total coating.

Thirty one ideas were generated, which were then evaluated, investigated, examined for technical feasibility and ranked according to priority for action. Work is in progress for implementation.

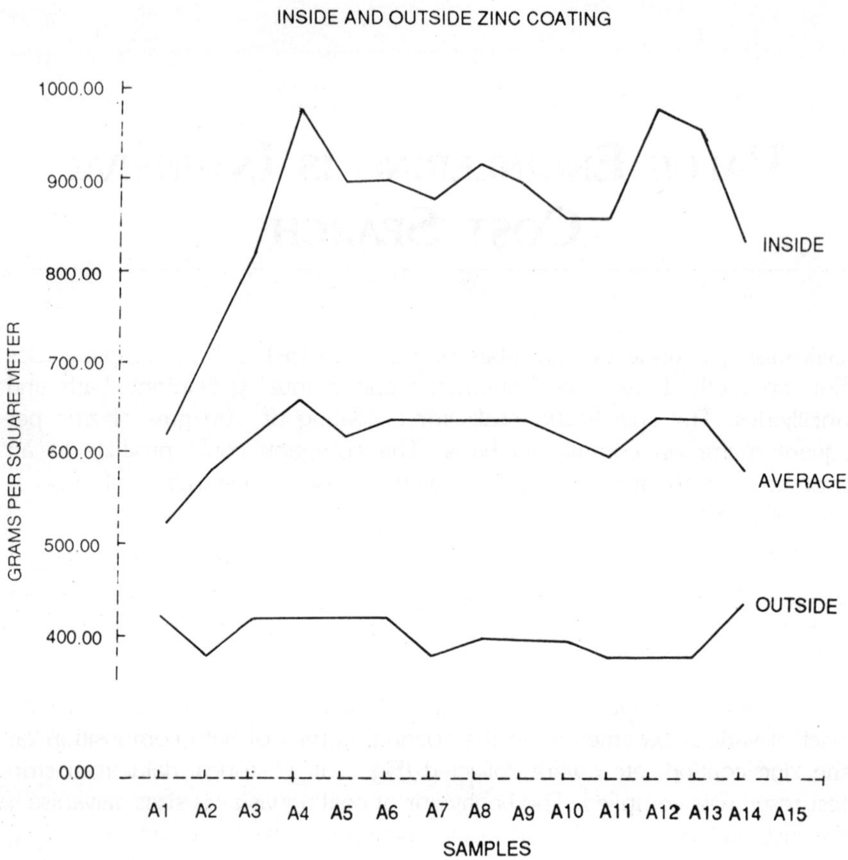
INSIDE AND OUTSIDE ZINC COATING
1000.00
900.00
800.00
700.00
600.00
500.00
400.00
0.00
GRAMS PER SQUARE METER
INSIDE
AVERAGE
OUTSIDE
A1 A2 A3 A4 A5 A6 A7 A8 A9 A10 A11 A12 A13 A14 A15
SAMPLES

Fig. 56.

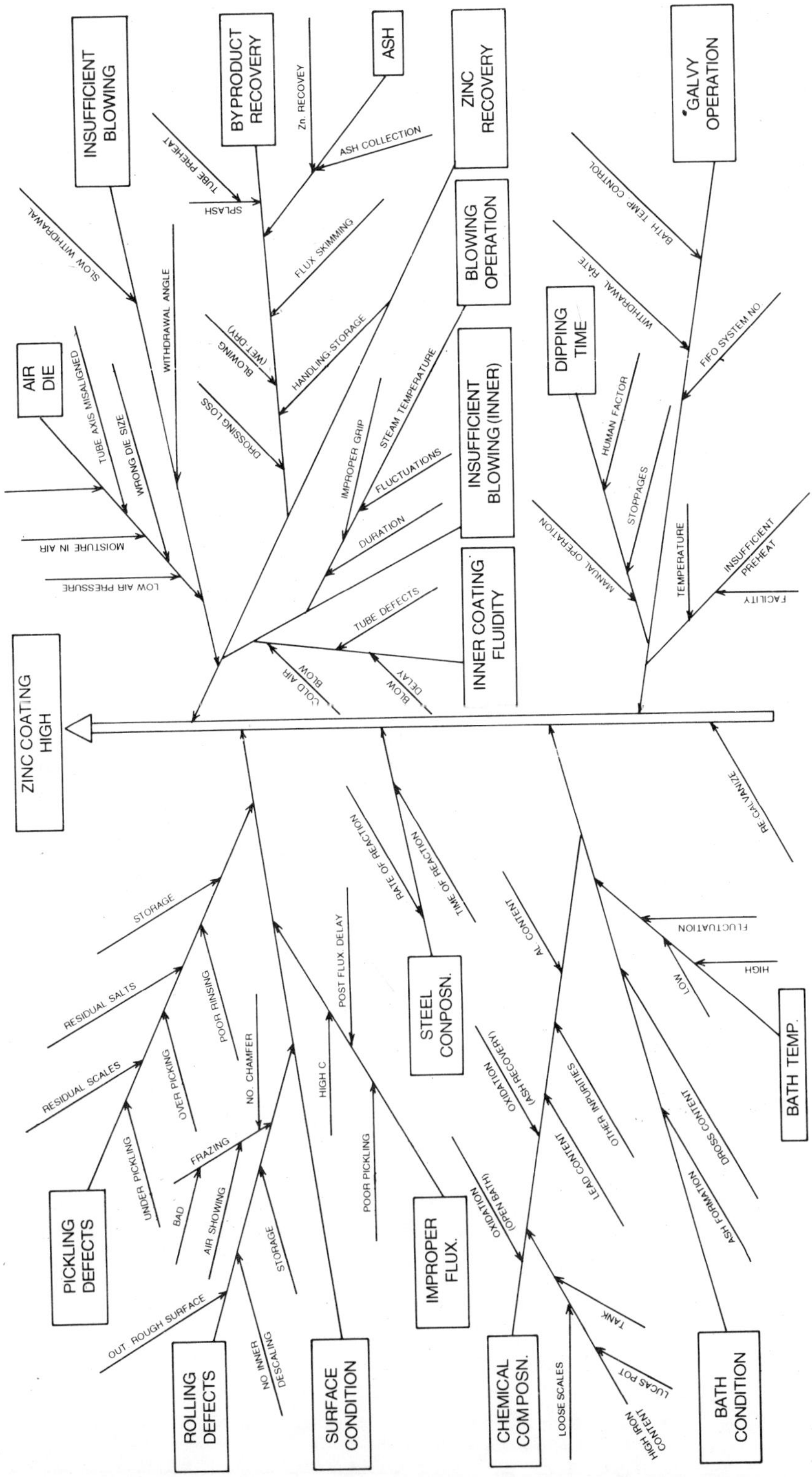
ZINC COATING HIGH
AIR DIE
TUBE AXIS MISALIGNED
WRONG DIE SIZE
MOISTURE IN AIR
LOW AIR PRESSURE
INSUFFICIENT BLOWING
SLOW WITHDRAWAL
WITHDRAWAL ANGLE
BYPRODUCT RECOVERY
TUBE PREHEAT
SPLASH
Zn. RECOVEY
ASH
ASH COLLECTION
FLUX SKIMMING
BLOWING (WET-DRY)
HANDLING STORAGE
DROSSING LOSS
ZINC RECOVERY
BLOWING OPERATION
STEAM TEMPERATURE
IMPROPER GRIP
INSUFFICIENT BLOWING (INNER)
FLUCTUATIONS
DURATION
INNER COATING FLUIDITY
TUBE DEFECTS
COLD AIR BLOW
BLOW DELAY
GALVY OPERATION
BATH TEMP. CONTROL
WITHDRAWAL RATE
FIFO SYSTEM NO
DIPPING TIME
HUMAN FACTOR
STOPPAGES
MANUAL OPERATION
TEMPERATURE
INSUFFICIENT PREHEAT
FACILITY
PICKLING DEFECTS
STORAGE
RESIDUAL SALTS
RESIDUAL SCALES
POOR RINSING
OVER PICKING
UNDER PICKLING
ROLLING DEFECTS
NO. CHAMFER
FRAZING
BAD
AIR SHOWING
STORAGE
OUT ROUGH SURFACE
NO INNER DESCALING
SURFACE CONDITION
HIGH C
POST FLUX DELAY
POOR PICKLING
IMPROPER FLUX.
STEEL CONPOSN.
RATE OF REACTION
TIME OF REACTION
CHEMICAL COMPOSN.
AL CONTENT
OXIDATION (ASH RECOVERY)
OTHER INPURITIES
LEAD CONTENT
OXIDATION (OPEN BATH)
TANK
LUCAS POT
HIGH IRON CONTENT
LOOSE SCALES
BATH CONDITION
DROSS CONTENT
ASH FORMATION
BATH TEMP.
FLUCTUATION
HIGH
LOW
RE-GALVANIZE

Fig. 57.

Value Engineering Finds Value in Discards

An automobile manufacturer used to discard off-cuts produced in their Forge and Press Shop as scrap (Mark 3, 6 and 7). However, cost was recovered selling the scrap as remeltable material.

A Value Engineering study of the process was made. Earlier the billet stock, Mark 1, was cut to two sizes. One size was forged to shape, Mark 2, crown wheel pressed out in one press and then the off-cut punched out (Mark 3); the other, to shapes, Mark 4 and 5 in another press, with similar off-cuts (Mark 6 and 7, not shown). The quality of steel used was 20MnCr5, an expensive and not easily available material. Each large off-cut was 5 Kg. in weight. Total yearly discard was 150 t. The study found valuable use for the large off-cut (Mark 3) itself, to forge the other part, Rear Axle Flange, Mark 4; and then again from its off-cut, a Groove Nut, Mark 5, both required for production of vehicles.

After the Value Engineering change the ultimate scrap generation was very little. Raw material requirement for the Rear Axle Flange and Groove Nut forgings was brought down to half the normal procurement, of billet stock.

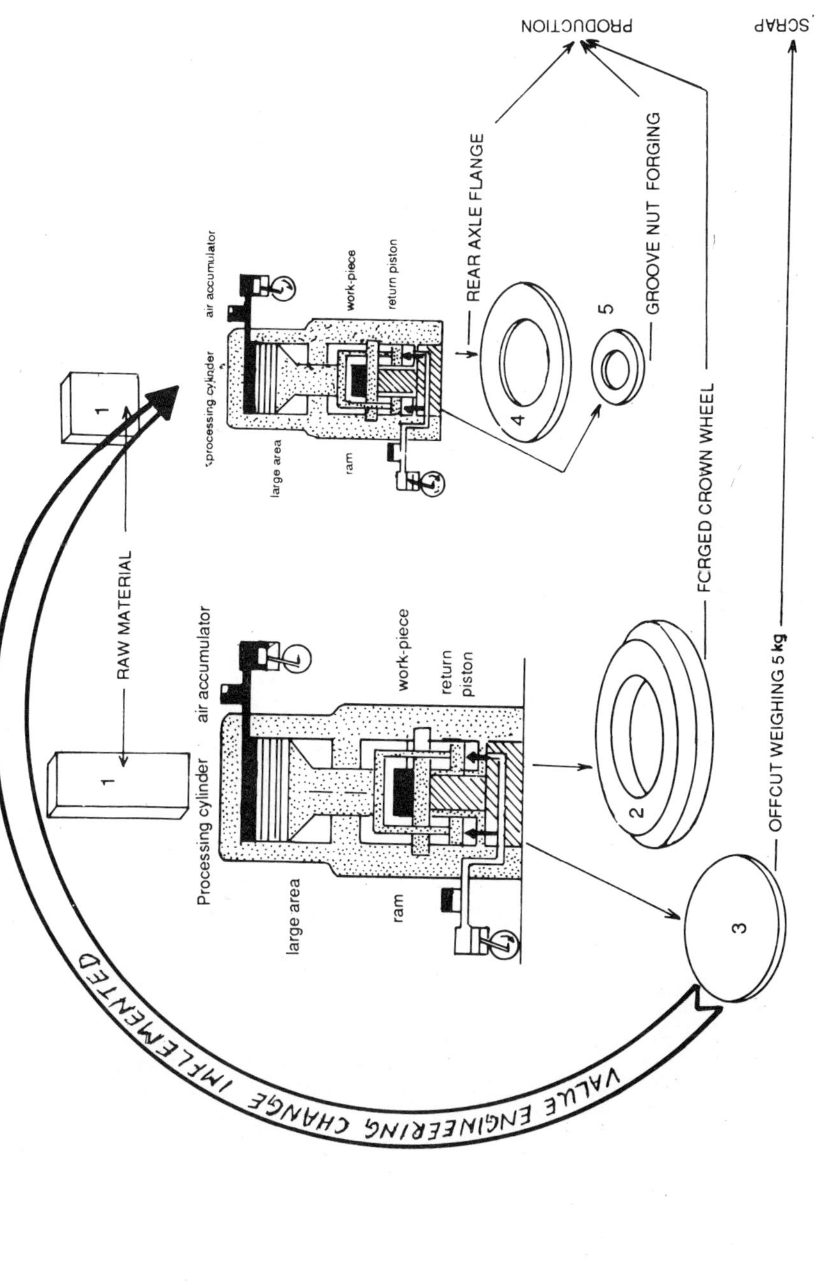
RAW MATERIAL
1
1
Processing cylinder
air accumulator
large area
ram
work-piece
return piston
processing cylinder
air accumulator
large area
ram
work-piece
return piston
2
3
4
5
REAR AXLE FLANGE
GROOVE NUT FORGING
FCRGED CROWN WHEEL
OFFCUT WEIGHING 5 kg
PRODUCTION
SCRAP
VALUE ENGINEERING CHANGE IMPLEMENTED

Fig. 58

Value Engineering Uses Vendor Assistance and Expertise

A major industry successfully used its strengths as complementary to the low level of skills, but lower unit costs and the capacities available, in the few indegenous small industries that existed, as well as those coming up. Earlier, many of the items of spares, components, consumables and stores used to be either made in their Shops complex, or purchased from outside sources, including imports. For import substitution, items were ordered on sources found and developed locally. Along with it, for lessening load in own Shops complex also, some orders were being similarly farmed out. The orders were for complete work and supplies in the finished state, to specs. Noticing that these sources were unable to make quality patterns for the castings, lacked sophisticated machine tools for the finishing and accuracy required, could not afford the expensive heat treatment facilities and the skills for the work involved, thus causing cost to escalate and qualities to suffer, orders were placed selectively for ONLY THE PORTIONS OF THE JOB that they can complete satisfactorily and well with their skills and equipment. Thus, for casting, the major company loaned their patterns; for forgings, the steel was supplied; for machined items, rough work alone was done by the local engineering parties; and so on. The modern machine tools in the major industry, their high grade heat treatment facilities, and the highly skilled and trained personnel completed the rest of the work. Besides the cost advantage, the workload on their Shops complex was also reduced.

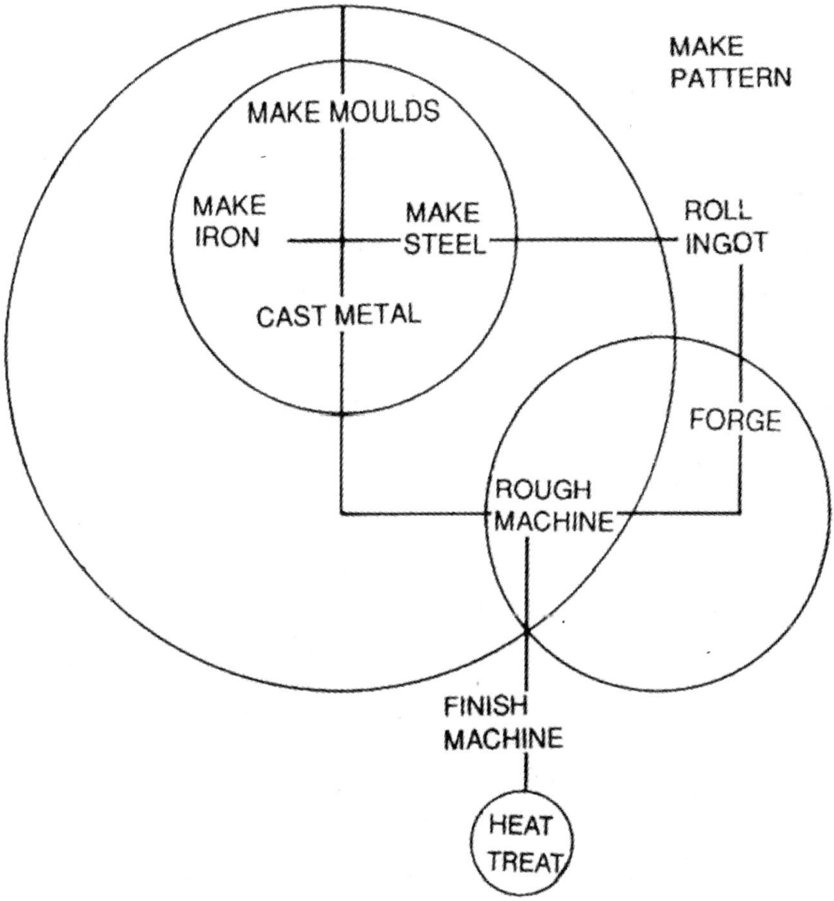
MAKE PATTERN
MAKE MOULDS
MAKE IRON
MAKE STEEL
ROLL INGOT
CAST METAL
FORGE
ROUGH MACHINE
FINISH MACHINE
HEAT TREAT

Fig. 59.

BIBLIOGRAPHY

MILES, Lawrence D., TECHNIQUES OF VALUE ANALYSIS AND ENGINEERING, 1972, McGraw-Hill.

MUDGE, Arthur E., VALUE ENGINEERING, A Systematic Approach, 1971, McGraw-Hill.

ZIMMERMAN Larry W. and HART, Glen D., VALUE ENGINEERING, A PRACTICAL APPROACH FOR OWNERS, DESIGNERS AND CONTRACTORS, 1982, Van Nostrand.

DELL ISOLA, Alphonse J., VALUE ENGINEERING IN THE CONSTRUCTION INDUSTRY, 1975, Van Nostrand

TUFTY, Harold G., COMPENDIUM ON VALUE ENGINEERING, 1983, The Indo American Society.

RAVEN, A.D., PROFIT IMPROVEMENT BY VALUE ANALYSIS, VALUE ENGINEERING AND PURCHASE PRICE ANALYSIS, 1971, Cassell & Company Ltd.

DRUCKER, Peter F., MANAGEMENT, TASKS, RESPONSIBILITIES, PRACTICES, 1975, Allied Publishers Private Ltd.

AKIYAMA, Kaneo, Prof., FUNCTION ANALYSIS — SYSTEMATIC IMPROVEMENT OF QUALITY AND PERFORMANCE, 1991, Productivity Press Inc.

FALLON, Carlos, VALUE ANALYSIS TO IMPROVE PRODUCTIVITY, 1971, Wiley - Interscience.

FREIDMAN, Thomas L. THE WORLD IS FLAT, 2005, Farrar, Straus & Giroux.

VALUE ENGINEERING IN MANUFACTURING, 1967, American Society of Tool and Manufacturing Engineers, Prentice Hall Inc.

SAVE, CONFERENCE PROCEEDINGS, INTERACTIONS and VALUE WORLD, The Society of American Value Engineers.

INVEST, National Conference Proceedings/Regional Conference Proceedings, The Indian Value Engineering Society.

JPC, International/Local Conference Proceedings, The Jamshedpur Productivity Council.

IW, Industry Week, Penton Publication, USA.

TIME, The Weekly News Magazine, USA.

Index